First World War

and Army of Occupation

War Diary

France, Belgium and Germany

24 DIVISION
Headquarters, Branches and Services
Commander Royal Engineers
25 August 1915 - 25 June 1919

WO95/2196/2

The Naval & Military Press Ltd
www.nmarchive.com
Published in association with The National Archives

Published by

The Naval & Military Press Ltd

Unit 10 Ridgewood Industrial Park,
Uckfield, East Sussex,
TN22 5QE England
Tel: +44 (0) 1825 749494

www.naval-military-press.com
www.nmarchive.com

Contents

Document type	Place/Title	Date From	Date To
Miscellaneous	WO95/2196/2		
Heading	24th Division Divl Engineers C.R.E. Aug 1915-Jun 1919		
Heading	24th Division H.Q. 24th Division CRE Vol I Aug & Sep 15 June 19		
War Diary	Black Down	25/08/1915	30/08/1915
War Diary	Havre	31/08/1915	31/08/1915
War Diary	Montreuil	01/09/1915	01/09/1915
War Diary	Offin	02/09/1915	21/09/1915
War Diary	Bomy	22/09/1915	23/09/1915
War Diary	Busnes	24/09/1915	24/09/1915
War Diary	Bethune	25/09/1915	26/09/1915
War Diary	Vermelles	26/09/1915	27/09/1915
War Diary	Sailly-La-Bourse	27/09/1915	29/09/1915
War Diary	St. Hilaire	30/09/1915	30/09/1915
Heading	H.Q. 24th Div. CRE Vol 2 Oct 15		
Heading	H.Q. R.E. 24th Divn. Oct 1915		
War Diary		01/10/1915	24/10/1915
War Diary	Reninghelst	25/10/1915	31/10/1915
Heading	24th Division H.Q. 24th Div. CRE Vol 3 Nov 15		
War Diary	Reninghelst	01/11/1915	22/11/1915
War Diary	Steenvoorde	23/11/1915	23/11/1915
War Diary	Broxeele	24/11/1915	24/11/1915
War Diary	Salperwick	25/11/1915	30/11/1915
Heading	CRE. 24th Div. Vol 4		
War Diary	Salperwick	01/12/1915	19/12/1915
War Diary	Elverdinghe	20/12/1915	21/12/1915
War Diary	Salperwick	22/12/1915	28/12/1915
War Diary	Reninghelst	29/12/1915	30/12/1915
War Diary	Salperwick	31/12/1915	31/12/1915
Heading	CRE. 24th Div. Vol 5 Jan 1916		
Heading	CRE 24th Div. Vol 6		
War Diary	Salperwick	01/01/1916	05/01/1916
War Diary	Reninghelst	06/01/1916	27/01/1916
War Diary	Ypres	28/01/1916	28/01/1916
War Diary	Reninghelst	29/01/1916	29/02/1916
Miscellaneous	Operation Order. by Lieut Column A.J. Craven R.E. C.R.E. 24th Division	12/03/1916	12/03/1916
Operation(al) Order(s)	C.R.E's Operation Order No. 20	15/03/1916	15/03/1916
Operation(al) Order(s)	Operation Order No. 21 by Lieut Colonel A.J. Craven R.E. C.R.E. 24th Division	14/03/1914	14/03/1914
Operation(al) Order(s)	Operation Order No 22 by Lieut Col A.J. Craven RE C.R.E. 24th Division		
Heading	C.R.E. 24th DW Vol 7		
War Diary	Reninghelst	01/03/1916	20/03/1916
War Diary	Fletre	21/03/1916	29/03/1916
War Diary	St Jans Cappel	30/03/1916	31/03/1916
Miscellaneous	C.R.E's Ox	08/03/1916	08/03/1916
War Diary	St Jans Cappel	01/04/1916	18/04/1916
War Diary	Bailleul	19/04/1916	30/06/1916

Operation(al) Order(s)	C.R.E's Operation Order No. S.E. 6	15/06/1916	15/06/1916
Operation(al) Order(s)	Operation Order No. 23 By Ct. Col A.J. Craven R.E. C.R.E. 24th Div	18/06/1916	18/06/1916
Operation(al) Order(s)	Operation Order No. 24 by Lt Col A.J. Craven R.E. C.R.E. 24th Div.	21/06/1916	21/06/1916
War Diary	Bailleul	01/07/1916	04/07/1916
War Diary	Locre	05/07/1916	10/07/1916
War Diary	Bailleul	11/07/1916	22/07/1916
War Diary	St Jans Cappel	23/07/1916	25/07/1916
War Diary	Cavillon	26/07/1916	31/07/1916
Operation(al) Order(s)	Operation Order No 26 by Col A.J. Craven R.E. C.R.E. 24th Div	01/07/1916	01/07/1916
Miscellaneous			
Operation(al) Order(s)	Operation Order No. 27 by Lt Col AJ Craven R.E. C.R.E. 24th Division		
Operation(al) Order(s)	Operation Order No. 28 by Lt Col AJ Craven R.E. C.R.E. 24th Div	10/07/1916	10/07/1916
Operation(al) Order(s)	Operation Order No. 29 by Lt Col AJ Craven R.E.	12/07/1916	12/07/1916
Operation(al) Order(s)	Operation Order No. 30 by Lt Col AJ Craven R.E. C.R.E. 24th Divn		
Heading	24th Divisional Engineers C.R.E. 24th Division August 1916		
War Diary	Cavillon	01/08/1916	02/08/1916
War Diary	Citadel 21/2 Miles N. of Bray	03/08/1916	05/08/1916
War Diary	Citadel	06/08/1916	10/08/1916
War Diary	Minden Post	11/08/1916	23/08/1916
War Diary	Forred Tree	23/08/1916	27/08/1916
War Diary	Buire	28/08/1916	30/08/1916
War Diary	Eii Central Sheet 62d	30/08/1916	31/08/1916
Operation(al) Order(s)	Operation Order No. 32 by Lt Col Craven R.E. C.R.E. 24th Division	07/08/1916	07/08/1916
Operation(al) Order(s)	Operation Order No. 33 by Lt Col Craven R.E. C.R.E. 24th Division	09/08/1916	09/08/1916
Operation(al) Order(s)	Operation Order No. 34 by Lieut Col A.J Craven R.E. C.R.E. 24th Division	10/08/1916	10/08/1916
Operation(al) Order(s)	Operation Order No. 35	17/08/1916	17/08/1916
Operation(al) Order(s)	Operation Order No. 36 by Lt Col A.J Craven R.E. C.R.E. 24th Division	17/08/1916	17/08/1916
Operation(al) Order(s)	Operation Order No. 38 by Lt Col A.J Craven R.E. C.R.E. 24th Division	17/08/1916	17/08/1916
Operation(al) Order(s)	Operation Order No. 39 by Lt Col A.J Craven R.E. C.R.E. 24th Division	20/08/1916	20/08/1916
Miscellaneous	Operation Order No. by Lt Col A.J Craven R.E. C.R.E. 24th Division		
Operation(al) Order(s)	Operation Order No.41 by Lt Col A.J Craven R.E. C.R.E. 24th Division	29/08/1916	29/08/1916
Heading	Royal Engineers 24th Division. C.R.E. 24th Division. September 1916		
War Diary	E.11 Central Sheet 62d	01/09/1916	17/09/1916
War Diary	Pont Remy	18/09/1916	20/09/1916
War Diary	Bruay	21/09/1916	25/09/1916
War Diary	Camblain L'Abbe	26/09/1916	30/09/1916
Operation(al) Order(s)	Operation Order No. 42 by Lieut Colonel A.J. Craven R.E. C.R.E. 24th Division.	02/09/1916	02/09/1916
Operation(al) Order(s)	Operation Order No. 44 by Lieut Colonel A.J. Craven R.E. C.R.E. 24th Division.	13/09/1916	13/09/1916

Miscellaneous	Operation Order No. 42 by Lieut Colonel A.J. Craven R.E. C.R.E. 24th Division.	02/09/1916	02/09/1916
Operation(al) Order(s)	Operation Order No. 43 by Lieut Colonel A.J. Craven R.E. C.R.E. 24th Division.	04/09/1916	04/09/1916
Operation(al) Order(s)	Operation Order No. 44 by Lieut Colonel A.J. Craven R.E. C.R.E. 24th Division.	13/09/1916	13/09/1916
Operation(al) Order(s)	March Order No. 45 by Lieut Colonel A.J. Craven R.E. C.R.E. 24th Division.	16/09/1916	16/09/1916
Miscellaneous	March Order No. 43 by Lieut Colonel A.J. Craven R.E. C.R.E. 24th Division.		
Operation(al) Order(s)	Operation Order No. 46 by Lieut Colonel A.J. Craven R.E. C.R.E. 24th Division.	22/09/1916	22/09/1916
Miscellaneous			
War Diary	Camblain L'Abbe	01/10/1916	31/10/1916
Operation(al) Order(s)	Operation Order No. 47 by Lieut Colonel A.J. Craven R.E. C.R.E. 24th Division.	24/10/1916	24/10/1916
Operation(al) Order(s)	Amendment to C.R.E's Operation Order No. 47	26/10/1916	26/10/1916
Miscellaneous	Movement Table to Accompany C.R.E. 24th Division Operation Order No.		
War Diary	Braquemont	01/11/1916	12/02/1917
War Diary	Labeuvriere	13/02/1917	28/02/1917
Operation(al) Order(s)	Operation Order No. 49 by Lieut Colonel A.J. Craven, R.E. C.R.E. 24th. Division.	08/02/1917	08/02/1917
Miscellaneous	March Tables Divisional R.E.		
Operation(al) Order(s)	Correction to C.R.E's Operation Order No. 49 of 8/2/17	09/02/1917	09/02/1917
Miscellaneous	March Tables Divisional R.E.		
Operation(al) Order(s)	Operation Order No. 50. by Major C.A. Rivers Moore. R.E.	26/02/1917	26/02/1917
Miscellaneous	March Table-Table "C"		
Miscellaneous	Table "D"		
Operation(al) Order(s)	Amendment to C.R.E's Operation Order No. 50	27/02/1917	27/02/1917
War Diary	Labeuvriere	01/03/1917	05/03/1917
War Diary	Barlin	06/03/1917	31/03/1917
Miscellaneous	Report on Operations Nos. 1 & 2. Night 22/23 March 1917	23/03/1917	23/03/1917
Miscellaneous	Operation No. 1 Calonne Sector.		
Heading	C.R.E. 24th Division April 1917		
War Diary	Barlin	02/04/1917	02/04/1917
War Diary	Barlin & Sains En Gohelle	03/04/1917	16/04/1917
War Diary	Sains En Gohelle	16/04/1917	28/04/1917
War Diary	Bomy	29/04/1917	30/04/1917
Operation(al) Order(s)	Operation Order No. 51 by Lieut Colonel A.J. Behrens. R.E. C.R.E. 24th. Division.	18/04/1917	18/04/1917
Miscellaneous	March Table 24th Divisional R.E.		
Operation(al) Order(s)	Correction to C.R.E's Operation Order No. 51 of 18/4/17	19/04/1917	19/04/1917
Miscellaneous	March Table. 24th. Divisional R.E.		
Operation(al) Order(s)	Operation Order No. 52 by Lieut Colonel T.T. Behrens. R.E. C.R.E. 24th. Division.	23/04/1917	23/04/1917
Operation(al) Order(s)	Operation Order No. 53 by Lieut Colonel T.T. Behrens. R.E. C.R.E. 24th. Division.	26/04/1917	26/04/1917
War Diary		01/05/1917	31/05/1917
Miscellaneous	24th Division No. Nd/34	07/07/1917	07/07/1917
Miscellaneous	Q 24th. Divisional Headquarters.	05/07/1917	05/07/1917
Operation(al) Order(s)	Operation Order No. 54 by Lieut Colonel T.T. Behrens. R.E. C.R.E. 24th. Division.	09/05/1917	09/05/1917

Miscellaneous	March Tables "A" for Field Companies. R.E.		
Operation(al) Order(s)	Operation Order No. 55 by Lieut Col T.T. Behrens. R.E. C.R.E. 24th. Division.		
Operation(al) Order(s)	Operation Order No. 56 by Lieut Col T.T. Behrens. R.E. C.R.E. 24th. Division.	11/05/1917	11/05/1917
Miscellaneous	March Table "A" for Field Company R.E. and 12th Sherwood Foresters (Pioneers).		
Operation(al) Order(s)	Operation Order No. 57 Lieut Col. T.T. Behrens. R.E. C.R.E. 24th. Division.	12/05/1917	12/05/1917
Miscellaneous			
Operation(al) Order(s)	Operation Order No. 58 by Lieut Colonel T.T. Behrens, R.E. C.R.E. 24th. Division.	14/05/1917	14/05/1917
Operation(al) Order(s)	Operation Order No. 59 by Lieut Colonel T.T. Behrens, R.E. C.R.E. 24th. Division.	25/05/1917	25/05/1917
Operation(al) Order(s)	Operation Order No. 60 by Lieut Colonel T.T. Behrens, R.E. C.R.E. 24th. Division.		
Miscellaneous	Q 24th Divisional Headquarters.	05/07/1917	05/07/1917
War Diary		01/06/1917	30/06/1917
Operation(al) Order(s)	Operation Order No. 62 by Lieut Colonel T.T. Behrens R.E. C.R.E. 24th. Division.	26/06/1917	26/06/1917
Operation(al) Order(s)	Operation Order No. 63 by Lieut Colonel T.T. Behrens R.E. C.R.E. 24th. Division.		
Miscellaneous	Second Army Offensive C.R.E's Instructions No. 2	04/06/1917	04/06/1917
Miscellaneous	Second Army Offensive C.R.E's Instructions No. 3	04/06/1917	04/06/1917
Miscellaneous	List of Loads.		
Miscellaneous	Second Army Offensive. C.R.E's Instructions No. 4. Pioneers.	04/06/1917	04/06/1917
Miscellaneous	Q.O. For May		
War Diary		01/07/1917	31/07/1917
Operation(al) Order(s)	Operation Order No. 64 by Lieut Col. T.T. Behrens. R.E. C.R.E. 24th. Division.	08/07/1917	08/07/1917
Miscellaneous	March Table A. To accompany C.R.E. Operation Order No. 64. Issued 8th. July 1917		
Operation(al) Order(s)	Operation Order No. 65. by Col Lieut T.T. Behrens R.E. C.R.E. 24th. Division.	16/07/1917	16/07/1917
Operation(al) Order(s)	Operation Order No. 66. by Col Lieut T.T. Behrens R.E. C.R.E. 24th. Division.	19/07/1917	19/07/1917
Operation(al) Order(s)	C.R.E's Order No. H.Q. 4. Move of Headquarters R.E. 24th. Division.	13/07/1917	13/07/1917
Operation(al) Order(s)	C.R.E's Order No. H.Q. 5. Move of Headquarters R.E. 24th. Division.	17/07/1917	17/07/1917
Miscellaneous	Fifth Army Offensive. C.R.E's. Instructions No. 1. Tasks Allotted To R.E. Companies For This Operation.	21/07/1917	21/07/1917
Miscellaneous	Fifth Army Offensive. C.R.E's. Instructions No. 2. Pioneers.	21/07/1917	21/07/1917
Miscellaneous	Fifth Army Offensive. C.R.E's. Instructions No. 3. Royal engineers & Pioneers.	25/07/1917	25/07/1917
War Diary		01/08/1917	31/08/1917
Heading	24 Div R.E. H.Q. September 1917 Vol 25		
War Diary		01/09/1917	30/09/1917
Operation(al) Order(s)	Operation Order No. 68. by Major J.H. Prior R.E. A/C.R.E. 24th Division.	03/09/1917	03/09/1917
Miscellaneous	Operation Order No. 69. By Lieut. Col. A.D. Walker. C.R.E. 24th. Division.	12/09/1917	12/09/1917
Operation(al) Order(s)	C.R.E. 24th Division. Operation Order No. 70	13/09/1917	13/09/1917

Miscellaneous	Programme of Reliefs R.E. 24th Division Operation Order No. 70		
Heading	War Diary Oct 1917 C.R.E. 24th Div Vol 26		
War Diary		01/10/1917	31/10/1917
Heading	War Diary C.R.E. 24th Division From Nov 1st to Nov 30th 1917 Vol 27		
War Diary		01/11/1917	30/11/1917
Heading	24th Divisional Headquarters I.C. War Diary for Month of December 1917 Vol 28		
War Diary		01/12/1917	31/12/1917
Heading	C.R.E. 24th Division. War Diary for Month of January 1918 Vol 29		
War Diary	In The Field	01/01/1918	31/01/1918
Heading	H.Q. R.E. War Diary for month of February 1918 Vol 30		
War Diary	In The Field	01/02/1918	28/02/1918
Heading	24th H.Q. R.E. War Diary for month of March 1918 Vol 31		
War Diary	Meraucourt	01/03/1918	12/03/1918
War Diary	Bouvincourt	13/03/1918	22/03/1918
War Diary	Brie	23/03/1918	23/03/1918
War Diary	Marchelepot	24/03/1918	24/03/1918
Miscellaneous	Rosieres	25/03/1918	25/03/1918
War Diary	Demuin	26/03/1918	28/03/1918
War Diary	Castel	29/03/1918	29/03/1918
War Diary	Cottenchy	30/03/1918	31/03/1918
Operation(al) Order(s)	Operation Order No. 72. by Lieut. Col. A.D. Walker R.E. C.R.E. 24th Division.	10/03/1918	10/03/1918
Miscellaneous	March Table "A"		
Heading	War Diary Headquarters, Royal Engineers, 24th Division. April 1918		
War Diary	Cottenchy	01/04/1918	04/04/1918
War Diary	Bouillet	04/04/1918	05/04/1918
War Diary	St. Valery.	06/04/1918	15/04/1918
War Diary	La Thieuloye	17/04/1917	30/04/1917
Heading	War Diary Month of May 1918 H.Q.R.E. Vol 33		
War Diary	La Thieuloye	01/05/1918	02/05/1918
War Diary	Sains En Gohelle	03/05/1918	31/05/1918
Operation(al) Order(s)	C.R.E's. Order No. 441		
Heading	HQ. R.E. War Diary for month of June 1918 Vol 34		
War Diary	Sains En Gohelle	01/06/1918	31/07/1918
Heading	War Diary H.Q. R.E. August 1918 Vol 36		
War Diary	Sains En Gohelle	01/08/1918	31/08/1918
Heading	War Diary H.Q. R.E. 24th Division September 1918 Vol 37		
War Diary	Sains-En-Gohelle	01/09/1918	30/09/1918
Heading	H.Q. R.E. 24th. Division. War Diary October. 1918 Vol 38		
War Diary	Lucheux	01/10/1918	05/10/1918
War Diary	Moeuvres	06/10/1918	06/10/1918
War Diary	Cantaing Mill	07/10/1918	07/10/1918
War Diary	Nine Wood	08/10/1918	08/10/1918
War Diary	Mount Sur L'Oeuvre	09/10/1918	09/10/1918
War Diary	Cambrai	10/10/1918	12/10/1918
War Diary	Avesnes	13/10/1918	17/10/1918
War Diary	Cambrai	18/10/1918	25/10/1918

War Diary	St. Aubert	26/10/1918	31/10/1918
Heading	War Diary H.Q. R.E. 24th Divn. November 1918 Vol 39		
Miscellaneous			
War Diary	In The Field	01/11/1918	30/11/1918
Heading	War Diary HQ. R.E. 24th Div Vol 40		
War Diary	In The Field	01/12/1918	31/01/1919
War Diary	Tournai	01/02/1919	31/03/1919
War Diary	Sin. (France)	01/04/1919	25/06/1919

24TH DIVISION
DIVL ENGINEERS

C. R. E.

AUG 1915-JUN 1919

Q

24th Division

121
7431

H.Q. 24th Division C.R.E.

Vol: I

Aug & Sept. 15

June '19

Instructions regarding War Diaries and Intelligence Summaries are contained in F. S. Regs., Part II. and the Staff Manual respectively. Title pages will be prepared in manuscript.

WAR DIARY

or

~~INTELLIGENCE SUMMARY.~~

(Erase heading not required.)

Army Form C. 2118.

H.Q. Divl. R.E XXIV Divn

Place	Date	Hour	Summary of Events and Information	Remarks and references to Appendices
BLACK-DOWN.	25/8/15	5 P.M.	Received Divisnl. order dated 25-8-15 that War Diaries shd be kept from 21-8-15, the date fixed as "first day of mobilization"	
"	26/8/15		Preparation for departure. Checking stores & equipment and returning surplus stores and those from "Trench Warfare" exercise on CHOBHAM COMMON	
"	27/8/15		Same as previous day. At 12.0 noon received instructions fixing time of departure for the several units of Divisnl. Engineers	
"	28/8/15		Same as previous days and closing ledgers & making up accounts.	
"	29/8/15		Same as previous day. The 103rd Fd Coy R.E. left Blackdown for SOUTHAMPTON, entraining at FARNBORO at 12.30 A.M. The 1st ½ Coy having left an hour earlier.	
"	30/8/15		Completed winding up accounts etc. H.Q. D.R.E. left FARNBORO 1.20 P.M. reaching SOUTHAMPTON at 3.10 P.M. and embarked on S.S. MT TEMPLE. The C.R.E being O.C. ship. Other troops on board ⅓ Div. Ammn. Coln. H.Q. 72nd Bde Signal Sectn & Train Co. Transport of	

Instructions regarding War Diaries and Intelligence Summaries are contained in F. S. Regs., Part II. and the Staff Manual respectively. Title pages will be prepared in manuscript.

WAR DIARY
or
~~INTELLIGENCE SUMMARY.~~
(Erase heading not required.)

H.Q. D.R.E XXIV Divn

Army Form C. 2118

Place	Date	Hour	Summary of Events and Information	Remarks and references to Appendices
	30/8/15	etc	9th EAST SURREYS. 8th BUFFS.	
		6.0 PM	Sailed from SOUTHAMPTON.	
HAVRE	31/8/15	9.0 AM	Arrived LE HAVRE. & received orders to disembark at 7.0 AM.	
		11.30 AM.	Disembarkn completed. Unit remained in docks	
		4.0 PM	Marched to station Pt 4 & commenced entraining	
		6.15 PM	Entraining completed. (C.R.E O.C Train other troops B. Baty 106th Bde R.F.A	
		8.0 PM.	Left LE HAVRE.	
	1/9/15	6.A.M	Reached ABBEVILLE where orders were recd to detrain at MONTREUIL	
MONTREUIL		10.30 AM	Detrained at MONTREUIL where " " " march to OFFIN	
		2.30 PM	Arrived at OFFIN where 103rd Fd Co had just arrived, & here went into Billets Hd Qrs R.E at the Chateau (propr Mr ~~[illegible]~~ FOURNIER. the Maire of OFFIN)	
OFFIN	2/9/15		Visited MARESQUEL & reported to H.Q. Group A.	
"	3/9/15		104th & 129th Fd Coys reach LOISON having detrained at HESDIN	
			Visited H.Q. 24th Divn & orders received 1 Cy R.E. Divl Pioneers and 1 Battn Infy to move to ST MICHEL ST LENOEUX & HOMBERT respectively	[illegible]

2353 Wt. W2544/1454 700,000 5/15 D. D. & L. A.D.S.S./Forms/C. 2118.

Instructions regarding War Diaries and Intelligence Summaries are contained in F. S. Regs., Part II. and the Staff Manual respectively. Title pages will be prepared in manuscript.

WAR DIARY
or
~~INTELLIGENCE SUMMARY~~.
(Erase heading not required.)

Army Form C. 2118

H.Q.D.R.E.
XXIV Divn

Place	Date	Hour	Summary of Events and Information	Remarks and references to Appendices
OFFINY	6.9/15	Contd	129th Fd Co Contd marking out wks on line. Dl Pioneers commenced digging in the afternoon.	
	7/9/15		Inspected line. 129th Fd Co & Divl Pioneers (800 men) working. Adjt made arrangements at BEAURAINVILLE for storage of material for defences consigned by order of E in C.	
	8/9/15		Met Col EDMONDS at SEMPY Mill. inspected line with him & O.C. 129th Fd Co & received instns to get out scheme of defence of hamlet of St WANDRILLE.	
	9/9/15		Met M. L. SCRIBOT at BOIS DES AGACHES drew up agreement & gave orders to Capt. WHITTALL R.E. 129th Fd Co R.E. that the 12 "portions" on the North East end of the wood were to be cut forthwith. O.C. 104th Fd Co preparing defensive scheme for St WANDRILLE.	[illegible]

2353 Wt. W2544/1454 700,000 5/15 D. D. & L. A.D.S.S./Forms/C. 2118.

Instructions regarding War Diaries and Intelligence Summaries are contained in F. S. Regs., Part II. and the Staff Manual respectively. Title pages will be prepared in manuscript.

WAR DIARY
or
~~INTELLIGENCE SUMMARY.~~
(Erase heading not required.)

Army Form C. 2118

H·Q·D·R·E
XXIV Divn

Place	Date	Hour	Summary of Events and Information	Remarks and references to Appendices
	10/9/15		Attending lecture on use of Gas protection helmets at ROYON, thence with O.C. 104th to St WANDRILLE position	
	11/9/15		Divisional field day. 103rd & 104th Cos taking part in operations. afterwards met Col EDMONDS and accompanied him on inspection of defensive position	
	12/9/15		Sunday	
	13/9/15		Met E in C XI Corps who inspected 104th & 129th at work on St WANDRILLE CHAUSSEE BRUNEHAUT line. 104th Fd Co having marched out from LOISON to lay out ~~defensive~~ defences of St WANDRILLE where they are bivouacking for the night.	
	14/9/15		Divisl. Field Day. Stopped by bad weather.	
	15/9/15		Visited defence line around BAILLEUL with 2 officers from each Coy. under guidance of Br. Gen HEATH.	
	16/9/15		Col EDMONDS inspected CHAUSSEE BRUNEHAUT line	[signature] Lt Col

OFF17

Army Form C. 2118

Instructions regarding War Diaries and Intelligence Summaries are contained in F. S. Regs., Part II. and the Staff Manual respectively. Title pages will be prepared in manuscript.

WAR DIARY

or

~~INTELLIGENCE SUMMARY.~~

(Erase heading not required.)

Place	Date	Hour	Summary of Events and Information	Remarks and references to Appendices
OFFIN	17/9/15		Inspected stores at BEAURAINVILLE and visited 129th Co. at St MICHEL	
			Received orders to stop work on CHAUSSEE-BRUNEHAUT line	
"	18/9/15		Visited G.H.Q. saw E in C, Col HARVEY & S.W.O. on return journey inspected French back line under construction.	
	19/9/15		Visited the front S of LA BASSEE with the G.O.C., G1 & Brigadiers	
"	20/9/15		103rd Fd Co moved to Pt St MICHEL, 129th to LEBIEZ, 104th to St MICHEL	
			Attended Conference at Div H.Q. details of proposed move explained and discussed. Orders received to march on night of 21st 10.30 P.M.	
"			Ordered to send "Pontoon Sections" of ~~?~~ all Fd Cos together by separate route. Wrote explaining that such sections did not exist & pointing out difficulties in organizing a divisl bridging train at	
"			such short notice with companies so scattered.	
"	21/9/15		Arranged with G.S.1 that the pontoon wagons of 104th & 103rd each accompanied by one section should join 129th for the march until concentration was completed.	[illegible]

2353 Wt. W2544/1454 700,000 5/15 D. D. & L. A.D.S.S./Forms/C. 2118.

Instructions regarding War Diaries and Intelligence Summaries are contained in F. S. Regs., Part II. and the Staff Manual respectively. Title pages will be prepared in manuscript.

WAR DIARY
or
~~INTELLIGENCE SUMMARY.~~
(Erase heading not required.)

Army Form C. 2118.

Place	Date	Hour	Summary of Events and Information	Remarks and references to Appendices
	~~22 9/15~~ 21 9/15		H.Q marched at 3.0 P.M. from OFFIN to LEBIEZ, left LEBIEZ at 5.30 P.M. C.R.E. in command of Divisl. H.Q.	
BOMY	22 9/15	12.30 A.M.	Reached BOMY, billeted there.	
		6. P.M	Marched from BOMY in command of Divisl. H.Q.	
	23 9/15	3. AM	Reached BUSNES, billeted there. Visited R.E. park BERGUETTE arranged to draw 13000 sand bags and 300 detonators Electric No 13. Visited the Fd Coys. 103rd at HAM-EN-ARTOIS 104th at ISBERGUES ~~BERGUETTE~~. 129th LA MIQUELLERIE.	
BUSNES	24 9/15		Visited BERGUETTE: ascertained stores ordered previous day had been sent by some error to the sub park. By XI corps order a lorry load of scantlings for bridging was sent to BUSNES also one G.S. wagon per Co to carry this material. One wagon sent by D.A.C. arrived loaded with explosives which had to be left in charge of Mayor of BUSNES. Wagons loaded with timber & distributed to Coys. Attended conference by corps commander at LILLERS. details of proposed attack explained.	[illegible]

2353 Wt. W2544/1454 700,000 5/15 D. D. & L. A.D.S.S./Forms/C. 2118

Army Form C. 2118

Instructions regarding War Diaries and Intelligence Summaries are contained in F. S. Regs., Part II. and the Staff Manual respectively. Title pages will be prepared in manuscript.

WAR DIARY
or
~~INTELLIGENCE SUMMARY.~~
(Erase heading not required.)

Place	Date	Hour	Summary of Events and Information	Remarks and references to Appendices
	24/9/15		Contin^d	
BETHUNE		6.30 P.M.	Left BUSNES, marched to BETHUNE in command of Divis^l H.Q. arrived 11.0 P.M. Billeted at BETHUNE	
	~~25~~ 25/9/15	11.0AM	Received orders to march forward to new Divis^l H.Q. at LE RUTOIRE Farm. Column was halted ~~#~~ W. of VERMELLES for several hours. Reached LE RUTOIRE 10.0 P.M. found it full of wounded & was told that Div^l H.Q. was at VERMELLES Field Coys had all been ordered to remain at cross r^ds near LE RUTOIRE. Road from VERMELLES to cross r^ds much congested with transport. Returned to VERMELLES and reported at Div^l H.Q	
VERMELLES	26/9/15	1.0AM.	~~R~~ Sent with D.A.A. & Q.M.G. & Adj^t R.E. to clear block on r^d as far as possible and reduce chance of losses by shell fire in day light by sending back all unessential transport of the division all entrenching tools & ~~[illegible]~~ S.A.A. not carried in limbered wagons to be dumped by roadside. Experienced great difficulty in getting transport back owing to artillery coming up at the time & consequent congestion especially at the bridges over the trenches.	[illegible signature]

2353 Wt. W2544/1454 700,000 5/15 D. D. & L. A.D.S.S./Forms/C. 2118.

Instructions regarding War Diaries and Intelligence Summaries are contained in F. S. Regs., Part II. and the Staff Manual respectively. Title pages will be prepared in manuscript.

WAR DIARY

or

~~INTELLIGENCE SUMMARY.~~

(Erase heading not required.)

Army Form C. 2118.

Place	Date	Hour	Summary of Events and Information	Remarks and references to Appendices
	26 cont'd.		During the night 25-26 a few shells fell in VERMELLES.	
		12 noon	OC 104 ordered to push forward behind 72nd Bde & assist in consolidating any positions won	
			OC 129th Coy ordered to continue repairs & improvements to road	
		1.30pm	Orders sent by Div HQ for 129th Fd Co to man trenches at cross roads near Le RUTOIRE	
		3pm	Received orders to arrange for collecting & feeding of stragglers of Infantry Battns to organise them under Infantry Reserve officers & send them into the firing line	
			Commenced doing so ~~cancelling~~ above (APM to look after stragglers) & then	
VERMELLES		7 pm	Received orders that 103 + 129th Fd Cos were to move forward at once into advanced line & assist in making good & holding trenches – OC 129th Coy had been given orders direct	
			Proceeded to bivouac of 103rd Fd Co who had been moved back ~~[illegible]~~ about 2 miles West of VERMELLES – they had had no food for 36 hours; was able to obtain some from cookers left behind by Infantry – then marched off with them but was stopped at VERMELLES & ordered back with the Company to bivouac	[illegible]

2353 Wt. W2544/1454 700,000 5/15 D. D. & L. A.D.S.S./Forms/C. 2118.

Army Form C. 2118.

Instructions regarding War Diaries and Intelligence Summaries are contained in F. S. Regs., Part II. and the Staff Manual respectively. Title pages will be prepared in manuscript.

WAR DIARY
or
INTELLIGENCE SUMMARY.

(Erase heading not required.)

Place	Date	Hour	Summary of Events and Information	Remarks and references to Appendices
			near FOSSE at ANNEQUIN on the VERMELLES-BETHUNE Road	
	27	2 am	Reached bivouac named above – 104th & 129th arrived later –	
			Reason for return was that the Div[n] had been relieved in the trenches by the Guards Brigade –	
SAILLY-LA BOURSE.			104th reported 2 Sappers wounded 2 missing –	
	28	10 am	Changed billets to point just S of ~~Sailly~~ SAILLY LA BOURSE	
		6 pm	Received orders that dismounted men were to proceed by train to unknown destination – O.C. to command mounted troops & transport leaving at 8 p.m.	
		8 pm	Marched off – Units of mounted Column did not assemble in proper time or order (owing to short notice) Heavy rain all march	
			Reached ANNEZIN ~~no~~ proper billeting arrangements had been made	
	29	2 am		
		12 noon	Marched off – (Unable to start before owing to roads being blocked by other Divisions	
		6 pm	Reached ST. HILAIRE	

2353 Wt. W2544/1454 700,000 5/15 D. D. & L. A.D.S.S./Forms/C. 2118.

Army Form C. 2118.

Instructions regarding War Diaries and Intelligence Summaries are contained in F. S. Regs., Part II. and the Staff Manual respectively. Title pages will be prepared in manuscript.

WAR DIARY
or
INTELLIGENCE SUMMARY.
(Erase heading not required.)

Place	Date	Hour	Summary of Events and Information	Remarks and references to Appendices
7	30		Visited 103rd Co. at HAM-EN-ARTOIS, 104 at MOLINGHEM & 129 at MAZINGHEM.	
St. HILAIRE				
			[illegible] Lt Col RE CRE. 24th Div.	

2353 Wt. W2544/1454 700,000 5/15 D. D. & L. A.D.S.S./Forms/C. 2118.

121/7608

H.Q. 24th Div: CRE.

Vol 2

Oct. 15

H. Q. R.E. 24th Divn.

Oct. 1915

Army Form C. 2118.

Instructions regarding War Diaries and Intelligence Summaries are contained in F. S. Regs., Part II. and the Staff Manual respectively. Title pages will be prepared in manuscript.

WAR DIARY
or
INTELLIGENCE SUMMARY.
(Erase heading not required.)

Place	Date	Hour	Summary of Events and Information	Remarks and references to Appendices
	1/10	10 am	Dismounted portion ~~Entrained~~ entrained ST. HILHAIRE – MOUNTED TROOPS & Transport by road to WALLON CAPPEL. ~~Billeted there~~	
		5 pm	~~billet~~ Arrived WALLON CAPPEL billeted there	
	2/10	~~9 a~~ 10 am	Left WALLON CAPPEL.	
		1 pm	Arrived STEENVOORDE billeted there – Dismounted men arrived by train & billeted in neighbourhood –	
	3/10	–	Maj Gen Capper CB took over Command of Division – which now transferred to 5th Corps – (II Army) – Went to RENNINGHELST to see CRE 17th Div, which division we are to replace in the trenches – Obtained information & visited locality ~~in~~	
	4/10		Accompanied GOC on his inspection of units of Div –	
	5/10		Spent day ~~visit~~ with CRE 17th Div – Went over portion of front to be taken over, with Maj Fleming RE & GSO2 17th Div.	
			Division moved to RENNINGHELST.	
			104th Fd Co moved to RENNINGHELST – 103rd to POPERINGHE – ~~[illegible]~~	[initials]

2353 Wt. W2544/1454 700,000 5/15 D. D. & L. A.D.S.S./Forms/C. 2118.

Instructions regarding War Diaries and Intelligence Summaries are contained in F. S. Regs., Part II. and the Staff Manual respectively. Title pages will be prepared in manuscript.

WAR DIARY
or
INTELLIGENCE SUMMARY.
(*Erase heading not required.*)

Army Form C. 2118.

Place	Date	Hour	Summary of Events and Information	Remarks and references to Appendices
	6/10		103rd moved to RENNINGHELST & attached to 3rd Div for training 104th attached to 43rd Bde for training – & 129 to 6th Div & E of POPPERINGHE. Took over Stores & Workshops previously ~~[illegible]~~ run by 17th Div.	
	7/10		Visited C.E. at ABEELE & also II Army workshops & stores at same place	
	8/10		Visited 129th Coy at POPERINGHE & accompanied G.O.C. round defences.	
	9/10		Routine work	
	10/10		M. Lantzius Belgian Interpreter reported for duty Inspected left sector of defences with G.S.1	

2353 Wt. W2544/1454 700,000 5/15 D. D. & L. A.D.S.S./Forms/C. 2118.

Instructions regarding War Diaries and Intelligence Summaries are contained in F. S. Regs., Part II. and the Staff Manual respectively. Title pages will be prepared in manuscript.

WAR DIARY
or
~~INTELLIGENCE SUMMARY.~~
(Erase heading not required.)

Army Form C. 2118.

Place	Date	Hour	Summary of Events and Information	Remarks and references to Appendices
	11th		Setting out scheme for hutting	
	12th		Inspection of G.H.Q. 2 & Priority wks	
	13th		visited defences of VOORMEZEELE with General JELF. 103rd Fd Co moved to same camp as 104th	
	14th		104th & 129 Fd Coys took over Right & Centre sectors of front respectively. 73rd I. Bde relieved 43rd Bde on these sectors during night 14th–15th.	
	15th	4.0 AM.	Enemy exploded large mine in left sector of defence N. of old crater in trench 29. Charge estimated at 3000 lbs. Considerable portion of trench filled in & much damage done. Casualties 50	
		12.0 noon	103rd Fd Co took over from 56th Co R.E., and during the night 15th–16th 72nd Bde relieved 1 Bde of 9th Division	
	16th	1.0 A.M.	Party of R.E. under Lt R.A.B. Smith put out wire entanglements	

2353 Wt. W2544/1454 700,000 5/15 D. D. & L. A.D.S.S./Forms/C.2118.

Army Form C. 2118.

Instructions regarding War Diaries and Intelligence Summaries are contained in F. S. Regs., Part II. and the Staff Manual respectively. Title pages will be prepared in manuscript.

WAR DIARY
or
~~INTELLIGENCE SUMMARY.~~
(Erase heading not required.)

Place	Date	Hour	Summary of Events and Information	Remarks and references to Appendices
			~~Rom~~ outside crater under heavy fire but without casualties. Party under Lt. J. Allen preparing & clearing portion of fire and support trench as well as communication trenches. Work was continued as far as possible during the day time	
	16th		C.R.E. visited II Army workshops HAZEBROUCK to draw periscopes urgently required.	
	17th		One section (No 2) 103rd Fd Co ordered to assist in mining operations on left sector as Bde mining section found to be too inexperienced. Work of repair of damaged portion of that sector continued. C.R.E. reconnoitred tramway location in R & Centre sectors with O.C. 129th & 104th Cos also part of G.H.Q. 2.	
	18th		Captn LOGAN put in charge of Hutting.	
	19th		17th Bde relieved 72nd Bde on left sector. 72nd Bde took over centre sector & 73rd Right sector went with G.O.C round G.H.Q 2 line & wk. "H. D."	

2353 Wt. W2544/1454 700,000 5/15 D. D. & L. A.D.S.S./Forms/C. 2118.

Army Form C. 2118.

Instructions regarding War Diaries and Intelligence Summaries are contained in F. S. Regs., Part II. and the Staff Manual respectively. Title pages will be prepared in manuscript.

WAR DIARY
or
~~INTELLIGENCE SUMMARY.~~
(Erase heading not required.)

Place	Date	Hour	Summary of Events and Information	Remarks and references to Appendices
	20		Went round left sector with G.O.C. 103rd Co doing good work but much remains to be done on this part of the line. Draft arrived of 5 men to 103rd, 7 to 104th, 13 to 129th	
	21		Office work + went round camps of West Kent Regt, East Surrey Pioneers, London Regt + 106 Bde RFA Amn Col re hutting	
	22		Inspected Camps with G.O.C. 24th Divn	
	23		Hutting & searching for site for rifle range	
	24		ABEELE POPERINGHE. VLAMERTINGHE. with Capt WHITTALL RE about stores. Arranged purchase of 500000 bricks. we to provide the coal. Inspected wood to be purchased for spars. Attended demonstration by Lt MARTIN RE of Jack pushed mining tools	

2353 Wt. W2544/1454 700,000 5/15 D. D. & L. A.D.S.S./Forms/C. 2118.

Army Form C. 2118

Instructions regarding War Diaries and Intelligence Summaries are contained in F. S. Regs., Part II. and the Staff Manual respectively. Title pages will be prepared in manuscript.

WAR DIARY
or
~~INTELLIGENCE~~ SUMMARY.

(*Erase heading not required.*)

Place	Date	Hour	Summary of Events and Information	Remarks and references to Appendices
RENINGHELST	OCT 25		Made arrangements for parade ground for his Majesty the Kings visit. Enemy blew mine opposite T1. 30 ft of our gallery damaged. 3 men buried no serious injuries	
	26		went into details of organisation of Brigade mining section & mining generally	
	27		His Majesty the King visited RENINGHELST.	
	28		Inspecting camps. Demonstration of BARRET borer by 2 Lt MARTIN. R.E. The experiment promises well though on this occasion not entirely successfull. The communication trench blown, very good. but the head of the pipe came out of the ground before reaching the enemy's parapet. this was through lack of the proper head, and bad coupling up of pipes.	

Instructions regarding War Diaries and Intelligence Summaries are contained in F. S. Regs., Part II. and the Staff Manual respectively. Title pages will be prepared in manuscript.

WAR DIARY
or
INTELLIGENCE SUMMARY.
(Erase heading not required.)

Army Form C. 2118.

Place	Date	Hour	Summary of Events and Information	Remarks and references to Appendices
REMINGHELST	Oct. 29		Settling alignment of tramway of central sector	
	30		Orders received that O.C. Tunnelling Co. was responsible for all mining operations, brigade sections abolished. 240 infantry to be supplied to each tunnelling company by the divisions on whose front they work. These men to be seconded & eventually transferred to tunnelling co. if found suitable.	
			Issued orders for Lt. ALLEN of 2 section 103rd Fd Co who had been in the trenches for mining work for 18 days to return to rest billets.	
	31		Water Board meeting V Corps	
			Conference at D.H.Q. on Defence Scheme	

1/11/15

Lt. COL. R.E.
C. R. E. 24th DIV.

2353 Wt. W2544/1454 700,000 5/15 D. D. & L. A.D.S.S./Forms/C. 2118.

24th Division

H.Q. 24th Div:
CRE.

Vol 3

121
7624

Nov. 15.

Army Form C. 2118.

WAR DIARY
or
~~INTELLIGENCE SUMMARY~~.
(Erase heading not required.)

Instructions regarding War Diaries and Intelligence Summaries are contained in F. S. Regs., Part II. and the Staff Manual respectively. Title pages will be prepared in manuscript.

Place	Date	Hour	Summary of Events and Information	Remarks and references to Appendices
RENINGHELST	NOV 1		Inspecting Central sector with O.C. 129th Fd. Co. arranging details of work IE (SEPTEMBER POST)	
	2		Inspecting G.H.Q 2 Line. C.E. visited RENINGHELST	
	3		visited R.A. Camps with C.R.A. and decided as to requirements & order of urgency there of. Heavy rain during last few days has done great damage to the trenches which are in places untenable	
	4		Visited trenches in right sector. damage by rain very great, due to difficulties of drainage, borrow pits too near parapets and in many cases to poor work & lack of maintenance, sandbagging especially was	
	[illegible]		indifferent; VOORMEZEELE Switch is sited too near to BOLLAARDT BEEK	
	5		Second experiment by 2nd Lt. MARTIN R.E. with BARRET JACK borer which was pushed successfully under barbed wire, but experimenter had apparently not carefully taken measurements & the explosion only	

2353 Wt. W2541/1454 700,000 5/15 D. D. & L. A.D.S.S./Forms/C. 2118.

Army Form C. 2118

WAR DIARY
or
INTELLIGENCE SUMMARY.
(Erase heading not required.)

Instructions regarding War Diaries and Intelligence Summaries are contained in F. S. Regs., Part II. and the Staff Manual respectively. Title pages will be prepared in manuscript.

Place	Date	Hour	Summary of Events and Information	Remarks and references to Appendices
RENINGHELST.	Nov.		affected a few feet of the obstacle. A demonstration was also given of boring through our own parapet & along surface of the ground to enemy's entanglement, crossing a 30 ft. gap without losing direction	
	6		accompanied G.S.1 & Lt. KENT of Specialists Co. R.E. GAS. round left & centre sectors of line & discussed possibilities of use of gas. In the present state of the trenches it would be impracticable to make any excavation in the toe of the parapet to take the cylinders. The centre sector of the line was in an specially bad state. in some places the parapet was practically non existent & one had to clamber across in the open. Enemy's trenches appear to be similarly affected & neither side was doing much sniping	

2353 Wt. W2544/1454 700,000 5/15 D. D. & L. A.D.S.S./Forms/C. 2118.

Instructions regarding War Diaries and Intelligence Summaries are contained in F. S. Regs., Part II. and the Staff Manual respectively. Title pages will be prepared in manuscript.

WAR DIARY

or

~~INTELLIGENCE SUMMARY.~~

(*Erase heading not required.*)

Army Form C. 2118.

Place	Date	Hour	Summary of Events and Information	Remarks and references to Appendices
RENINGHELST	7		Visiting Huts & selecting sites with Capt. LOGAN R.E.	
	8		With G.O.C. to VOORMEZEELE he decided not to alter the trace of I.E. (September Post) but to provide machine guns on flanks & to put the old French trench into working order so as to form an intermediate line from the canal opposite LANKHOF Chateau to V4. Inspected V.E Switch & defences of V-E which G.O.C. approved.	
	9.		~~Nothing exceptional to report~~ except Lts HIBBERT & BRISCO entered & investigated enemys gallery opposite Trench 33. shot one German, & then blew in enemys mine	
	10.		With G.S.O. 3 round strongpoints & arranging details to be carried out under his supervision at ROSENHILL & KRUIS(S)TRAAT HOEK. The latter was being considerably shelled & many of the latter being blind.	
	11		To Corps H.Q. to see about cutting timber in 6th Corps Area. Visited RE Park & wkshops ABEELE & saw trial of smoke bombs made after Canadian design. Manufacture easy but requires some organization & plant.	

Army Form C. 2118.

Instructions regarding War Diaries and Intelligence Summaries are contained in F. S. Regs., Part II. and the Staff Manual respectively. Title pages will be prepared in manuscript.

WAR DIARY
or
~~INTELLIGENCE SUMMARY.~~
(Erase heading not required.)

Place	Date	Hour	Summary of Events and Information	Remarks and references to Appendices
	11		Bombs difficult to ignite & cylinder very liable to burst. This leads to the mixture bursting into flame instead of producing smoke. Casing too flimsy & thin. 2nd Army P.K. are undertaking production on a large scale & will no doubt improve pattern.	
	12		Round camps with G.O.C. : more rain	
	13		Routine work.	
	14		Attended Water Board, representatives of all divisions of 5th Corps present. Meeting also discussed roads. Owing to difficulties in obtaining materials repairs have been delayed & it has become necessary to limit the direction of traffic on many roads to avoid ~~crossings~~ passing*. Extra police will be required to enforce regulations when published by the army. Als * vehicles having to go off the pavé on to the muddy sides	

Army Form C. 2118.

Instructions regarding War Diaries and Intelligence Summaries are contained in F. S. Regs., Part II. and the Staff Manual respectively. Title pages will be prepared in manuscript.

WAR DIARY

or

~~INTELLIGENCE SUMMARY.~~

(*Erase heading not required.*)

Place	Date	Hour	Summary of Events and Information	Remarks and references to Appendices
RENINGHELST.	15		Inspected trenches 32–35 recently taken over from 9th Divn. Owing to configuration of the ground the recent rains have not damaged them so much as our other trenches. Excellent work being done by 1st Fusiliers. Heavy shelling of one of our forward batteries in I 25 d two emplacements appearing to have had direct hits. Visited work at LA CHAPELLE. Drainage requires attention. ~~Good~~ machine guns & shelters could be put in the ~~far~~ farm itself.	
	16		Conference with B.G. 72nd Inf Bde as to modification of Trench line needed owing to apparent impossibility of keeping present line in repair, also as to sites for M.G. in support of present line and as to difficulties in connection with finding working parties, the ~~impression~~ supervision of which by young infantry officers & N.C.O.S. of the New Army is far from satisfactory. There seems to be an idea that it is the R.E. N.C.O.S. & Sappers job to do this.	

2353 Wt. W2544/1454 700,000 5/15 D. D. & L. A.D.S.S./Forms/C. 2118.

Army Form C. 2118.

Instructions regarding War Diaries and Intelligence Summaries are contained in F. S. Regs., Part II. and the Staff Manual respectively. Title pages will be prepared in manuscript.

WAR DIARY
or
~~INTELLIGENCE SUMMARY.~~
(*Erase heading not required.*)

Place	Date	Hour	Summary of Events and Information	Remarks and references to Appendices
RENINGHELST	17		Inspected L sector of R section with O.C. 129th. Arrangements for providing working parties leave much to be desired. Parties turn up very late & not in full numbers. Trenches in many places thigh deep in mud. Much could be done to ~~xxx~~ prevent trenches getting into such a bad state by a little care & attention on the part of the garrison in keeping them drained. Orders received that division goes into Army Reserve being relieved by 3rd Division between 20th & 25th inst.	
	18.		Conference with G.O.C. & Brigadiers on recommendations to be submitted to 3rd Division for steps to be taken to modify defences so as to enable line to be held by reduced numbers during winter. Visit C.R.E. 3rd Divn to discuss handing over.	
	19.		103rd Fd Co. Withdrawn from line	
	20.		C.R.E. 3rd Division came here ~~x~~ to discuss engineering questions in connection with this section. 103rd Fd Co marched with Composite Brigade to EEKE on being relieved by Fd Co of 3rd Division	

2353 Wt. W2544/1454 700,000 5/15 D. D. & L. A.D.S.S./Forms/C. 2118.

Army Form C. 2118.

Instructions regarding War Diaries and Intelligence Summaries are contained in F. S. Regs., Part II. and the Staff Manual respectively. Title pages will be prepared in manuscript.

WAR DIARY
or
~~INTELLIGENCE SUMMARY.~~
(Erase heading not required.)

Place	Date	Hour	Summary of Events and Information	Remarks and references to Appendices
RENINGHELST	21		Winding up. 129th withdrew sections from front line	
"	22		~~Handed over to C.R.E.~~ 3rd Division. Left RENINGHELST and Proceeded by road via POPERINGHE and ABEELE to STEENVOORDE.	
STEENVOORDE	23		Left STEENVOORDE and marched to BROXEELE via ~~S~~ CASSEL. 103rd arrived at TILQUES	
BROXEELE	24		Left BROXEELE & marched to ~~S~~ TILQUES but no suitable billets being available went on to SALPERWICK.	
SALPERWICK	25		~~Ha~~ Visited G.H.Q. reported to E in C & arranged with S.W.O. for stores for training 103rd moved to MONNECOVE 129th arrived at TILQUES	
"	26		~~B~~ Visited Companies. 104th arrived at MOULE.	

2353 Wt. W2544/1454 700,000 5/15 D. D. & L. A.D.S.S./Forms/C. 2118.

Army Form C. 2118

Instructions regarding War Diaries and Intelligence Summaries are contained in F. S. Regs., Part II. and the Staff Manual respectively. Title pages will be prepared in manuscript.

WAR DIARY
or
~~INTELLIGENCE SUMMARY.~~

(Erase heading not required.)

Place	Date	Hour	Summary of Events and Information	Remarks and references to Appendices
SALPERWICK	27		Making arrangements in connection with Divisional Technical School.	
			104th moved from MOULE to find billets at GUEMY.	
"	28		To St OMER making enquiries as to local resources	
"	29		Visited Companies	
		2.0 pm.	Lecture to Technical school on trenches	
		7.30	Dined with G.O.C.	
	30.		Visited by Secretary R.E. Comee & I.R.E.S. went round Companies with them, discussed modifications to vehicles & question of technical equipment. Interview with D.D.R. re obtaining material etc from ~~AUDRUICQ~~ AUDRUICQ.	

[signature]
Lt. COL. R.E.
C. R. E. 24th DIV.

30 NOV 1915

2353 Wt. W2544/1454 700,000 5/15 D. D. & L. A.D.S.S./Forms/C. 2118.

Instructions regarding War Diaries and Intelligence Summaries are contained in F. S. Regs., Part II. and the Staff Manual respectively. Title pages will be prepared in manuscript.

WAR DIARY
or
~~INTELLIGENCE SUMMARY.~~
(*Erase heading not required.*)

Secret

Army Form C. 2118

Place	Date	Hour	Summary of Events and Information	Remarks and references to Appendices
SALPERWICK	DECEMBER 1		TO BOULOGNE ~~to interview~~ to interview French Officer in charge of Forests with a view to obtaining permission to cut in state woods. Arranged for cutting in FORET DE TOURNEHEM. Also purchasing stores for Training	
"	2		to AUDRUICQ where O/c Railway Stores agreed to supply limited amount of material & tools for 24 Division	
"	3			
"	4		To G.H.Q to see Col. EDMONDS To Gas Training depot at HELFAUT. Inspecting bridges on S.T OMER - CLAIRMARAIS Rd. and found traffic has shaken the abutments in two cases	
"	5		Routine wk.	
"	6		To VLAMERTINGHE to enquire into arrangements made by C.R.E. 14th Division in view of possibility of 24th Division taking over from 14th. Major KING returned from leave	C/R

Army Form C. 2118.

WAR DIARY
or
~~INTELLIGENCE SUMMARY.~~
(Erase heading not required.)

Instructions regarding War Diaries and Intelligence Summaries are contained in F. S. Regs., Part II. and the Staff Manual respectively. Title pages will be prepared in manuscript.

Place	Date	Hour	Summary of Events and Information	Remarks and references to Appendices
SALPERWICK	Decr 7		Lt. Col. CRAVEN R.E. went on leave. Major KING R.E. took over duties of C.R.E.	
			To 129th Fd Co RE	
			To St. OMER to arrange re pickets in TOURNEHEM forest. Detonators etc for grenade school.	
			GUEMY to 104th Fd Co.	
"	8		Saw G.O.C. Motored to 103rd Fd Co R.E. 17th & 72nd Inf. Bdes., D.A.C. & G.O.C.R.A. re horse standings	
			To SETQUES & arranged for a few loads of ashes for D.A.C.	
"	9		Saw G.O.C. Motored to BLEU MAISON to report on condition of Road which was badly cut up by lorries. Arranged with C.E. G.H.Q., C.E. 2nd Army and Col. LIDDELL for Engineer PONTS et CHAUSSEES to repair	
"	10		Saw G.O.C. lectured to Technical School.	[initials]

2353 Wt. W2514/1454 700,000 5/15 D. D. & L. A.D.S.S./Forms/C. 2118.

Army Form C. 2118.

Instructions regarding War Diaries and Intelligence Summaries are contained in F. S. Regs., Part II. and the Staff Manual respectively. Title pages will be prepared in manuscript.

WAR DIARY

or

~~INTELLIGENCE SUMMARY.~~

(Erase heading not required.)

Place	Date	Hour	Summary of Events and Information	Remarks and references to Appendices
SALPERWICK	Dec 11		With G.S.O.2 to inspect Technical Schools of 6th 14th 49th Division. Looked at proposed H.Q. for 24th Division in the anticipated sector of front. Attended conference at H.Q. 6th Corps.	
"	12		Saw G.O.C. To AUDRUICQ to arrange for each Fd Co to construct a portable wooden hut on the principle of the "HUMPHREYS". To NAUDAUSQUES to inspect mules of 103rd & 104th prior to handing over to 3rd Division in exchange for L.D. Horses.	
"	13		With G.O.C, inspecting bad road near MAISON BLEU. Some larger metal has been put down and also straw but road is still unsatisfactory for heavy M.T. Thence to see infantry Co attack trenches near TOURNEHEM. Then to St. OMER. with G.O.C. for electric stores for Cinema.	
"	14		With G.O.C. to Gas demonstration near RECQUES Thence to AUDRUICQ to see progress with portable huts.	AH

2353 Wt. W2544/1454 700,000 5/15 D. D. & L. A.D.S.S./Forms/C. 2118.

Army Form C. 2118

WAR DIARY
or
~~INTELLIGENCE SUMMARY.~~
(*Erase heading not required.*)

Instructions regarding War Diaries and Intelligence Summaries are contained in F. S. Regs., Part II. and the Staff Manual respectively. Title pages will be prepared in manuscript.

Place	Date	Hour	Summary of Events and Information	Remarks and references to Appendices
	Decr			
SALPERWICK	14		Lt Col A.T. CRAVEN returned from leave and resumed duty as C.R.E.	
"	15		To a lecture on machine guns at NAUDAUSQUES inspected wk of 104th Co	
"	16		Routine wk and inspecting 129th Fd Co	
"	17		Visited 103rd Fd Co and parties working at ARDRUICQ	
"	18		Inspected work at Technical School.	
"	19		G.H.Q. to arrange for supply of signalling discs	
ELVERDINGHE	20		To new area (49th Div) went round defences up to canal bank, unable to proceed further owing to shelling.	
do	21		Went round portion of "C" line with C.R.E (49th) and discussed work of section generally. Visited field Co camps and divisl workshops. Returned to SALPERWICK.	

2353 Wt. W2544/1454 700,000 5/15 D. D. & L. A.D.S.S./Forms/C. 2118.

Army Form C. 2118

Instructions regarding War Diaries and Intelligence Summaries are contained in F. S. Regs., Part II. and the Staff Manual respectively. Title pages will be prepared in manuscript.

WAR DIARY
or
~~INTELLIGENCE SUMMARY.~~
(Erase heading not required.)

Place	Date	Hour	Summary of Events and Information	Remarks and references to Appendices
SALPERWICK	Dec. 15 22		Visited Field Companies. Received verbal orders as to move which would commence on 26th	
"	23		Routine work.	
"	24		Visited H.Q. 49th Divn "Q" Branch and 6th Corps R.E. Park & also Corps workshops at POPERINGHE. Visited C.E. 6th Corps who was on leave, but obtained information on system of work in Corps from his S.O.	
"	25.		Recieved operation orders regarding move to 49th Divisional area. Conference of O.C.s, Fd Cos to explain details of move at 11.0 P.M received message that all orders for move were cancelled & communicated this to Companies	
"	26		Visited Technical School and 129th Fd Co	
"	27.		orders received that Division would relieve 17th Divn	
"	28		visited 103, 104 & 129th and H.Q. 72nd Bde	
RENINGHELST	29		To RENINGHELST to confer with C.R.E. 17th Divn visited R.E. Parks, campsite in new area. Saw C.E. V corps	

2353 Wt. W2544/1454 700,000 5/15 D. D. & L. A.D.S.S./Forms/C. 2118.

Instructions regarding War Diaries and Intelligence Summaries are contained in F. S. Regs., Part II. and the Staff Manual respectively. Title pages will be prepared in manuscript.

Army Form C. 2118.

WAR DIARY

or

~~INTELLIGENCE SUMMARY.~~

(*Erase heading not required.*)

Place	Date	Hour	Summary of Events and Information	Remarks and references to Appendices
	Dec.	15.		
RENINGHELST	30		at RENINGHELST. visited front line with C.R.E. 17th Divn returned SALPERWICK	
SALPERWICK	31		Explained details of move to O.C. Coys and gave them information obtained during visit to new area	
			Orders for move altered – departure of all RE. postponed to 3rd (mounted party were to have gone by road on 1st) dismounted by bus on 3rd	
			[signature] Lt. Col. R.E. C.R.E. 24th Div. 31/12/15	

2353 Wt. W2544/1454 700,000 5/15 D. D. & L. A.D.S.S./Forms/C. 2118.

C.R.E. 24th Div.
Vol. 5
Jan. '16 –

C.R.E. 24th Div:

Vol: 6

Instructions regarding War Diaries and Intelligence Summaries are contained in F. S. Regs., Part II. and the Staff Manual respectively. Title pages will be prepared in manuscript.

WAR DIARY
or
~~INTELLIGENCE SUMMARY~~.
(*Erase heading not required.*)

Army Form C. 2118.

Place	Date	Hour	Summary of Events and Information	Remarks and references to Appendices
SALPER-WICK	1/1		Routine work & arrangements for move – Received orders for move	
"	2/1		Issue orders for move of Div RE – Lt Wallace RAMC proceeded on leave – temporarily replaced by Lt Knight RAMC 1 officer 7 OR of RE of 17th Division arrived to take over from 29th Div Fd Companies –	
"	3/1		Dismounted portions of 70 Cos by bus to RENINGHELST & 3 sections of each Coy billeted in YPRES. Mounted portion by road (in 3 marches) to RENINGHELST Adjutant accompanied former party – Med Officer the latter.	
"	4/1		Settling bills &c Field Coy in trenches with 17th Div. RE.	
"	5/1		With GOC. to CLAIRMARAIS to see Pensions making hurdles & duckwalks in forest – Progress fair	
RENING-HELST	6		RE. HQ by march to RENINGHELST (in 2 days) CRE by motor Rritter – took over from CRE 17th Div	

2353 Wt. W2544/1454 700,000 5/15 D. D. & L. A.D.S.S./Forms/C. 2118.

Instructions regarding War Diaries and Intelligence Summaries are contained in F. S. Regs., Part II. and the Staff Manual respectively. Title pages will be prepared in manuscript.

WAR DIARY
or
INTELLIGENCE SUMMARY.
(Erase heading not required.)

Army Form C. 2118.

Place	Date	Hour	Summary of Events and Information	Remarks and references to Appendices
RENING-HELST	7/1		Div RE HQ [illegible] re-arrived – Visited Camps, dumps &c	
"	8/1		Visited YPRES & ZILLEBEKE Dugouts &c.	
"	9/1		Routine work & arranging hutting scheme –	
"	10/1		Visited A&B Camps & old hutting dumps – TO ZILLEBEKE with GOC & DAQMG.	
"	11/1		Visited Fd Co camps & Billets in YPRES & KRUISTRAAT	
"	12/1		TO hutting dumps – C, E & F Camps	
"	13/1		TO YPRES & front line of left sector (& of right section) with GSO1 & OC 103rd Fd Co	
"	14/1		With DAAG to select camp for Grenade School – with ADMS to Divisional Baths at POPERINGHE, 72 &	

2353 Wt. W2544/1454 700,000 5/15 D. D. & L. A.D.S.S./Forms/C. 2118.

Instructions regarding War Diaries and Intelligence Summaries are contained in F. S. Regs., Part II. and the Staff Manual respectively. Title pages will be prepared in manuscript.

WAR DIARY
or
INTELLIGENCE SUMMARY.
(Erase heading not required.)

Army Form C. 2118.

Place	Date	Hour	Summary of Events and Information	Remarks and references to Appendices
	14 Contd		72 Field Ambulance, Divisional Rest Station	
RENINGHELST	15/1		Inspecting dump - Battle Head Quarters which was shelled - Dugouts & Splinter proof huts at BELGIAN CHATEAU To ZILLEBEKE & GORDON FARM with G.O.C. to reconnoitre new line of defence	
"	16/1		TO ABEELE to ~~[illegible]~~ see C.E. & visited 2nd Army Workshops & Park & Quarter Siding Timber store	
"	17/1		Hutting dumps & camps	
"	18/1		Round front trenches in left section of right sector with O.C. 104 F[d] Co -	
"	19/1		Round Back area of Right sector with O.C. 129 F[d] Co	
"	20/1		L[t] J.B. Whitfield 104 F[d] Co Killed (gunshot wound) while inspecting working parties in C7 - TO YPRES to see G.O.C. 17th Bde	

2353 Wt. W2544/1454 700,000 5/15 D. D. & L. A.D.S.S./Forms/C. 2118.

Army Form C. 2118.

Instructions regarding War Diaries and Intelligence Summaries are contained in F. S. Regs., Part II. and the Staff Manual respectively. Title pages will be prepared in manuscript.

WAR DIARY
or
INTELLIGENCE SUMMARY.
(Erase heading not required.)

Place	Date	Hour	Summary of Events and Information	Remarks and references to Appendices
RENINGHELST	21/1		With GSO, round proposed substitute for ZILLEBEKE Switch –	
"	22/1		To wood near PROVEN where BELGIANS (4) are making fascines – to Divisional baths –	
			To HQ 73rd Bde to see Brig. Gen. & with him to IK, IL Moated GRANGE line – Lt KYNNERSLY acts for him – Adjt proceeded on leave.	
"	23/1		Meeting of Brigadiers &c at YPRES – Routine work – Lt Watson joined 104 Fd Co	
"	24/1		Visited Pioneers camp, hutting & trench dumps – Camps E & F –	
"	25/1		Routine work	
"	26/1		Water Board meeting – Inspected Divisional Rest Camp with drainage officer also Divl Baths with AQMG –	

2353 Wt. W2544/1454 700,000 5/15 D. D. & L. A.D.S.S./Forms/C. 2118.

Instructions regarding War Diaries and Intelligence Summaries are contained in F. S. Regs., Part II. and the Staff Manual respectively. Title pages will be prepared in manuscript.

WAR DIARY
or
INTELLIGENCE SUMMARY.
(Erase heading not required.)

Army Form C. 2118.

Place	Date	Hour	Summary of Events and Information	Remarks and references to Appendices
RENINGHELST	27/1		To YPRES – saw O.C. 103rd Fd Co – Routine work.	
YPRES	28/1		To Left Section of Left Sector. Progress much hampered but continuous shelling – O.C. 103rd has insufficient men available owing to his day work in back area. Instructed O.C. 129th to do all work behind X, Y, A line – Conferred with B.G. 72nd Brigade & arranged to commence support line along his front & concentrate on that –	
RENINGHELST	29/1		To Hutting Dumps – Trench Dump – Camps A B. E & F. Freight for YMCA hut – To 129th Fd Co Camps – saw experimental wire entanglement &c –	
"	30/1		Conference of G.O.C. Brigadiers &c at YPRES.	

2353 Wt. W2544/1454 700,000 5/15 D. D. & L. A.D.S.S./Forms/C. 2118.

Instructions regarding War Diaries and Intelligence Summaries are contained in F. S. Regs., Part II. and the Staff Manual respectively. Title pages will be prepared in manuscript.

WAR DIARY
or
INTELLIGENCE SUMMARY.
(Erase heading not required.)

Army Form C. 2118.

Place	Date	Hour	Summary of Events and Information	Remarks and references to Appendices
~~31/1/16~~ RENINGHELST	31/1		TO POPERINGHE to meet Belgian official who had been in charge of YPRES Water Supply – with him along pipe line from DICKEBUSCH LAKE to YPRES – in connection with proposal to utilise supply for troops in YPRES. L^T MYER returned from leave.	
			[illegible] L^T Col R.E. CRE 24 Div^n – 31/1/16	

Instructions regarding War Diaries and Intelligence Summaries are contained in F. S. Regs., Part II. and the Staff Manual respectively. Title pages will be prepared in manuscript.

WAR DIARY
or
~~INTELLIGENCE SUMMARY~~.
(Erase heading not required.)

CRE 24th Div.

Army Form C. 2118.

Place	Date	Hour	Summary of Events and Information	Remarks and references to Appendices
	Feb. 1916			
RENINGHELST.	1		The difficulty in obtaining timber is becoming very serious. Endeavouring to purchase locally without success	
"	2		To HAZEBROUCK and BAILLEUL visiting 2nd Army workshops & purchasing stores.	
"	3		with C.E. 2nd Army to visit left sector	
"	4		Routine.	
"	5		arranged to purchase timber from MERVILLE	
"	6		Meeting of Brigadiers in YPRES	
"	87		with C.E. 2nd Army round Right sector.	
"	8.		Routine	
"	9		Selecting sites for M.G. emplts.	
"	10		Wiring begun on ZILLEBEKE moat line. 350 infy with RE supervision wired about 800 yds 10 yds deep. work well organized by MAJOR KING O.C. 104th Fd Co.	

2353 Wt. W2544/1454 700,000 5/15 D. D. & L. A.D.S.S./Forms/C. 2118.

Army Form C. 2118.

Instructions regarding War Diaries and Intelligence Summaries are contained in F. S. Regs., Part II. and the Staff Manual respectively. Title pages will be prepared in manuscript.

WAR DIARY
or
~~INTELLIGENCE SUMMARY.~~
(Erase heading not required.)

Place	Date	Hour	Summary of Events and Information	Remarks and references to Appendices
RENINGHELST	Feb. 11		Wiring of ZILLEBEKE Moat line completed to 1200 yds	
	12		Orders received for Capt. LOGAN R.E. to report to C.S.M.E.	
	13		Heavy bombardment of right sector. G.O.C. ordered work in trenches to be handed over to Brigadiers with one section of Fd. coys. as pioneers to assist. Remainder of Fd. Coys to concentrate on M.G. emplacements in 2nd line.	
	14		Major KING sent on leave as he was shewing signs of over strain. Capt. LOGAN proceeded to ENGLAND. 2 mines exploded on left sector, very heavy bombardment of Right sector. Enemy attempted to attack but were repulsed by Lewis gun fire and heavily punished by Artillery barrage. Reconnoitred alignment for new communication trench to Right sector.	
	15		Heavy shelling. "Stand To" ordered. ~~5 shells fell~~ 2 sections of 104 placed at disposal of Reserve Bde. 5 shells fell in 104th camp	

Instructions regarding War Diaries and Intelligence Summaries are contained in F. S. Regs., Part II. and the Staff Manual respectively. Title pages will be prepared in manuscript.

WAR DIARY
or
~~INTELLIGENCE SUMMARY.~~
(Erase heading not required.)

Army Form C. 2118.

Place	Date	Hour	Summary of Events and Information	Remarks and references to Appendices
RENINGHELST.	Feb 15		Killing 10 horses & mules & wounding 12. These shell probably aimed at 9.2 Howitzer which had come into action less than 100 yds from the camp	
	16.		Conference of Fd. Co. commanders to standardize M.G. emplts. and dug outs	
	17.		Q.M.G. visited Dumps with C.E. 2nd Army. accompanied C.E. V Corps round Camps and visited Corps siding at Ouderdom. OUDERDOM.	
	18.		Lectured at Technical School. 103rd Camp bombed. 1 killed 5 wounded. Inspected the work on M.G. Emplacts.	
	19.		Visited Left sector	
	20		Conference of Brigadiers in YPRES. orders received that left sector would be taken over by 6th Division on night 25/26. B.G.C.S. arrange relief of Fd Coys. ordered 103rd Fd Co to rest billets on completion of relief.	
	21		Major CLOUGHTON R.E. who had been sent out from home for instructional tour. Bgde H.Q dug outs ZILLEBEKE having been heavily shelled visited site to arrange to make mined dug outs	

2333 Wt. W2544/1454 700,000 5/15 D. D. & L. A.D.S.S./Forms/C. 2118.

Instructions regarding War Diaries and Intelligence Summaries are contained in F. S. Regs., Part II. and the Staff Manual respectively. Title pages will be prepared in manuscript.

WAR DIARY
or
~~INTELLIGENCE SUMMARY~~.
(*Erase heading not required.*)

Army Form C. 2118.

Place	Date	Hour	Summary of Events and Information	Remarks and references to Appendices
RENINGHELST.	Feb. 16 21		Received orders to take in hand reclaiming of G.H.Q 2 line	
	22		Took drainage officer to G.H.Q 2 line & arranged drainage scheme to be carried out under his supervision by entrenching Batt	
	23		Routine	
	24		Round G.H.Q 2 line 103rd Fd Co having handed over to 1st London Fd Co left YPRES & returned to rest billets	
	25		Round G.H.Q 2 line with G.O.C. who decided to hold LILLE Rd line. arranged with O.C. R.A.R.E. to make timbered M.G emplacements. Reported that Lt ALLEN 103rd slipped in camp & injured his leg & sent to hospital	
	26		Aeroplane bombs fell on RENINGHELST. Routine. 2nd Lt GREATHEAD reported for duty with 103rd Wiring of LILLE Rd line begun	
	27		Conference of Brigadiers	
	28		104th Fd Coy camp shelled at night 1 horse wounded one man wounded Capt R.A.B. SMITH only officer in camp (others at work) had all animals removed to safer place. ~~Company ordered to remove its camp~~	
	29		Working party of 400 infantry wiring [illegible] in front of LILLE Rd and reclaiming G.H.Q 2 line. 104th Co ordered to move camp	

1/3/16 [signature] Lt Col RE CRE 24 Div

2353 Wt. W2544/1454 700,000 5/15 D. D. & L. A.D.S.S./Forms/C. 2118.

SECRET.

Operation Order. "B" No 19.
by
Lieut Colonel A. J. Craven R.E. Copy No. 1
C. R.E. 24th Division

1. The 103rd Field Company RE will relieve the 129th Field Company R.E. in the LEFT. SECTOR on the night of the 13th – 14th March.

2. 103rd Field Company RE will take over billet at present occupied by 129th Field Company RE in YPRES but leaving one section in "rest billet"

3. 129th Field Company RE will proceed to rest billets and take over all works in back area at present carried out by 103rd Field Company RE.

4. Detail of transfer to be arranged by Os C. Companies concerned with the concurrence of the B.G.C. LEFT. SECTOR.

5. Completion of transfer to be reported to C.R.E.

6.

P.T.O.

6. This order to be acknowledged.

Wal. Moyer

Lieut + Adj: RE
for C.R.E. 24th Division

Issued at. 11 p.m.

12 3/16

Copy No 1 War Diary
2 H.Q. 24th Division
3 A.A. Q.M.G
4 File
5 72nd Infantry Brigade
6 O.C. 103rd Field Company RE.
7. O.C. 129th Field Company RE
8. 73rd Infantry Brigade.

Secret. "C" Copy No. 2.

C.R.E.'s Operation Order No. 20.

1. The 3rd Canadian Division will relieve the 24th in the present section of the line.

2. The Field Coys. will move with Brigades as follows:–
   103rd Fd. Co. R.E. — 72nd Inf. Bde.
   104th " " " — 17th " "
   129th " " " — 73rd " "
   March orders will be issued by B.G.C.

3. One section from each Field Co. will remain behind until further orders

4. Officers selected to remain with these sections must be experienced in trench work and must know the line well

5. As the companies leave, these sections will move to the camps now occupied by 103rd Fd. Co. R.E.

O.O. No. 20 Contd.

6. Capt WHITTALL R.E. will remain in charge of the Divisional R.E. Park until relieved.

7. Special orders will be issued as to the transport of Stores surplus to normal equipment.

15/3/16 Col. Major [illegible]

Copy No. 1 War Diary
2 Record
3 103rd F.C. Coy R.E.
4 104th " "
5 127th " "
6 71st Infy. Bde
7 72nd " "
8 73rd " "
9 H.Q. "G"
10 " " "Q"

Please acknowledge.

SECRET. "D" Copy no.

Operation Order No 21.
by
Lieut: Colonel A J. Craven R.E.
C.R.E. 24th Division

Order No 20 para No 5 is cancelled.

1. The sections of Field Companies left behind will be located as follows:-

103rd Fd Coy 1 section YPRES.
104th Fd Coy 1 section ZILLEBEKE.
129th Fd Coy 1 section in present camp.

2. Arrangements for reliefs have been made direct with acting CRE. 3rd Canadian Division

3. Ration arrangements:-
The sections left in this area will, after departure of their companies, draw their own rations from the refilling point on the POPERINGHE-BUSSEBOOM. Road.
This arrangement will hold good until 23rd inst:. (rations for 24th).
Arrangements are being made for rations to be drawn on 24th
25th

25th and 26th from 3rd Canadian Division.

4. O.s. C. Field Companies will arrange for the detached sections to rejoin their companies on the 26th inst:.

17/3/16 [signature]

~~Lt. and Adjt. R.E.~~
~~24th Division.~~
for CRE 24th Divn.

Issued at.

Copy no 1 War Diary
2 "G"
3 "Q"
4 103rd Fd. Coy RE.
5 104th Fd. Coy RE.
6 129th Fd. Coy RE.
7 Act. CRE. 3rd Canadian Div:
8. Record

E

SECRET

Copy No. 16

Operation Order No 22
by
Lieut: Col: A. J. Craven RE.
CRE. 24th Division

1/ The 24th Division will relieve the 1st Canadian Division in the trenches as follows.

RIGHT SECTOR	17th I.B.
CENTRE SECTOR.	73rd I.B.
LEFT SECTOR.	72nd I.B.

2/. Field Companies RE will relieve Field Companies CE as follows:–

~~RIGHT~~ LEFT	SECTOR	103rd Fd Coy	relieves	3rd Fd Coy CE
CENTRE	–"–	129th –"–	——	1st –"–
~~LEFT~~ RIGHT	–"–	104th –"–	——	2nd –"–

3/. O.C. Field Companies will at once get into touch with O.C. of the CE. Field Companies they are to relieve and make mutually suitable arrangements for carrying out the relief – They will report to CRE and to the I.B. H.Q. Concerned the date on which the transfer will be carried out.

P. T. O.

4/. The billets of the Field Companies C.E. are as follows:-

1st Field Company B4 b 7.7.
2nd Field Company B4 a 8.4.
3rd Field Company M35 d 9.8.

All companies have telephones.

5/. Each Field Company will send an advance party of at least 2 officers and 8 N.C.Os. to the Field Company it is to relieve on the following dates:-

129th Fd Coy 22nd March
103rd -"- 25th March
104th -"- 28th March

. Report of completion of transfer to be sent to CRE by wire

Please acknowledge.

Issued at.

[signature]

Copy No 1 H.Q.
2 Q.
3 CRE 1st Can Div
4 17th I.B.
5. 72nd I.B.
6 73rd I.B.
7 103rd Fd Coy RE
8. 104th Fd Coy RE
9 129th Fd Coy RE
10 Record
11 War Diary

CRE 24

DW

Vol 7

Army Form C. 2118.

Instructions regarding War Diaries and Intelligence Summaries are contained in F. S. Regs., Part II. and the Staff Manual respectively. Title pages will be prepared in manuscript.

WAR DIARY or INTELLIGENCE SUMMARY. C.R.E. 24th Division

(Erase heading not required.)

Place	Date	Hour	Summary of Events and Information	Remarks and references to Appendices
REMINGHELST	March 1		2Lt. NICHOLS. G.S. reported for duty with 104th Fd Co. All night working parties cancelled owing to contemplated operations. Made arrangements for obtaining & transport of bricks urgently required for bursters for Belgian chateau dugouts where several casualties had occurred through shell fire.	
	2		BLUFF recaptured by 3rd Division. C.E. 2nd Army visited REMINGHELST to discuss improvement of 2nd (R.S.) line and issued instructions for daily wire to be sent of progress thereon. Arranged for working party from resting Brigade to erect entanglement and reclaim trenches. H.Q. & 2 sections 104th Fd Co moved to new camp on OUDERDOM – VLAMERTINGHE Rd. 2 sections 103rd Fd Co detailed to hold themselves at disposal of B.G.C. Reserve I.B.	

2353 Wt. W2544/1454 700,000 5/15 D. D. & L. A.D.S.S./Forms/C. 2118.

Army Form C. 2118.

Instructions regarding War Diaries and Intelligence Summaries are contained in F. S. Regs., Part II. and the Staff Manual respectively. Title pages will be prepared in manuscript.

WAR DIARY
or
~~INTELLIGENCE SUMMARY.~~
(Erase heading not required.)

Place	Date	Hour	Summary of Events and Information	Remarks and references to Appendices
RENINGHELST	3		Routine	
"	4		Visited R.E. Park and Hutting Dump.	
"	5.		Meeting of Brigadiers. Orders given by G.O.C. for discontinuation of Grenade School.	
"	6		Routine	
"	7		Conferred with C.R.E. 50th Division in connection with transfer of his left sector to this Division. Inspected detachments in YPRES.	
"	8		Visited new portions of 50th Division trenches to be handed over to 104th by 7th Fd Co RE. 103rd Fd Co taking over back area. Orders issued accordingly as attached. (marked 'A')	
"	9.		Went round L sector with G.O.C. who decided on line of M.G. emplacements along LILLE Rd. Visited camps C.D and A. with o/c Hutting.	

2353 Wt. W2544/1454 700,000 5/15 D. D. & L. A.D.S.S./Forms/C. 2118.

Army Form C. 2118.

Instructions regarding War Diaries and Intelligence Summaries are contained in F. S. Regs., Part II. and the Staff Manual respectively. Title pages will be prepared in manuscript.

WAR DIARY
or
~~INTELLIGENCE SUMMARY.~~

(Erase heading not required.)

Place	Date	Hour	Summary of Events and Information	Remarks and references to Appendices
REMINGHELST	10		Visited FESTUBERT with C.E. V Corps to inspect Artillery Observation Posts. These consisted of double brick towers inside partially ruined buildings	
"	11		Attended demonstration of FLAMMEN WERFER which proved a failure owing to machine not working.	
			Went round Canal line, LILLE Rd and ZILLEBEKE with O.C. 103rd.	
"	12		Capt. MISSEN, R.E. ordered to join 29th (A.P) Coy R.E.	
			Conference in Ramparts where G.O.C. gave out that 24th Divn would relieve 1st Canadian Div.	
			Visited Swan Chateau with G.O.C. & G.S.O.1. as Corps have decided that its defence should be organized.	
			103rd ordered to relieve 129th in L sector as Orders attached and marked "B"	
"	13		Inspected L sector	

2353 Wt. W2544/1454 700,000 5/15 D. D. & L. A.D.S.S./Forms/C. 2118.

Instructions regarding War Diaries and Intelligence Summaries are contained in F. S. Regs., Part II. and the Staff Manual respectively. Title pages will be prepared in manuscript.

WAR DIARY

or

~~INTELLIGENCE SUMMARY.~~

(Erase heading not required.)

Army Form C. 2118.

Place	Date	Hour	Summary of Events and Information	Remarks and references to Appendices
RENINGHELST	14.		to ABEELE to inspect sample trench bridges & artillery bridges submitted by divisions	
			with O.C. 124th regarding defences of SWAN CHATEAU	
			129 handed over 2 section night 13/14th to 103rd	
	15.		went round LILLE Rd line and G.H.Q. 2	
			Orders received accelerating move to new area move to be completed on 21st inst.	
			with O.C. 103rd Fd and M.G.O 17th I.B. to Moated Grange and Yeomanry Post selecting M.G. emplacements also 6" R.S.8.	
			Preliminary orders as to move issued as O.O. 20 marked "C" attached.	
	16		Major MALCOLM acting C.R.E. 3rd Canadian Divn came to RENINGHELST to discuss transfer. Took him to Hutting dump Trench Dumps and 129th Camp.	

Army Form C. 2118.

Instructions regarding War Diaries and Intelligence Summaries are contained in F. S. Regs., Part II. and the Staff Manual respectively. Title pages will be prepared in manuscript.

WAR DIARY
or
~~INTELLIGENCE SUMMARY.~~
(Erase heading not required.)

Place	Date	Hour	Summary of Events and Information	Remarks and references to Appendices
RENINGHELST 17.	17		Took acting C.R.E. 3rd Canadian Divn round a portion of Left sector and back line. Issued revised orders as to location of R.E. sections left in line as O.O. No 21 marked "D" attached.	
	18		Preparations for transfer. Captn IZAT R.E. O.C. 103 slightly wounded in thigh. Lt KYNNERSLEY in command of Coy. Received instructions that Lt Col. ANDERSON had been appointed C.R.E. 3rd Canadian Divn.	
	19		Lt Col. ANDERSON arrived at RENINGHELST. Took him round ZILLEBEKE. M.G. line, LILLE Rd line & G.H.Q. 2. Received orders as to relief of 1st Canadian Divn by 24th Divn.	
	20		Handing over to C.R.E. 3rd Canadian Divn.	

2353 Wt. W2544/1454 700,000 5/15 D. D. & L. A.D.S.S./Forms/C. 2118.

Army Form C. 2118.

Instructions regarding War Diaries and Intelligence Summaries are contained in F. S. Regs., Part II. and the Staff Manual respectively. Title pages will be prepared in manuscript.

WAR DIARY
or
~~INTELLIGENCE SUMMARY.~~
(Erase heading not required.)

Place	Date	Hour	Summary of Events and Information	Remarks and references to Appendices
~~21~~ FLETRE	21		H.Q.R.E. marched to FLETRE.	
			Visited C.R.E. 1st Canadian Divn; went round	
			Divisl R.E. Park & visited C.E. Canadian Corps	
	22		Went with C.R.E. 1st Canadian Divn, round left sector of new line	
	23		O.O. No 22 marked "E" attached issued as to relief of 1st 2nd & 3rd	
			~~Canadian~~ Fd Coys.	
			Round centre sector with O.C. 1st Fd Co C.E.	
	24		Visited Chief Engr Canadian Corps, also corps workshops & Park	
	~~25~~		Lt Shaw R.E. 104th Fd Co R.E. ordered to join ~~[illegible]~~	
			11th Labour Battn RE	
	25		Went round R sector with O.C. 2nd Fd Co C.E. and O.C.	
			104th Fd Co R.E.	

2353 Wt. W2544/1454 700,000 5/15 D. D. & L. A.D.S.S./Forms/C. 2118.

Instructions regarding War Diaries and Intelligence Summaries are contained in F. S. Regs., Part II. and the Staff Manual respectively. Title pages will be prepared in manuscript.

WAR DIARY
or
~~INTELLIGENCE SUMMARY~~.
(Erase heading not required.)

Army Form C. 2118.

Place	Date	Hour	Summary of Events and Information	Remarks and references to Appendices
FLETRE	26		Round 103rd Fd. Co. Camps at DRANOUTRE inspected new School site. Inspected LA CRÊCHE with a view to its suitability for new Divisl. H.Q. found it to be fully occupied by 9th Div. troops	
"	27		To St. JANS CAPPEL to see C.R.E. 1st Canadian Division re taking over	
"	28		Round Right Sector of Front with O.C. 104th Adjt. inspected Divisl. Baths at DRANOUTRE and NEUVE-EGLISE.	
"	29		To BAILLEUL to confer with C.E. Canadian Corps BAILLEUL decided upon as Divisn. H.Q. with possible need of [illegible] huts.	

Instructions regarding War Diaries and Intelligence Summaries are contained in F. S. Regs., Part II, and the Staff Manual respectively. Title pages will be prepared in manuscript.

WAR DIARY
or
~~INTELLIGENCE SUMMARY.~~
(Erase heading not required.)

Army Form C. 2118.

Place	Date	Hour	Summary of Events and Information	Remarks and references to Appendices
St JANS CAPPEL	30		To MIEPPE with C.E. V Corps. moved in to new quarters at St JANS CAPPEL Prospected for site of new Divisl. R.E. park.	
"	31		visited L sector with B.G.C 72nd Inf. Bde. Lt Kingsnorth wounded by rifle Grenade	

[illegible]
Lt. COL. R.E.
C. R. E. 24th DIV.

2353 Wt. W2544/1454 700,000 5/15 D. D. & L. A.D.S.S./Forms/C. 2118.

Copy No 1. SECRET.

CRE's Orders O.O. 18

"A"

1. The 17th Inf. Bde will ~~[illegible]~~ relieve the 150th Inf. Bde on the night of 8th/9th and 9th/10th March. Command will pass to B.G.C. 17th Inf. Bde on completion of relief on night of 9th/10th March

2. The Boundary between the 24th and 50th Divisions will be as under:—
From the junction of A 3 and A 4 Trenches at I 30 b. 0 4. — I 24 c. 2. 2 - road junction at I 22 d (Central) - along road to road junction at I 28 a 1.9 — due West to road bend at I 19 c 6 0 — H. 24. c 3. 5

3. The Boundary between the Right and Left Brigade of the 24th Division will be as follows:—
From junction of GOUROCK ROAD with B 3. (GOUROCK ROAD inclusive to Right Brigade) - I 24 b 3. 8. — I 24 b 1½. 5 — I 24 a ½. 7. —. Thence along track past YEOMANRY POST to I 18 d 6. 1½ Thence to N.W. corner of ZILLEBEKE LAKE I 21 b 0. 5. — I 20 a 5. 4.

4 The 104th Fd COY. R.E. will take over the R.E. work in our new Right sector from the Field Coys of the 50th Division on the night of 8th/9th March

5. O.C. 104th Fd Co. R.E. will hand over the work of which he is at present in charge to O.C. 103rd Fd Co. with the exception of the completion of ZILLEBEKE YPRES Line. Arrangements for transfer to be made direct between O.C.'s companies concerned.

6. Completion of taking over of work in New Sector to be reported to the C.R.E.

7. Please acknowledge.

[signature]

Lt. & Adjt. R.E.

8/3/16 for C.R.E.

24th Division

Copies to 1. Record
2. "G"
3. 17th Inf. Bde
4. 72nd " "
5. 73rd " "
6. 103rd Fd Co. R.E.
7. 104th " "
8. 129th " "

Secret

Instructions regarding War Diaries and Intelligence Summaries are contained in F. S. Regs., Part II. and the Staff Manual respectively. Title pages will be prepared in manuscript.

WAR DIARY
or
~~INTELLIGENCE SUMMARY~~.
(Erase heading not required.)

Army Form C. 2118.

C.R.E. 1 Vol 8
24th Division

Place	Date	Hour	Summary of Events and Information	Remarks and references to Appendices
~~BAILLEUL~~ St JANS CAPPEL	APRIL 1		Round 72nd I.B. area with G.S.O. 1 and O.C. 103 prospecting for M.G. Emplacements. 2nd Lt FRANCIS temporarily transferred to 103rd Fd Co from 104th	
"	2		Attended conference of Brigadiers and visited DRANOUTRE & NEUVE EGLISE with ADMS in connection with water supply & Baths	
"	3		Visited camps & dumps of 129th & 104th Fd Cos Divisl R.E. Park NIEPPE & Corps Park STEENWERCKE	
"	4		Visited C.E. V Corps BAILLEUL went round front line & defended localities of Centre Sector with O.C. 129.	

2353 Wt. W2544/1454 700,000 5/15 D. D. & L. A.D.S.S./Forms/C. 2118.

Instructions regarding War Diaries and Intelligence Summaries are contained in F. S. Regs., Part II. and the Staff Manual respectively. Title pages will be prepared in manuscript.

WAR DIARY
or
~~INTELLIGENCE SUMMARY.~~
(Erase heading not required.)

Army Form C. 2118.

Place	Date	Hour	Summary of Events and Information	Remarks and references to Appendices
~~BAILLEUL~~ S^T JANS CAPPEL	5		Capt F. P. HEATH. R.E. appointed to command 103rd Fd Co reported arrival.	
			2nd Lt SPARROW joined 103	
"	6		Visited rear ~~[illegible]~~ defences of 72nd I.B.	
			Visited front line & localities A.B. of R. sector with O.C. 104th	
"	7		Visited Divl R.E. Park & NEUVE EGLISE	
			Prospected for new site for Divl Park, That at NIEPPE being inconveniently situated & outside our area	
"	8		Inspected WULVERGHEM Switch & Subsidiary Line & examined work done there by Pioneers.	
"	9		Attended Corps Water Board Conference	
			Visited 73 I.B. ~~[illegible]~~ shelters in S. slope of Hill 63. which were inadequately protected from artillery fire & arranged for erection of steel dug outs & construction of mined casemates for garrison	

2353 Wt. W2544/1454 700,000 5/15 D. D. & L. A.D.S.S./Forms/C. 2118.

Army Form C. 2118.

Instructions regarding War Diaries and Intelligence Summaries are contained in F. S. Regs., Part II. and the Staff Manual respectively. Title pages will be prepared in manuscript.

WAR DIARY
or
~~INTELLIGENCE SUMMARY~~.

(Erase heading not required.)

Place	Date	Hour	Summary of Events and Information	Remarks and references to Appendices
ST JANS CAPPEL	10		With C.E., O.C. Water patrols & water expert inspecting water supply on Hill 63 and near BULFORD Huts with G.O.C. and O.C. Pioneers inspected WULVERGHEM Switch, subsidiary line & locality No 1.	
"	11		Went round front line with G.S.O.1	
"	12.		Visited Divisl R.E. Park & Hutting work with O.C. Hutting.	
"	13		Went round L sector with O.C. 103rd	
"	14		Accompanied B.G.C. 73 I B round rear defences of his area	
"	15		Visited No 2 R.E. Park STRAZEELE & inspected work in centre sector with O.C. 129th	
"	16		Attended conference of Brigadiers and inspected camps & dumps at ROMARIN.	

2353 Wt. W2544/1454 700,000 5/15 D. D. & L. A.D.S.S./Forms/C. 2118.

Army Form C. 2118.

Instructions regarding War Diaries and Intelligence Summaries are contained in F. S. Regs., Part II. and the Staff Manual respectively. Title pages will be prepared in manuscript.

WAR DIARY
or
~~INTELLIGENCE SUMMARY.~~
(Erase heading not required.)

Place	Date	Hour	Summary of Events and Information	Remarks and references to Appendices
ST JANS CAPPEL	17		Routine.	
BAILLEUL	18		H.Q. 24th Divn moved to BAILLEUL	
"	19.		Inspected proposed site for camp of 175th Co R.E. Visited 129th Co Divl R.E. Park & works on Hill 63.	
"	20		Visited centre sector & especially considered new defences for MIDLAND FARM.	
"	21		Visited 104 & inspected work on R. sector. Inspected ALDERSHOT camp.	
"	22		Routine	
"	23		attended conference of Brigadiers	
"	24		Visited camps at DRANOUTRE & NEUVE EGLISE with A.D.M.S. with C.R.E. 9th Divn PLOEGSTEERT & Hill 63 in connection with water supply.	
"	25		Visited infantry camps above NEUVE EGLISE with M. BOCQUET water expert & arranged for sinking wells near NEUVE EGLISE Baths & opening one up at KORTEPYP.	

Instructions regarding War Diaries and Intelligence Summaries are contained in F. S. Regs., Part II. and the Staff Manual respectively. Title pages will be prepared in manuscript.

WAR DIARY
or
INTELLIGENCE SUMMARY.
(Erase heading not required.)

Army Form C. 2118.

Place	Date	Hour	Summary of Events and Information	Remarks and references to Appendices
BAILLEUL	26		With C.R.A. visiting O.P.S with a view to making arrangements for strengthening them	
"	27		to Divis'l R.E. Park. 129 & 104 camps and R section Defences.	
			Definite orders received to begin work on Divis'l Rest Station	
"	28		Conducted Army Commander. C.E. Second Army & C.E. V Corps round works on S. slopes of Hill 63. accompanied C.E. V Corps on his inspection of camps of 129th & 104th Fd Cos.	
"	29		With G.O.C. to Hill 63 & locality No 1. inspected site of new D.R.S & work on water supply at NEUVE EGLISE & DRANOUTRE.	
"	30	~~10~~ 12.45 A.M	~~visited~~ ~~conference of~~ Gas attack on left & centre sections ~~which~~ This was repulsed, 103rd had been warned of attack by Brigade & sent back to camp before it took place. Orders to concentrate at concentration points in left section issued 1.50 A.M. direct to companies by Divis'l Staff.	

Army Form C. 2118.

Instructions regarding War Diaries and Intelligence Summaries are contained in F. S. Regs., Part II. and the Staff Manual respectively. Title pages will be prepared in manuscript.

WAR DIARY
or
INTELLIGENCE SUMMARY.

(Erase heading not required.)

Place	Date	Hour	Summary of Events and Information	Remarks and references to Appendices
BAILLEUL	30		103rd Fd Coy marched to concentration point. 104th & 129th received orders not to march until further orders. Orders to stand down issued at 2.50 A.M. Conference of Brigadiers. Visited 104 & 129 Fd Coy camps.	

Val. [illegible]
Lt. and Adjt. R.E.
24th Division.
for C.R.E.

Instructions regarding War Diaries and Intelligence Summaries are contained in F. S. Regs., Part II. and the Staff Manual respectively. Title pages will be prepared in manuscript.

WAR DIARY
or
~~INTELLIGENCE SUMMARY.~~
(Erase heading not required.)

Army Form C. 2118.

C.R.E 24th Div Vol 9

Place	Date	Hour	Summary of Events and Information	Remarks and references to Appendices
BAILLEUL	May 1		Visited Divisional Rest station Camp with Major Edwards (O C Div rest station)	
			Visited Divisional baths and Water Supply	
			Tunnelling Conference decided that defensive mining was to be carried out by Div^l Pioneers under direction of O.C 171st Coy R.E.	
	2.		With O C 171st Coy R.E to front line left sector to arrange details for defensive mining which is to be carried out by Pioneers under supervision of 171st Coy R.E. 1 officer and 80 Other Ranks required from Pioneers.	
	3		Investigated case of 6 men of 129th Coy R E who were gassed in gas attack on 30.4.16	
	4		Went round works with O.C 104th Coy R E prior to handing over on going on leave	
	5.		Lt Col A.J. Craven R.E went on leave, Major W.A. de C KING took over duties of acting C.R.E	
			~~attended~~ Lectured at Divisional school	
			Visited Divisional Water supply and 104th Coy R.E	
			Lieut MARVIN R.E. 129th Field Coy awarded military cross	
	6		Visited Hill 63 with O.C 104th Coy R E and discussed O P in BARREL HOUSE	

2353 Wt. W2514/1454 700,000 5/15 D. D. & L. A.D.S.S./Forms/C. 2118.

Instructions regarding War Diaries and Intelligence Summaries are contained in F. S. Regs., Part II. and the Staff Manual respectively. Title pages will be prepared in manuscript.

WAR DIARY

or

~~INTELLIGENCE SUMMARY~~.

(Erase heading not required.)

Army Form C. 2118.

Place	Date	Hour	Summary of Events and Information	Remarks and references to Appendices
BAILLEUL	May 7		Visited trial well near ROMARIN gravel pit with M. BOUQUET	
			Visited wells at BULFORD, NIEPPE and NEUVE EGLISE with Capt MAULE (O i/c Vth Corps water patrol)	
	8		Visited three company dumps	
			Visited sites for proposed dug outs behind 103rd Coy lines	
	9		Inspected water supply at BULFORD	
	10		Visited Pioneer camp to arrange secret work	
			Visited back area of right sector	
	11		Visited 104th Coy R.E camp with Major HENDERSON R E	
			Visited Hill 63 and telephone shelters in front line of right sector	
	12		Visited Water supply DRANOUTRE and O.C 103rd Coy R E	
			Reconnoitred route for movement of troops out of view of enemy	
			Visited Pioneers	
			Inspected proposed site for experimental mine crater	
			Saw B.G.C 17th I.B and O.C 104th Coy R.E	
			Lieut. R.H WHITFIELD 104th Field Coy R.E killed.	

2353 Wt. W2544/1454 700,000 5/15 D. D. & L. A.D.S.S./Forms/C. 2118.

Army Form C. 2118.

Instructions regarding War Diaries and Intelligence Summaries are contained in F. S. Regs., Part II. and the Staff Manual respectively. Title pages will be prepared in manuscript.

WAR DIARY
or
~~INTELLIGENCE SUMMARY.~~

(Erase heading not required.)

Place	Date	Hour	Summary of Events and Information	Remarks and references to Appendices
BAILLEUL	May 13		Visited NEUVE EGLISE with G.S.O 3	
			Visited 104th Field Coy R.E.	
	14		Routine	
			Lieut VAL MYER R E adjutant went on leave	
			Lieut B RUSSEL 129th Coy R.E took over duties of acting adjutant	
	15		Lt Col A J. CRAVEN R.E. returned from leave	
			Routine.	
	16		Orders transferring Lieut VAL MYER RE to Special Works Park received	
			Major W.A de C KING resumed command of 104th Coy R.E	
			Visited site of New Divisional R.E Park, R E Park NIEPPE and 103rd Field Coy R E	
	17		Visited Divisional Water Supply	
			Visited 103rd Fd Coy and 72nd I. B H Q.	

2353 Wt. W2544/1454 700,000 5/15 D. D. & L. A.D.S.S./Forms/C. 2118.

Instructions regarding War Diaries and Intelligence Summaries are contained in F. S. Regs., Part II. and the Staff Manual respectively. Title pages will be prepared in manuscript.

WAR DIARY
or
~~INTELLIGENCE SUMMARY~~.

(Erase heading not required.)

Army Form C. 2118.

Place	Date	Hour	Summary of Events and Information	Remarks and references to Appendices
BAILLEUL	May 18		Visited BULFORD CAMP and KORTE PYP	
			Visited water supply with C.E V^th^ Corps	
			Visited baths at DRANOUTRE and NEUVE EGLISE	
			Visited 103rd and 129th Field Coys R.E	
	19		Routine	
	20		Visited 103rd Coy R.E, NEUVE EGLISE and proposed new road for ammunition supply and New Divisional R.E. Park	
			Went round Subsidiary line with G.O.C and O.C Pioneers	
	21		Attended conference of Brigadiers	
			Visited C R E 3rd Div, 103rd Field Coy and Divisional Rest Station	
	22		Lieut VAL MYER R.E returned from leave and resumed duties of adjutant	
			With O C 104th Coy R.E round front line and back area right section	
			Inspected Water Supply	
	23		With O C 103rd Coy R.E round front line Left Section	
			Inspected dug outs in back area of Division	

2353 Wt. W2544/1454 700,000 5/15 D. D. & L. A.D.S.S./Forms/C. 2118.

Army Form C. 2118.

Instructions regarding War Diaries and Intelligence Summaries are contained in F. S. Regs., Part II. and the Staff Manual respectively. Title pages will be prepared in manuscript.

WAR DIARY
or
~~INTELLIGENCE SUMMARY~~.

(Erase heading not required.)

Place	Date	Hour	Summary of Events and Information	Remarks and references to Appendices
BAILLEUL	May 24		With G S O 2 selected site for practising crater warfare Saw O C 171st Coy R.E in this connection	
	25		Captain G CHEETHAM RE reported for duty as adjutant from 90th Field Coy R.E	
	26		With O.C 129th Fd Coy R E round front line and back area Centre Section	
	27		Capt G CHEETHAM RE took over duties of adjutant from Lieut VAL MYER RE transferred to special works park.	
	28		2nd Lieut J.H HANCOCK RE reported for duty with 129th Field Coy R E Routine and office work	
	29		Routine and office work	
	30		With G O C and G.S.O I round subsidiary line	
	31		Routine and office work Visited Vth Corps Park BAILLEUL	

[signature]
Lt. COL. R.E.
C. R. E. 24th DIV.

Instructions regarding War Diaries and Intelligence Summaries are contained in F. S. Regs., Part II. and the Staff Manual respectively. Title pages will be prepared in manuscript.

WAR DIARY
or
INTELLIGENCE SUMMARY.
(Erase heading not required.)

C.R.E 24th Div

Army Form C. 2118.

Vol 10

Place	Date	Hour	Summary of Events and Information	Remarks and references to Appendices
	June			
BAILLEUL	1st		Visited 103rd 104th and 129th Field Coys and Div R.E Park Road near NEUVE EGLISE Divisional Rest Station and KORTE PYP Huts	
			East Riding Field Coy R.E arrived for work on O.Ps	
	2nd		Visited 103rd Field Coy R.E and witnessed practice for minor operations	
			Inspected pioneer work near NEUVE EGLISE	
			Visited right sector with G.S.O 1 to select route of new Comm. Trench and O.Ps	
	3rd		2nd Lieut C ROBERTS R.E attached to 104th Field Coy for training, from 2nd Entrenching battalion.	
			Routine and office work	
	4th		Inspected work on mining for practice crater, reservoir at DRANOUTRE and water supply	
			King's birthday gazette:- C.R.E promoted brevet Lt. Col Major W.A de C KING R.E (104th Field Coy) D.S.O Capt A. IZAT late 103rd Field Coy M.C One W.O 104th Field Coy D.C.M Three N.C.Os and Men Military Medal	

Instructions regarding War Diaries and Intelligence Summaries are contained in F. S. Regs., Part II. and the Staff Manual respectively. Title pages will be prepared in manuscript.

WAR DIARY
or
INTELLIGENCE SUMMARY.
(Erase heading not required.)

Army Form C. 2118.

C.R.E. 24th Div

Place	Date	Hour	Summary of Events and Information	Remarks and references to Appendices
BAILLEUL	June 5th		Attended conference of Brigadiers Visited 104th and 129th Field Coys and new Div R.E. Park	
	6th		Round right sector with O.C. 104th Field Coy. Selected sites for dugouts in rear of locality 3.	
	7th		Visit from officers of special brigade Visited 167th A.T. Coy R.E. and East Riding Field Coy R.E.	
	8th		Visited 103rd Field Coy and 72nd I.B. and 104th Field Coy R.E. Received instructions to make preparations for Gas Attack.	
	9th		Assembled Field Coy commanders at BOMARIN to issue instructions regarding preparations for Gas Attack Conferred with C.R.E. 41st Div regarding joining up support lines etc Visited R.E. Park and 129th Field Coy R.E. Saw representatives of Special brigade re arrangements for Gas Attack Arranged with 2nd Army Workshops to supply boxes for gas cylinders.	
	10th		Routine 50 Boxes for gas cylinders provided and delivered to Bde areas.	

2353 Wt. W2544/1454 700,000 5/15 D. D. & L. A.D.S.S./Forms/C. 2118.

Instructions regarding War Diaries and Intelligence Summaries are contained in F. S. Regs., Part II. and the Staff Manual respectively. Title pages will be prepared in manuscript.

WAR DIARY
or
INTELLIGENCE SUMMARY.
(*Erase heading not required.*)

Army Form C. 2118.

CRE 24th Div

Place	Date	Hour	Summary of Events and Information	Remarks and references to Appendices
BAILLEUL	June 11th		Attended meeting of Brigadiers	
			Visited 103rd, 104th Field Coys, NEUVE EGLISE road, water supply KORTE PYP and Div R.E Park	
			Conferred with C.R.E 50th Div and arranged to connect up trench tramways systems	
			Eighty boxes for gas cylinders provided and delivered to Brigade areas	
	12th		Went round right sector with O.C 104th Field Coy R.E	
			Eighty boxes for gas cylinders provided and delivered to brigade areas	
			Gas cylinder boxes were succesfully put in, smaller size containing two cylinders much more convenient as it interferes less with pickets of revetments	
	13th		Went round left sector with O.C 103rd Field Coy.	
	14th		Received intimation that 73rd I.B would be relieved by an Australian I.B and would then relieve a Brigade of 50th Div holding line on the left of our present front 129th Field Coy to remain in our present area until relieved by	

Instructions regarding War Diaries and Intelligence Summaries are contained in F. S. Regs., Part II. and the Staff Manual respectively. Title pages will be prepared in manuscript.

WAR DIARY
or
INTELLIGENCE SUMMARY.
(Erase heading not required.)

Army Form C. 2118.

C R E 24th Div

Place	Date	Hour	Summary of Events and Information	Remarks and references to Appendices
BAILLEUL	June 14th		by an Australian Field Coy	
			One field coy 50th Div will remain in new area until 129th Field coy can relieve	
			Visited 129th Field coy, Div R.E Park and Picket Office MONT ROUGE, ordered	
			2,000 sticks for cylinder carriers	
	15th		Visited C R E 50th Div	
			Went round O.Ps on Hill 63 with O.C East Riding Field Coy	
			Visited 103rd and went round back area with O.C	
	16th		Went with C R A and lectured to each R.F.A Bde on use of materials and construction of Gun Pits and dugouts.	
			German Gas attack on Div. Front.	
			Gas casualties :- 2 men killed and 7 gassed 103rd Field Coy 2nd Lieut C ROBERTS wounded and gassed, 2nd Lieut R A HARDINGE slightly gassed at duty 104th Field Coy.	
	17th		1/1st East Riding Field Coy left the Div	
			Routine and office work.	

2353 Wt. W2544/1454 700,000 5/15 D. D. & L. A.D.S.S./Forms/C. 2118.

Army Form C. 2118.

Instructions regarding War Diaries and Intelligence Summaries are contained in F. S. Regs., Part II. and the Staff Manual respectively. Title pages will be prepared in manuscript.

WAR DIARY
or
INTELLIGENCE SUMMARY.
(Erase heading not required.)

C.R.E 24th Div

Place	Date	Hour	Summary of Events and Information	Remarks and references to Appendices
BAILLEUL	18th		Routine and Office work	
	19th		Round front at present held by 150th Bde 50th Div with C.R.E 50th Div. One section of 6th Aust Field Coy arrived as advanced party at 129th Field Coy billets. Centre sector taken over by 7th Aust Bde. One section 129th Field Coy RE moved to LOCREHOF (Operation Order No 23 attached)	
	20th		H Q and 3 sections 6th Aust Field Coy arrived and took over billets of 129th Field Coy which moved to LOCREHOF Visit from C.E. 1st ANZAC to dis-cuss work in area to be taken over by that corps. Took him to Hill 63 Major BOVET R E arrived to represent ANZAC CORPS and superintend work. Orders issued for Divisional Pioneers to hand over work to 1st Australian Pioneers preparatory to moving to another camp in the neighbourhood of LOCRE Arranged for 1st Australian Field Coy to take over work on R.A. O Ps and for Australian Infantry to provide working parties for them and start work on Comm Trenches and Fire Trenches on Hill 63	

2353 Wt. W2514/1454 700,000 5/15 D. D. & L. A.D.S.S./Forms/C. 2118.

Instructions regarding War Diaries and Intelligence Summaries are contained in F. S. Regs., Part II. and the Staff Manual respectively. Title pages will be prepared in manuscript.

WAR DIARY
or
INTELLIGENCE SUMMARY.
(Erase heading not required.)

Army Form C. 2118.

C.R.E 24th Div

Place	Date	Hour	Summary of Events and Information	Remarks and references to Appendices
BAILLEUL	June 21st		Round 73rd I.B area with O C 129th Field Coy Visited B.G.C 73rd I.B	
	22nd		Routine 2nd Lieut J.T Godfrey R.E joined 104th Field Coy for duty.	
	23rd		Visited 72nd I.B area with O.C 103rd Field Coy R.E. Two sections of the 1st Australian Field Coy relieved 2 sections of 104th Field Coy R.E which started to take over work on O.Ps	
	24th		104th Field Coy R.E less 2 sections moved into ALDERSHOT Camp and took over O.Ps from 1st Aust Field Coy [illegible] First Aust Field Coy took over work on line in centre section (Operation Order No 24 attached) Second Lieut B WATSON rejoined 104th Field Coy Went to LOCRE reconnoitring roads and selecting site for new Div R.E Park	
	25th		104th Field Coy handed over O.Ps to 5th Aust Field Coy and moved to rest billets near BAILLEUL 2nd Lieut R.C BROWN joined 104th Field Coy Capt R.A B SMITH rejoined 104th Field Coy Saw B G.C 72nd Brigade and O.C 103rd Field Coy	

2353 Wt. W2544/1454 700,000 5/15 D. D. & L. A.D.S.S./Forms/C. 2118.

Instructions regarding War Diaries and Intelligence Summaries are contained in F. S. Regs., Part II. and the Staff Manual respectively. Title pages will be prepared in manuscript.

WAR DIARY
or
INTELLIGENCE SUMMARY.

(Erase heading not required.)

Army Form C. 2118.

C.R.E 24th Div

Place	Date	Hour	Summary of Events and Information	Remarks and references to Appendices
BAILLEUL	26th		Interview with C.R.E 50th Div	
			Saw C.R.E 1st Australian Div Re handing over.	
	27th		Went round right of left sector with O.C. 103rd Field Coy R.E	
	28th		Routine	
			Interview with C.R.E 41st Div re handing over portion of our present front	
			Hutting officer moved to MONT NOIR to construct H.Q of IX Corps	
	29th		With Chief Engineer IX Corps round front line and back area of 73rd I.B sector	
			Went to MONT NOIR to see work on IX Corps H.Q	
	30th		Visited trench mortar school BERTHEN	

[signature]

-2 JUL 1916

Lt. COL. R.E.
C. R. E. 24th DIV.

2353 Wt. W2544/1454 700,000 5/15 D. D. & L. A.D.S.S./Forms/C. 2118.

<u>Secret</u> Copy No 5

C.R.E's Operation Order No S.E 6

1. One Infantry Brigade of the 2nd ANZAC Division will relieve the 73rd Infantry Brigade in the centre sector of the 24th Div front.

This relief will be completed by the night of the 17th/18th June

2. The 129th Field Coy R.E will remain in its present area until relieved by a field Coy of the 2nd ANZAC Division at a date to be notified later.

G. Cheetham
Capt and Adjt. R.E.
24th Division.
for C.R.E

15.6.16

Copy No1. H.Q "G" 24th Div.
No2 "Q" "
No3 73rd I.B
No4 129th Field Coy R.E
No5 War Diary
No6 Record

Copy No 8

Operation Order No 23
By Lt. Col A J. Craven R.E
C.R.E 24th Div

1 The 129th Field Coy R.E will be relieved on 20th June by the 6th Australian Field Coy.
O.C 129th Field Coy will arrange details of handing over direct with O.C 6th Australian Field Coy.

2. The 129th Field Coy will relieve 2nd Northumbrian Field Coy (50th Div) on 19th and 20th June

3. Two sections of the 129th Field Coy will move to the billets of the 2nd Northumbrian Field Coy at Sheet 28 H 29 d.2.3 on 19th June

4. The 129th Field Coy less two sections will move to the billets of 2nd Northumbrian Field Coy on 20th June
Route:- Le ROMARIN (B.4a) - T 28 c.1.6. T 26 c.6.4 - T 25 d 5.3 - NEUVE EGLISE - DRANOUTRE - M 29 d ½ 4 - LOCRE HOF

An interval of 200x will be kept between sections and between the rear section and transport when passing through NEUVE EGLISE

5. The 129th Field Coy will take over work in the new area (present 109th Brigade Area) as follows:—

Left section of Area on night 19th/20th June
Right " " " " " 20th/21st June

6. The Medical Officer with his personnel and transport will move with the 129th Field Coy.

7. O.C 129th Field Coy will report completion of relief by wire

8. Acknowledge

G. Cheetham
Capt

18.6.16

Copy No 1. H.Q. G 24th Div
No 2 H.Q. Q "
No 3 73rd I.B
No 4 7th Australian I.B
No 5 C.R.E 50th Div
No 6 129th Field Coy
No 7 Record
No 8 Diary

10

Secret.

Copy No. 2

Operation Order No 74
by Lt Col A J. Craven R.E
C.R.E 24th Div.

Reference
Trench Map
1/20,000 Sheet
28 S.W

21.6.16.

1. The 2nd Australian Bde will relieve the 17th I.B in the right sector of the 24th Div Front
The relief will be completed by the 24th June

2. Command will pass from B.G.C 17th I.B to B.G.C 2nd Australian I.B on completion of relief in the trenches on the night 23rd/24th June.

3. The 104th Field Coy R.E will be relieved by the Field Coy RE, 1st Australian Division now at Aldershot Huts, taking over from the latter the work on O.P's now being carried out

4. On 22nd June [illegible] and [illegible] 104th Field Coy R.E. will report at [illegible] to the O.C. 1st Field Coy Australian Engineers who will arrange for them to be shown the work in progress.

5. On the same day (22nd June) 1 officer and 4 men of 1st Australian Field Coy will report at [illegible] to the O.C. 104th Field Coy who will arrange for them to be shown round the trench [illegible] by the [illegible].

6. On June 23rd two sections of 104th Field Coy R.E. will move [illegible] camp of 1st Australian Field Coy and two sections of the latter will move into the 104th Field Coy Camp. Time of arrival in both cases 3 p.m.

7. On June 24th the 104th Field Coy R.E. less 2 sections will move into camp at present occupied by 1st [illegible] Field Coy and the 1st Australian Field Coy less 2 sections will move into camp of 104th Field Coy.

8. The 104th Field Coy will leave behind a small detachment to show 1st Australian Field Coy all work in progress not already handed over. This detachment will rejoin its unit on June 25th

9. In accordance with the above orders the 1st Australian Field Coy will be responsible for work on O.Ps up to and including the night of 23/24 June after which the responsibility will rest with 104th Field Coy

10. Completion of transfer will be reported to C.R.E.

11. Acknowledge.

G. Cheetham
Capt
for C.R.E

Copy No1 to HQ (G)
No2 to HQ (Q)
No3 to 17th I.B
No4 to 2nd Australian I.B
No5 to C.R.A 24th Div.
No6 to ADMS 24th Div
No7 to 104th Fd Coy
No9 Record
No10 Diary

Instructions regarding War Diaries and Intelligence Summaries are contained in F. S. Regs., Part II. and the Staff Manual respectively. Title pages will be prepared in manuscript.

WAR DIARY
or
INTELLIGENCE SUMMARY.
(Erase heading not required.)

SECRET — Army Form C. 2118. — July

C.R.E 24th Div — Vol II

Place	Date	Hour	Summary of Events and Information	Remarks and references to Appendices
BAILLEUL	1st		Went with C.E IX Corps round KEMMEL defences. Visited LOCRE and DRANOUTRE	
	2nd		Routine	
	3rd		Routine 24th Div came under orders of IX Corps at 10.0 p.m	
	4th		24th Div HQ moved to LOCRE Handed over to S.O.R.E 1st ANZAC.	
LOCRE	5th		Conference of B.G.C s to dis-cuss work to be done in connection with contemplated offensive. With G.O.C and O.C Pioneers to KEMMEL HILL to select site for right Brigade HQ.	
	6th		Visited No 2 R.E. Park Vth Corps HQ and 103 Field Coy	
	7th		Received orders to relieve 1st ANZAC. Visited 73rd I.B with reference to Battle HQ Visited No 3 R.E. Park ABEELE Visit from assistant to controller of mines, arranged that 171st Tunnelling Coy would make tunnelled HQ for right sector.	
	8th		Issued orders for move (O.O 27 attached) 104th Field Coy R.E moved to LE DON Routine	

2353 Wt. W2544/1454 700,000 5/15 D. D. & L. A.D.S.S./Forms/C. 2118.

Army Form C. 2118.

Instructions regarding War Diaries and Intelligence Summaries are contained in F. S. Regs., Part II. and the Staff Manual respectively. Title pages will be prepared in manuscript.

WAR DIARY
or
INTELLIGENCE SUMMARY.
(Erase heading not required.)

CRE 24th Div

Place	Date	Hour	Summary of Events and Information	Remarks and references to Appendices
LOCRE	9th		Interview with O C 250th Tunnelling Coy about work on Tunnelled H Q.	
	10th		Div. H Q moved to BAILLEUL	
			Saw C.E 1st ANZAC about work to be done in ANZAC area	
BAILLEUL	11th		Visited work by Pioneers on KEMMEL HILL and preparatory work in right sector IX corps area. 73rd I.B took over centre section of line. 129th Field Coy took over R.E work in this section. (O O No 28 attached)	
	12th		104th Field Coy R E less one section and details moved from LEDON to LOCRE (O.O No 29 attached)	
			Visited centre sector with O.C 129th Field Coy	
	13th		Issued orders for each field Coy to use only one section to assist infantry on trench work remainder to be employed on special work such as O.Ps tunnelled dugouts etc.	
	14th		Visited O.Ps on Hill 74 and VIERSTRAAT with Lieut Kynnersley	
	15th		Routine.	
	16th		Visit from Controller of mines 2nd Army	
			Conference of Brigadiers	

2353 Wt. W2544/1454 700,000 5/15 D. D. & L. A.D.S.S./Forms/C. 2118.

Army Form C. 2118.

WAR DIARY
or
INTELLIGENCE SUMMARY.
(*Erase heading not required.*)

Instructions regarding War Diaries and Intelligence Summaries are contained in F. S. Regs., Part II. and the Staff Manual respectively. Title pages will be prepared in manuscript.

C.R.E 24th Div

Place	Date	Hour	Summary of Events and Information	Remarks and references to Appendices
BAILLEUL	17th		Visited preparatory work with O.C 104th Field Coy. Visited C E V Corps	
	18th		Visited 17th I B area with O.C 103 Field Coy R.E	
	19th		Orders received for the relief of the right and centre brigades by 20th Div and of left brigade by 50th Div Visited preparatory work on 50th Div area with O.C 250th Tunnelling Coy.	
	20th		129th Field Coy R.E relieved by 83rd Field Coy R.E (20th Div) and moved into rest area (C.R.E's O.O 30 attached) Handed over to C.R.E 20th Div.	
	21st		H.Q. R.E moved to St JANS CAPPEL 103rd Field Coy relieved by 2nd North'n Field Coy (50th Div) and moved to rest area 104th Field Coy relieved by 96th Field Coy (20th Div) and moved to rest area	
	22nd		Visited 2nd Army Shops HAZEBROUCK and No2 R.E. Park STRAZEELE arranged for supply of hand carts for Lewis Gunners.	

Instructions regarding War Diaries and Intelligence Summaries are contained in F. S. Regs., Part II. and the Staff Manual respectively. Title pages will be prepared in manuscript.

WAR DIARY
or
INTELLIGENCE SUMMARY.
(Erase heading not required.)

Army Form C. 2118.

C R E 24th Div

Place	Date	Hour	Summary of Events and Information	Remarks and references to Appendices
ST JANS CAPPEL	23rd		Routine	
	24th		Division started to move to 4th Army Area	
			Visited 103, 104, 129th Field Coys	
	25th		H.Q. R.E entrained BAILLEUL MAIN at 1.28 a.m for LONGUEAU and marched thence to CAVILLON	
			103rd Field Coy entrained BAILLEUL WEST at 2.30 a.m for LONGUEAU and marched thence to SAISSEMONT	
			104th Field Coy entrained BAILLEUL MAIN at 1.28 a.m for LONGUEAU and marched thence to SOUES	
			129th Field Coy entrained GODEWAERSWELDE at 2.30 a.m for LONGUEAU and marched thence to LE FAYEL MONTAGNE	
CAVILLON	26th		Visited 103, 104, and 129 Field Coys	
	27th		Visited C E IX Corps, H Q III Corps and 103, 104 and 129th Field Coys	
	28th		With G O C 24th Div to visit XIII corps, saw C E and went up to BOIS DES BILLONS	

2353 Wt. W2544/1454 700,000 5/15 D. D. & L. A.D.S.S./Forms/C. 2118.

Instructions regarding War Diaries and Intelligence Summaries are contained in F. S. Regs., Part II. and the Staff Manual respectively. Title pages will be prepared in manuscript.

WAR DIARY
or
INTELLIGENCE SUMMARY.
(Erase heading not required.)

Army Form C. 2118.

C.R.E 24th Div

Place	Date	Hour	Summary of Events and Information	Remarks and references to Appendices
CAVILLON	29th		Visited R.E Park LEALVILLERS and 103, 104, 129th Field Coys.	
	30th		Received Orders to move to area CORBIE – DAOURS Routine	
	31st		Division moved to XIII Corps area. Field Coys moved with Brigade groups under orders of B.G.Cs H.Q.R.E transport marched to ~~CAVILLON~~ CORBIE. Left CAVILLON at 11.30 p.m (30th) halted near DOUARS from 8.30 p.m to 12 noon arrived CORBIE 1.30 p.m March greatly delayed by continual checks in the column.	
			1/8/16 [signature] Lt Col RE CRE 24th Div	

2353 Wt. W2544/1454 700,000 5/15 D. D. & L. A.D.S.S./Forms/C. 2118.

Copy No 9.

Operation Orders No 26
by Lt Col A J Craven R E
C R E 24th Dvn

Reference
Trench Map 1/10000
Sht 28 S W

1. On the night of the 4th/5th July the 41st Div will take over the front South of R. DOUVE but excluding WINTER TRENCH (squares U 7 b and U 8 a) which remains in 1st ANZAC CORPS area and will continue to be held by 2nd Australian I. B.

2. The R E work in this area will be handed over by O C 1st Australian Field Coy to O C 233rd Field Coy 41st Dvn by ~~morning~~ noon ~~of~~ on July 1st.
Arrangements for transfer will be made direct between Field Coy commanders concerned subject to approval of B. G. Cs concerned.

3. The 41st Div will take over GRANDE MUNQUE and Brigade H Q at PETIT MUNQUE Farm from 2nd Aust. I. B.

2nd Aus I B H Q will move to PETIT PONT

4. The 2nd Aust I B will extend its front as far north as the WULVERGHEM-MESSINES road (Trench 140 inclusive) in relief of 7th Aust I B which is now holding trenches South of that road.

5. The R E work in this area will be handed over by O C 6th Aus Field Coy to O C 1st Aus Field Coy by the morning of July 4th
Arrangements for the transfer will be made direct between Field Coy commanders subject to approval of B G Cs concerned.

6. Command will pass on completion of relief as under:-
To G.O.C 1st Div The front South of R. DOUVE now held by 2nd Aust I.B on completion of infantry relief on night July 4th/5th

To B G C 2nd Aust. I B. The front between R. DOUVE and the WULVERGHEM MESSINES road on completion of infantry reliefs on night of July 5th/6th.

7 Completion of reliefs will be reported to C R E 24th Div

8 At 10.0 p.m. on 3rd July the 24th Div will come under the orders of the IX Corps.

At the same hour the command of troops in the 1st ANZAC Corps area (i.e. 2nd and 1st Aust. I Bs and other details) will pass from G O C 24th Div to G O C 1st ANZAC Corps.

9 Please acknowledge.

G. Cheetham
Capt
and Adjt. R.E.
24th Division.

1.7.16

Copy No 1 To H.Q. 2nd Divn
No 2 To H.Q. G
No 3 To 7th Aust I.B
No 4 To 2nd Aust I.B
No 5 To 1st Aust Field Coy
No 6 To 6th Aust Field Coy
No 7 To C.R.E. 41st Divn
No 8 To S.O.R.E. 1st ANZAC Corps
No 9 To Diary
No 10 Record.

Operation Order No 27
By Lt Col A J Craven R.E.
C.R.E. 24th Division

[illegible]
[illegible]

1. [illegible] I.B. [illegible] G.L. [illegible] J. [illegible] right [illegible] 9/7th [illegible]

2. [illegible] 129th Field Coy R.E. will [illegible] the [illegible] arrangements to [illegible] R.E. [illegible] concerned.

3. [illegible] I.B. [illegible] from its present [illegible] the WULVERGHEM-WYTSCHAETE road to the trench C.4. inclusive [illegible] the right 9/7th [illegible].

4. [illegible] Field Coy R.E. will [illegible] I.B. [illegible] WULVERGHEM-WYTSCHAETE [illegible] Field Coy R.E. [illegible] to be [illegible] by 3 [illegible].

[illegible] DONNE [illegible]
WINTER TRENCH [illegible] 133 [illegible]
[illegible]
[illegible] DONNE [illegible]
[illegible] LE R[illegible] [illegible]
[illegible] RED LODGE.
([illegible]).
[illegible]
[illegible] the
LE DON
[illegible]

8. [illegible] Trench 41 [illegible]
1st I.B. [illegible] C.3. and C.4. [illegible] to T.6.d.7.4.
and thence [illegible]
R. DOUVE.

9. Command will pass as under.
from G.O.C. 1st Australian Div.
to G.O.C. 2nd Div. at 6 a.m. 9 7/16.

from B.G.C. 1st Australian I.B. to
B.G.C. 17th I.B. on completion of relief
in trenches C.4 to D.4.

from B.G.C. 2nd Australian and
[illegible] Brigades to B.G.C.
17th I.B. on completion of relief on
front R. DOUVE. to trench C.3.

from B.G.C. [illegible] I.B. to B.G.C.
[illegible] Div. on completion of
relief in trenches G.1. to J. 3. R.

10. [illegible] of relief will be
reported by [illegible] to C.R.E.

11. Please acknowledge.

G. Cheetham

8-7-16. Capt.

and Adjt. R.E.

24th Division.

Copy No. 1 — H.Q. 24th Divn.
2 - Q.
3 - 17th I.B.
4 - 72nd I.B.
5 - 73rd I.B.
6 - 103rd Field Coy. R.E.
7 - 104th
8 - 129th
9 - C.R.E. [illegible] Div.
10 - C.R.E. 50th Div.
11 - War Diary.
12 - Record.

After Order 1.

The 103rd Field Coy. R.E. will continue the work on the artillery O.P.s

8-7-16. Capt.

Copy No 8

Operation Order No 28
By Lt Col A J Craven R.E
C.R.E 24th Div

Ref Trench Map 1/20,000 10.7.16
Sheet 28 S.W

1. On the night of July 11th/12th the 73rd I.B will take over the front from trench 140 exclusive to trench D5 inclusive

2. O.C 129th Field Coy R.E will be responsible for the R.E work on this front, employing not more than two sections on the work.

The work will be taken over from 103rd and 104th Field Coys by the night of the 12th/13th under arrangements to be made by O.C Coys concerned with the approval of B.G.Cs concerned.

3. Completion of relief will be reported to this office

4 Please acknowledge

J. Cheetham
Capt and Adjt. R.E.
24th Division.

Copy No 1 HQ 24th Div
No 2 HQ (Q) 24th Div
No 3 73rd I. B
No 4 103rd Field Coy R.E
No 5 104th
No 6 129th
No 7 ~~Diary~~ Record
No 8 ~~Record~~ Diary 1~~04th Field Coy R.E~~

Secret

Copy No 6

Operation Order No 29
By Lt Col A J. Craven R.E

Ref Trench Map 1/20,000 12.7.16
Sheet 28 S.W

1. The 104th Field Coy R.E less the details specified below will move to billets at LOCRE M23a 73 on the 13th inst under arrangements to be made by O.C. 104th Field Coy R.E

2. One section and any men required for special work in shops will be left at present camp to assist in the work in the 72nd Bde area

3. Completion of move to be reported to the C.R.E

4. Please acknowledge

G. Cheetham
Capt
and Adjt. R.E.
24th Division.

✓ Copy No 1 to HQ 24th Div
No 2 H.Q. G.
✓ No 3 72nd I B
No 4 104th Field Coy
✓ No 5 24th Div Train
No 6 Diary
No 7 Record

[illegible]

Copy No 11

Operation Order No 30
By Lt Col A J Craven R.E.
C.R.E. 24th Div.

Ref Map 27 S.E.
1/20000

1. The 24th Div will move into Rest Camp.

2. The portion of the line held by the 17th I.B will be taken over by a Bde of 50th Div.

3. The remainder of the line held by the 24th Div will be taken over by the 20th Div.

4. The work of defence work in the area now being held by the 17th I.B will be handed over by the 103rd Field Coy to 2nd Northumbrian Field Coy. They will move into the billets now occupied by the 129 Field Coy on 20th inst.

5. All other work will be taken over by R.E of 20th Div.

[illegible] F [illegible]

[illegible]

[illegible] F [illegible] (22 – 26 Lbs.)

2. [illegible]

[illegible]

4. F [illegible] C_4 [illegible]

[illegible] full [illegible]

[illegible]

[illegible] 5th [illegible]

[illegible] F [illegible] C_4 [illegible]

[illegible]

10. The M.O. i/c R.E. will be [illegible] and [illegible] [illegible] with [illegible] Field Coy.

11. Completion [illegible] will be reported to this office.

12. Please acknowledge.

G. Cheetham
Capt
and Adjt. R.E.
24th Division.

Copy No 1 G. 24th Div.
No 2 Q
No 3 17th I.B.
No 4 72nd
No 5 73rd
No 6 103 Field Coy
No 7 104
No 8 129
No 9 C.R.E. 50th Div
No 10 " 20th Div
11 Diary
12 R.E.

24th Divisional Engineers

C. R. E.

24th DIVISION

AUGUST 1 9 1 6

Instructions regarding War Diaries and Intelligence Summaries are contained in F. S. Regs., Part II. and the Staff Manual respectively. Title pages will be prepared in manuscript.

WAR DIARY
or
INTELLIGENCE SUMMARY.
(*Erase heading not required.*)

Army Form C. 2118.

Vol 12

Ap 1916

C R E 24th Div

Place	Date Aug. ~~Sept~~	Hour	Summary of Events and Information	Remarks and references to Appendices
CAYILLON	1		104th Field Coy moved with 17th I B group to Sand pit valley	
			103rd Field Coy moved with 72nd I.B group to Sand pit valley	
			Visited C.R.E 30th Division and 30th Div R.E Park. Arranged to take over the latter the next day	
	2nd		Divisional H Q moved to the CITADEL 2½ miles N of BRAY SUR SOMME	
			All three companies moved into camps at SAPPER CORNER just N. of BRAY	
			Took over 30th Div R.E Park and workshops at BRAY. Capt WHITTALL 129th field Coy R.E Placed in charge	
CITADEL 2½ miles N. of BRAY	3rd		Visited No 6 R.E Park MERICOURT and MM Dump, also C E XIII Corps	
	4th		Received orders to start work on A and B lines behind front line in TRONES and BERNAFAY woods with one company R E 2 companies pioneers and one infantry battalion working party	
			Ordered 103 Field Coy to move into bivouacs in old British line N W of CARNOY	
	5th		103 Field Coy moved to Bivouac in old British line N W of CARNOY leaving transport at SAPPER CORNER	

2353 Wt. W2544/1454 700,000 5/15 D. D. & L. A.D.S.S./Forms/C. 2118.

Instructions regarding War Diaries and Intelligence Summaries are contained in F. S. Regs., Part II. and the Staff Manual respectively. Title pages will be prepared in manuscript.

WAR DIARY
or
INTELLIGENCE SUMMARY.
(Erase heading not required.)

Army Form C. 2118.

CRE 24th Div

Place	Date Sept Aug	Hour	Summary of Events and Information	Remarks and references to Appendices
CITADEL	6th		Received orders to build a new Div HQ at FORKED TREE on the BRAY - ALBERT road. 129th Field Coy ordered to do so	
			104th Field Coy ordered to prepare a dummy position representing GUILLEMONT. Received orders to dig deep dug outs in MALTZ HORN TRENCH, work held up owing to projected attack by 2nd and 55th Divisions	
			Conferred with C.R.E 55th Div.	
	7th		Conferred with C R E 2nd Div.	
			Received orders to take over from 2nd Div and to hand over work to 3rd Div	
			Two sections 104th Field Coy to be ready to move with 17th I.B in relief of 6th Bde 2nd Div and to consolidate position gained by them	
			O.O 32 issued (attached)	
	8th		Orders to take over cancelled. Conferred with C R E 55th Div. 104th Field Coy moved to CARNOY	
	9th	4.15a.m	Orders received to relieve 55th Div in right sector of XIII corps	
		3p.m	orders received cancelling relief of 55th Div, the 17th I.B will relieve 6th I.B 2nd Div on night 9th/10th, 104th Field Coy to send one section to relieve one section 5th Field Coy on front line work. 72nd I.B to relieve 166th Bde 55th Div 103 Field Coy to relieve 2/2 W Lancs Field Coy with one section on front line work.	
			O O 33 issued (Attached)	

2353 Wt. W2544/1454 700,000 5/15 D. D. & L. A.D.S.S./Forms/C. 2118.

Instructions regarding War Diaries and Intelligence Summaries are contained in F. S. Regs., Part II. and the Staff Manual respectively. Title pages will be prepared in manuscript.

WAR DIARY
or
INTELLIGENCE SUMMARY.
(Erase heading not required.)

Army Form C. 2118.

C.R.E 24th Div

Place	Date	Hour	Summary of Events and Information	Remarks and references to Appendices
CITADEL	Aug. 10th		103rd Field Coy took over from 2/2 West Lancs Field Coy	
			O.O 34 issued ordering 129 Field Coy less two sections to move to camp at A13d5.9	
			in CARNOY VALLEY. H.Q 24th Div moved to MINDEN POST ½ mile W of CARNOY	
MINDEN POST	11th		Two battalions of the 73rd I.B moved up to provide parties for work on C.Ts	
			under O.C.S 103 and 104 Field Coys	
			129th Field Coy less 2 sections moved to CARNOY valley	
	12th		With O.C 104 Field Coy to see Bde H.Q mined dugouts	
	13th		With O.C 103 Field Coy to inspect work on C.T.s through BERNAFAY and TRONES	
			WOODS	
			Visit from C.R.E 35th Div	
			Attended conference held by Corps Commander	
			2nd Lieut F.E. SPARROW 129th Field Coy died of wounds	
	14th		Round the front line with O.C 104th Field Coy.	
			Visited B.G.C 17th I.B and Pioneers	
			24th Div O.O 76 received giving orders for an attack on GUILLEMONT	
	15th		Visited 104th Field Coy	
			Round front line with O.C 103 Field Coy R.E	
			500 infantry lent by 35th Div for work on our C.Ts under supervision of 104 Field Coy	

Instructions regarding War Diaries and Intelligence Summaries are contained in F. S. Regs., Part II. and the Staff Manual respectively. Title pages will be prepared in manuscript.

WAR DIARY
or
INTELLIGENCE SUMMARY.
(*Erase heading not required.*)

Army Form C. 2118.

C.R.E 24th Div

Place	Date	Hour	Summary of Events and Information	Remarks and references to Appendices
MINDEN POST	16th		With G.O.C to front line to reconnoitre GUILLEMONT.	
			Visited B.G.C 17th I.B and Pioneers.	
			500 infantry 35th Div worked on our C.Ts under supervision of 104th Field Coy	
			2 sections of 129th Field Coy moved up to CARNOY valley	
		10pm	O.O. No 77 received giving further instructions as to attack on GUILLEMONT	
	17th	1pm	Received 24th Div O O No 78. ordering 72nd I.B to attack enemy strong point in conjunction with an attack by 3rd Div on our right	
		3¼pm	C.R.E's O.O 35 issued attached.	
		5pm	Received 24th Div O.O 79 modifying O.O. 77	
		7pm	C.R.E's O.O 36 issued (attached) modifying O.O 35.	
		8pm	Received 24th Div O.O 79 (Addenda).	
	18th		Capture of Station and Quarry at GUILLEMONT reported. Right of attack held up by enemy strong point.	
			Brigadiers reported that 103rd Field Coy were sent up to consolidate the QUARRY and 104th to consolidate the station.	
	19th		Report received that 103rd Field Coy had done a certain amount of consolidation at the QUARRY but time available was very short as they were sent back by the infantry	

2353 Wt. W2544/1454 700,000 5/15 D. D. & L. A.D.S.S./Forms/C. 2118.

Instructions regarding War Diaries and Intelligence Summaries are contained in F. S. Regs., Part II. and the Staff Manual respectively. Title pages will be prepared in manuscript.

Army Form C. 2118.

WAR DIARY
or
INTELLIGENCE SUMMARY.
(Erase heading not required.)

C.R.E. 24th Div

Place	Date	Hour	Summary of Events and Information	Remarks and references to Appendices
MINDEN POST	19th (Cont)		by the infantry who said that the QUARRY had not yet been taken. The Brigade major however sent them up again.	
			Casualties to 103 Field Coy 4 O.R wounded	
		1.p.m	Received message saying that right Brigade would be relieved by 35th Div as far North as TRONES WOOD GUILLEMONT road on night 19th-20th	
			C.R.E ordered (EA222 attached) 2 sections 103rd Field Coy under 2nd in command to work on this point the following night, also ordered 2 sections of the 104th to improve and wire strong point at the station	
		10.0p.m	Ordered 129th Field Coy to relieve 103rd Field Coy on 20th (O.O 38 attached)	
	20th		100 infantry of 73rd I.B ordered to report to O.C. 129 Field Coy as carrying and working party.	
			Report received from Lieut. KYNNERSLEY 103 Field Coy about strong point at QUARRY while working on which 2nd Lieut R C BROWN was killed and from 104 Field Coy that Station strong point had been improved and good wire provided on North and East faces	
		4.30p.m	Asked for a further 50 men to be attached to 104 Field Coy as two more sections were going in. Refused because battalions were too weak	

2353 Wt. W2544/1454 700,000 5/15 D. D. & L. A.D.S.S./Forms/C. 2118.

Instructions regarding War Diaries and Intelligence Summaries are contained in F. S. Regs., Part II. and the Staff Manual respectively. Title pages will be prepared in manuscript.

WAR DIARY
or
INTELLIGENCE SUMMARY.
(Erase heading not required.)

Army Form C. 2118.

C.R.E 24th Division

Place	Date	Hour	Summary of Events and Information	Remarks and references to Appendices
MINDEN POST	20th Cont	4.40 p.m	Orders sent for 2nd Lieut WATSON 104th Field Coy (Supernumerary officer) to be temporarily attached to 129th Field Coy. 129th Field Coy relieved 103 Field Coy in right Brigade sector	
		7.10 p.m	Issued O.O. 39 (Attached)	
		7.50 p.m	Sent up one section 104th Field Coy to further improve station defences	
		10 p.m ~~[illegible]~~	At request of B.G.C 72nd I.B sent up 1 section 129th Field Coy to assist 8th Queens to connect up certain posts. This work was eventually not required	
	21st		Attack on GUILLEMONT without much success. Only work done by the R.E a short length of C.T near the "QUARRY"	
		7.0 p.m	24th Div O.O No 83 received	
	22nd		It is now clear that we never held the Quarry which has been occupied throughout by the enemy and not shelled by us	
	~~[illegible]~~		O.O No 84 received. The 24th Div to be relieved by the 20th Div on night 22nd 23rd	
			Field Coys moved back to BRAY handing over their camps to Field Coys 20th Div	
	23rd		Handed over to C.R.E 20th Div. Div Head Quarters moved back to FORKED TREE ½ mile from BRAY on the BRAY - ALBERT road.	

2353 Wt. W2544/1454 700,000 5/15 D. D. & L. A.D.S.S./Forms/C. 2118.

Army Form C. 2118.

WAR DIARY
or
INTELLIGENCE SUMMARY.
(Erase heading not required.)

Instructions regarding War Diaries and Intelligence Summaries are contained in F. S. Regs., Part II. and the Staff Manual respectively. Title pages will be prepared in manuscript.

C.R.E 24th Div

Place	Date	Hour	Summary of Events and Information	Remarks and references to Appendices
FORKED TREE	23rd		During the active operations just concluded, the chief difficulty experienced by the R.E was that of obtaining carrying parties for R.E stores from the Brigades. Carrying parties for all other stores were arranged for by Brigades, and R.E stores were apparently considered to be of minor importance. A considerable quantity of General stores was dumped at the most forward point to which transport could be taken in each Brigade area, but only a small amount was carried right forward.	
	24th		Received orders from C.E to erect huts at CITADEL and to take over work on rear defences from 35th Division. Ordered 104th Field Coy to erect huts and 129th to do defence work.	
	25th	1 a.m	Received 24th Div 0.0 85. The Division is to move to squares E13 and E14	
		6 a.m	Issued C.R.E's 0.0 40 (attached)	
			H.Q.R.E moved to BUIRE, division transferred to 15th Corps	
	26th		Visited C.E XV Corps	
	27th		Made arrangements for tarpaulin shelter for troops	

2353 Wt. W2544/1454 700,000 5/15 D. D. & L. A.D.S.S./Forms/C. 2118.

Army Form C. 2118.

Instructions regarding War Diaries and Intelligence Summaries are contained in F. S. Regs., Part II. and the Staff Manual respectively. Title pages will be prepared in manuscript.

WAR DIARY
or
INTELLIGENCE SUMMARY.

(*Erase heading not required.*)

Place	Date	Hour	Summary of Events and Information	Remarks and references to Appendices
BUIRE	28th		Visited C.R.E 14th Div from whom we are taking over shortly.	
			Commenced camps for 2 brigades; by evening 104th and 129th Field Coys had completed 21 shelters 38'x15'.	
	29th		Visited 33rd Div trenches with G.S.O2 who was wounded by a sniper.	
			Shelters continued. Total of 36 completed. 15 roofed but not provided with sides and about 20 partially erected	
			Received 24th Div O.O.s 88 and 89. The Division will take over a Brigade front 33rd Division on night of 30th/31st in addition to relief already ordered.	
		10.30pm	O.O 41 issued (Attached.	
	30th		Troops moved into area occupied by 33rd Div Visited C.R.E of that Div with a view to taking over	
			Major King commanding 104th Field Coy appointed C.R.E 38th Div and promoted temporary Lieut-Col	
			103rd Field Coy and 1 Coy Pioneers placed at the disposal of B.G.C 72nd I.B in the right sector	
			129th Field Coy and 1 Coy Pioneers placed at the disposal of B.G.C 73rd I.B in the left sector	

Army Form C. 2118.

WAR DIARY
or
INTELLIGENCE SUMMARY.
(Erase heading not required.)

Instructions regarding War Diaries and Intelligence Summaries are contained in F. S. Regs., Part II. and the Staff Manual respectively. Title pages will be prepared in manuscript.

C.R.E. 24th Div

Place	Date	Hour	Summary of Events and Information	Remarks and references to Appendices
E11 Central Sheet 62d	30th Cont.		104th Field Coy and rest of pioneers in reserve	
	31st		Moved to H.Q at E11 central and took over from C R E 33rd Div	
			Visited 104th Field Coy, B.G.C 72nd I.B and 73rd I.B and dumps	
			Enemy attacked our front. Repulsed on 72nd I.B front and on right of 73rd I.B, penetrated on left of 73rd I.B	

[signature]
Lt Col RE
CRE 24th Div

Secret

Operation Order Copy No. 9.
No 32
By Lt Col [illegible] Craven RE
CRE 24th Division

Ref.

Map 1/5000 GUICHY and GUILLEMONT.
and Map 1/20,000 57 d S.E.
57 c S.W.
62 d N.E.
62 c. N.W.

1. The XIII Corps is attacking GUILLEMONT and the trenches between it and DELVILLE WOOD on [illegible] August.

2. 24th Division relieves 2nd Div. as soon after the attack as circumstances permit. 17th I.B. will take over front held by 2nd Div. from railway inclusive at point reached by attacking line and DELVILLE WOOD.

3. The 2nd Division has orders to construct strong points at
The Station
Point T 19 a 4 2
Point S 18 d central
These works will be improved by 17th I.B.

(sd)

4. The work of consolidating captured positions will be continued immediately after relief has been effected. The importance of quickly consolidating must be impressed upon all ranks. Wiring in front and placing machine guns in position are matters of special importance.

5. The 17th Div H.Q. will be at A.8.b.2.9. Command of front will pass to 17th Div. on completion of relief.

6. Command of front and area at present held by 2nd Div will pass to G.O.C. 24th Div at 7 a.m. on 9th Aug at which hour 24th Div H.Q. will close at the CITADEL and open at MINDEN POST F.12.c.3.4.

7. 103rd Field Company will remain in its present camp.

8. 104th Fd Coy RE will march tomorrow at time ordered by 17th Div. Two sections of the company will proceed to the craters A.8.a where guides will be sent by C.R.E. 2nd Div to conduct them to the front

arrived to take over from 5th Field Coy, etc. must be coordinating.

The remainder of the company will proceed to take over the 226th Fd Coy Camp at A 13 c 8.0.

9. It is possible that more than 2 sections may have to be sent forward. O.C. 104th Fd Coy must be prepared to do so.

O.C. 104th Fd Coy will arrange direct with 17th Bde. for any carrying parties required.

10. The 124th Fd Coy less 2 sections will march at a time to be notified later and take over the camp of the East Lancs Fd Coy at A 13 a 5.9.

11. Pontoons and Trestles and all Transport not required will be left in the present camps where horses will also be left.

12. In the forward area units will not march in larger formations than sections.

13. O.C. 106th Fd Coy will send two

reporting to 17th Div. H Q in this area.

14. The 129th Fd Coy will detail an NCO to take charge of the 2nd Div dump at CARNOY. He will receive instructions from the Adjutant R.E.

15. Please acknowledge.

16. The Div RE Park at BRAY continues under 24th Div as heretofore.

G Chettiam

7/8/16

Capt & Adj RE
24th Div.

Issued at 11.30 pm.

Copy No.	
1	H.Q. 24th Div
2	G 24th Div.
3 (Extract)	17th Div.
4	103rd Fd Coy RE
5	104th — —
6	129th — —
7	CRE 2nd Div
8	Record
9	Diary.

1

Operation Order No 33 Copy No. 6

Secret

By Lt Col: A J Craven RE
CRE 24th Division

Ref map 1/20,000.
Sheets 57d SE
57c S.W.
62d N.E.
62c N.W.

9. 8. 16.

1. The 72nd I.B. will relieve the 166th Bde. on the night of 10/11th August under arrangements between B. G. Cs concerned

The area to be taken over will extend from S30b 7 3. – S30c 5½ 3 – A5b0. 2 – A4c 4 7 – A4a 0.0. to about the railway.

2. The 103rd Fd Coy will remain in their present camp and will take over with one section the work on the front line in this area, now being done by one section of the 2/2 W. Lancs Field Company whose H.Q are at Bde H.Q TALUS BOISE A4b central under arrangements to be made between O.Cs Companies.

3. Please acknowledge

G Cheetham
Capt & Adj RE
24th Div

Issued at 11.45 p.m.

Copies to.

No 1 H.Q. 24th Div
2 Q 24th Div
3 72nd I.B.
4 103rd Fd Coy RE.
5 CRE 55th Div
6 Diary
7 Record

Operation Order No 34 Copy No 6
by Lieut Col A. J. Craven RE
CRE 24th Division

Ref Map 1/20,000

10 Aug 1916

Sheets 62d NE.
62c N.W.

1. The 129th Fd Coy RE less two sections will move to the camp recently occupied by the East Anglian Field Company RE at A13d 5 9. The move to be complete by 12 noon on the 11th inst.

2. Pontoons, trestles and all transport not required will be left in their present camp where horses will also be left.

3. In the forward area the company will not march in larger formations than sections.

4. OC 129th Fd Coy will report personally to CRE at MINDEN POST on arrival

c/. Please acknowledge.

G Cheetham
Capt + Adj RE
24th Div.

Issued at 11.45 p.m.

Copies to

No 1 H.Q. 24th Div
2 Q 24th Div
3 73rd I.B.
4 129th Fd Coy RE
5 Record
6 Diary.

SECRET.

Operation Order No 35 Copy No 9

[illegible]

[illegible]

17-8-16.

Reference Map 1/10,000
Sheets 57C S.W.3
62C N.W.1.
and map 1/5000 GINCHY [illegible] GUILLEMONT.

1. The 24th Division will attack GUILLEMONT on 18th August.

2. The objective will be reached in three stages.

<u>1st Stage</u> The capture and consolidation of the German Defences along the line T25 b 1.4½ (inclusive) where touch will be maintained with the 3rd Division – T25 a 9.4 – T25 a 7½.7½ – T25 a 0.8½ – S24 b 4.2 – T19 a 1.6 – S18 d 5½.4 (where touch will be maintained with the 14th Division.

<u>2nd Stage</u> Establishing a line along the LONGUEVAL – GUILLEMONT road from S24 b 7.4 (M.G. House). – crossroads T19 c 6.3½ – S.E. corner of GUILLEMONT at T25 b 1.9 – T25 b 1.4½.

<u>3rd Stage</u> The capture of the whole of GUILLEMONT village and the German Trench between the village and

Point

point T19 d 7.3 connecting with the 3rd Division on the right and with the southern portion of GUILLEMONT on the left.

3. The attack will be carried out by the 73rd Inf. Bde and one battalion 72nd Inf. Bde on the right, and by the 17th Inf: Bde on the left.

4. The work of consolidation will be carried out with the greatest energy directly the objectives have been gained.

5. The 103rd Field Company R.E. will construct strong points at: about T25 a 9.4, the Quarry, T19 d 4.4, T19 a 9.1.

The company will come under the orders of B.G.C. 73rd I.B. who will issue instructions as to when each point is to be started.

6. 2 sections of the 104th Field Company RE will construct strong points at the STATION, and T19 c 4.9½ (about).

They will come under the orders of the B.G.C. 17th Inf: Bde, who will issue instructions as to when each point is to be started.

7. Each Brigade will detail 25 men per section

section of the Field Company allotted to them – with one officer per 50 men. This party will be used for carrying up material and for working and will be attached to the Field Company throughout the operations.

8. On completion of the strong points each section will return to the point of assembly – Completion to be reported to the C.R.E. through the Brigade.

9. The 129th Field Company R.E. and the 10th Field Company R.E. less 2 sections will be in Divisional Reserve – in their present camps – They must be ready to move within 15 minutes.

~~10~~ 11.

Each Field Company will send 2 orderlies to H.Q. Divn. R.E. and 2 to Brigade H.Q. In the case of the units in reserve the orderlies will be sent to 12th Bde H.Q.

10. All troops will wear fighting kit – 50 rounds of ammunition to be carried.

12. M.O. i/c R.E. will remain at Div:

Div H. Q.

13. Advanced Dressing Stations will be established at :-

THE BRIQUETERIE. (A 4. b.).
N. W. corner of BERNAFAY. WOOD (S28 b9.9).

Walking cases proceed to BRONFAY. FARM. (F 29 b).

14. acknowledge.

17/8/16.

[illegible]
Lt Col [illegible]
[illegible]

Issued at [illegible]

Copy No 1 [illegible] 24th Div
2 [illegible] Q.
3 17th Inf. Bde
4 72nd Inf. Bde
5 73rd Inf. Bde
6 103rd Fd. Coy RE
7 104th Fd. Coy RE
8 129th Fd. Coy RE
9 Diary
10 Record

SECRET. Copy No. 6

Operation Order No 36
by Lieut Col: A. J. Craven R.E.
C.R.E. 24th Division

Ref maps 1/10,000 17-8-16
Sheets 57c S.W.3
62c. N.W. 1.
and map 1/5,000 GINCHY. and GUILLEMONT.

1. C.R.E's O.O. No 35 of 17.8.16. is modified as follows

2. The boundary between the 24th and 3rd Division will be from point S. 30 b 6·2. to T25 b 1·4½. (Trench from T25 a 3·3 to T25 b1·4½ inclusive to 24th Division

3. The 72nd Brigade has been ordered to capture and consolidate the enemy strong point at S 30 b 6·2. tonight

4. The attack will be carried out on the 18th and 19th August as follows.

18th August

1st Objective

ZERO.

73rd I.B. The enemy defences from S 30 b 6·2 along the Sunken Road and including the trench which runs east of the east of the Sunken Road to T25 a 0·9. thence the trench to S24 d 8·5.

17th I.B. The enemy defences from S. 24 d 8·5 – S24 b 4·2 – M.G. HOUSE. (inclusive) – T19 a 1·6 – S18 d 5½·4

2nd Objective

ZERO + 2 hours

73rd I.B. The line T25 a 3·3 – T25 a 2·8 – T25 a 3½·9 – T19 c 3·2 thence round the Eastern and Northern edges of the QUARRY (T19c).

17th I.B. The STATION and defence round it from S24 d 6·8 – T19 c 1·9½ – S24 b 7·4.

19th August

ZERO

73rd I.B. The line T25 a 9½·4½ – cross roads T19 c 6·3½ thence along the GUILLEMONT – LONGUEVAL road as far North as the cross roads at T19 c 2·8½ (exclusive).

17th I.B. The enemy defences West of the cross roads at T19 c 2·8½ and North of BROMPTON ROAD

19th August (cont) ZERO + 1½ hours.

73rd I.B.

(a). To advance to the Eastern edge of the village from T25 b1·4½ – T19 a8·2 and establish a defensive line on the outskirts of the village.

(b). To push forward a line of outposts on the line T25 b1·4½ – CEMETERY – T19 b0·2½.

17th I.B.

To capture and consolidate the portion of the German Trench between the village and T19 a1·6 and the German trench on the BROMPTON ROAD between T19 c2·8½ and T19 a5·0.

5. Strong points will be established at the points named in CRE's Operation Order No 35.

6. ZERO hour on 18th + 19th August will be notified separately.

7 Acknowledge.

G Cheetham
Capt + Adj RE
for CRE 24th Div

Copy No 1 H.Q. 24th Div
2 103rd Fd Coy
3 104th Fd Coy
4 129th Fd Coy
5 Record
6 Diary

Issued at 7 p.m.

Secret

copy No. 5

Operation Order No 38
By Lt Col A J Craven R.E.
C.R.E. 24th Div.

17.8.16

1. The 129th Field Coy will relieve the 103rd Field Coy in the 72nd Brigade area tomorrow [illegible] 20th inst.
Detailed orders will be issued later.

2. Please acknowledge

G. Cheetham
Capt and Adj R.E.
for C.R.E. 24th Div

Issued at 10.0 p.m.

Copy No 1 to 72nd I.B.
No 2 to 129 Field Coy
No 3 to 103. Field Coy
No 4 to Diary
No 5 to Record.

Copy No 8

Operation Order No 37

Ref Map 1/5,000 by Lt Col A J Craven RE
GINCHY and CRE 24th Div
GUILLEMONT 20th Aug. 1916

1. The 24th Div will renew the attack on GUILLEMONT on August 21st

2. The objective will be as follows:–
SOUTH WEST corner of the orchard at T 25 a ½.8. – Trench junction at T 25 a 3½ 8
T 19 c 3 2 – road junction T 19 c 5.6 – T 19 a 5½ ½
T 19 a ½ 6

3. The attack by the 24th Div will be delivered as follows:–
Right Brigade (72nd I.B)
The attack by this Brigade depends on whether or not the enemy strong point at S 30 b 7.1½ which is being attacked today by the 35th Div has fallen
(a) If strong point has fallen
<u>Objective</u> (Attack to be made from the West)
The enemy defences within the area North of DOWN STREET (inclusive) – T 25 a 3½.8. – road junction T 19 c 4½.6 – road junction S 24 d 3.5 and to connect with 35th Div on right and 17th I.B on left

T 19 c 4½ 6

(b) If strong point has not fallen

1st Objective

Attack to be made from West

The area North of MOUNT STREET from T 19 c 3 2 - road junction T 19 c 4½ 6 - road junction S 24 d 8.5 and to form a defensive flank on the right along MOUNT STREET and to connect with 17th I.B on the left

2nd Objective (Attack to be made from NORTH)

The area between MOUNT STREET and DOWN STREET both inclusive and as far EAST as the line T 25 a 3½ 8 - T 19 c 3 2.

In the case of (b) Operation alone taking place the attack on the 2nd Objective will begin 30 minutes after "Zero" time.

Left Brigade (17th I.B)

Objective The area bounded by a line from road junction S 24 d 8.5 - road junction T 19 c 4½. 6 - T 19 a 5½. ½ - T 19 a. 0.7 and to connect with 72nd I.B on the right.

3

4. Strong posts will be established at:-
T 25 a 0.8.
T 25 a 3½.8. } By 72nd I.B
T 19 c 4½.6.

T 19 a 5½.½. By 17th I.B
The work of consolidation will be carried out with the greatest energy directly objectives have been gained.

5. The 104th Field Coy R.E is allotted to the 17th I.B for work on strong point.
The 124th Field Coy R.E is allotted to the 72nd I.B for work on strong points.
Accurate Orders as to assembly points and times at which R.E are to move forward will be obtained by O.C.s Field Coys from the Brigades to which they are attached.
The 103rd Field Coy is allotted to the Divisional Reserve, it will remain in its present position and be ready to move at 15 minutes notice.

6. The boundary between 17th and 72nd I.B will be:-
From road junction S.24 d.8.3 —
T 19 c 4½.6.

7. The R.E. will wear "Fighting Kit", 50 rounds of S.A.A. per man will be carried.

8. O.C. Field Coys. will apply to Brigades for parties to carry up wire and pickets and tools.

9. Carrying parties must be made to realise the urgent necessity of carrying through their tasks with as much vigour and determination as is required from troops detailed to assault the position.

9. The position of any wells found, with a report, giving the dimensions and depth of the water will be forwarded to this office as soon as possible after discovery.

10. Advanced dressing stations will be established at

The BRIQUETERIE (A 4 b)

N.W. corner of BERNAFAY WOOD (S 22 b 9 [illegible])

Walking cases will proceed to BRONFAY FARM (F 29 b)

11. Please acknowledge.

Issued at 7.10 p.m. G. Cheetham

Capt. [illegible] R.E.

[illegible]

Secret

Operation Order No 40 — Copy No 6

By Lt Col A J Craven RE
CRE 24th Division

Ref Map 1/20 000
Sheet 62d NE.

1. The division will move today to bivouacs in squares E 13 and E 14.

2. The 103rd, 104th & 129th Field Coys will march via MORLANCOURT – VILLE SUR ANCRE so as to clear MORLANCOURT by 3 p.m.

3. Billeting parties will meet the DAA and QMG at road junction E 14 c 3.0. at 10 a m

4. Working parties detailed for today will carry out their work and will rejoin their units at the new camp

5. Div H. Q will move at 10 am to BUIRE

7

6. Please acknowledge

G. Cheetham
Capt and Adj. R.E.
25.8.16 24th Div

Cpy No 1 H.Q 24th Div
No 2 Q
No 3 103rd Field Coy ✓
No 4 104th Field Coy ✓
No 5 129th Field Coy. ✓
No 6 Diary
No 7 Record
Issued at 6. a. m

S E C R E T   Copy No.. 11

Operation Order No, 41
by Lieut Colonel A.J. Craven R.E.
C.R.E. 24th Division.

Reference map 1/20,000 Sheet 62 c N.W., 62 d N.E. 57 c S.W.
and trench map 1/10,000.

1. The 24th Division will relieve the 14th and 33rd Divisions on the 30th August and the night 30th/31st August.

2. The 72nd I.B. will relieve the Brigade of the 24th Division in the line from ALE ALLEY T 13 a (exclusive) to the LONGUEVAL - FLERS road (exclusive) about S 12 a 8 2½.

3. The 103rd Field Company R.E. is placed at the disposal of B.G.C. 72nd I.B. for work on this front in advance of LEES support line.

Two sections of the 103rd Field Company R.E. will be billeted in the forward area under arrangements which will be made by the 72nd Brigade.

O.C. 103rd Field Company R.E. will arrange to take over work now being done by 89th Field Company R.E. in this area.

4. The 73rd I.B. will relieve the Brigade of the 33rd Division in the line between the LONGUEVAL - FLERS road inclusive at about S 12 a 8 2½ and the left of the 33rd Division which it is expected will then be on WOOD LANE S 11 a 1 5.

5. The 129th Field Company R.E. is placed at the disposal of B.G.C. 73rd I.B. for work on this front.

The 129th Field Company R.E. will take over the R.E. work in this area from the 222nd Field Company R.E.

Two sections of the 129th Field Company R.E. will be billeted in the forward area under arrangements which will be made by the 73rd Brigade.

6. The Field Companies will take over camps as follows on 30th August, arriving at their new camps before 12 noon.

103rd Field Company R.E. from 89th Field Company R.E.
F 10 a 9 8
104th Field Company R.E. from 61st Field Company R.E.
F 4 d 5 3
129th Field Company R.E. from 222nd Field Company R.E.
F 2 c 1 9

7. On arrival in the 14th Divisional area all troops of

the 24th

the 24th Division will come under the orders of G.O.C. 14th Division until 10 a.m. on 31st August.

8. Command of the front and area at present held by the 14th Division will pass to G.O.C. 24th Division at 10 a.m. on 31st August at which hour Divisional Headquarters will close at D 28 d 8 5 and re-open at E 11 central.

9. Completion of reliefs will be reported to C.R.E. 24th Division.

10. Acknowledge.

G Cheetham

29/8/1916

Captain & Adjt R.E.
for C.R.E. 24th Division.

Issued at 10-30 p.m.

Copy No, 1 to Headquarters G
2 " Q
3 17th I.B.
4 72nd I.B.
5 73rd I.B.
6 103rd Field Company R.E.
7 104th Field Company R.E.
8 129th Field Company R.E.
9 C.R.E. 14th Division
10 C.R.E. 33rd Division
11 Diary
12 Record

Royal Engineers

24th Division.

C. R. E.

24th Division.

S E P T E M B E R 1 9 1 6

Vol 13

Army Form C. 2118.

Instructions regarding War Diaries and Intelligence Summaries are contained in F. S. Regs., Part II. and the Staff Manual respectively. Title pages will be prepared in manuscript.

WAR DIARY
or
INTELLIGENCE SUMMARY.
(Erase heading not required.)

C. R. E. 24th Division

Place	Date	Hour	Summary of Events and Information	Remarks and references to Appendices
E. 11 central Sheet 62d	Sept 1st		Detailed 1 company of Pioneers to repair road from MONTAUBAN to QUARRY	
			Counter attack by 17th I. B. in Left Sector.	
			103rd Field Company reported following casualties during attack on 31st 2/Lieut GODFREY wounded (gas) slight. Killed 5. O.R. wounded 6. O.R.	
			Retook ORCHARD TRENCH but not TEA TRENCH. Heavy casualties on both sides.	
	2nd		129th Field Company ordered by Brigade to report to O.C. 3rd Rifle Bde. for instructions about strong-point at left of ORCHARD TRENCH, had difficulty in getting orders, eventually given guide who took them for about 3 hours, failed to find the appointed spot, returned to Brigade H.Q, got another guide who lost his way and as day was breaking, company returned without having done any work.	
			103rd Field Company working on dugouts in RIGHT SECTOR.	
			104th Field Company building huts for Reserve Brigade and general work.	
			By orders of G.O.C. ordered additional Company of Pioneers to be at disposal of B.G.C. Right Sector later G.O.C. instructed me to order that company to assist Left Sector and to hold portion of line owing to shortness of men.	
			2 Sections 104th and 3 sections 103rd at disposal of B.G.C. Right Sector.	
			Saw CREs N.Z. and 55th Division and arranged with them about constructing new Communication trench ordered by Corps, beginning tomorrow morning	
			Issued Operation Order no 42.	

2353 Wt. W2544/1454 700,000 5/15 D. D. & L. A.D.S.S./Forms/C. 2118.

Army Form C. 2118.

Instructions regarding War Diaries and Intelligence Summaries are contained in F. S. Regs., Part II. and the Staff Manual respectively. Title pages will be prepared in manuscript.

WAR DIARY
or
INTELLIGENCE SUMMARY.
(Erase heading not required.)

Place	Date	Hour	Summary of Events and Information	Remarks and references to Appendices
E 11 central Sheet 62 D.	3rd Sept		As part of an attack by 15th Corps and the French, 24th Division attacked at 12 noon without making much progress. Reported that 7th Division had entered GINCHY and had been driven out, also that French had done well. 1st Division on our left failed to achieve objective, this rendered our task impossible.	
			129th Field Company in Left Sector (2 sections) and 30 Pioneers erected a strong Block in WOOD LANE and wired it in with Concertina wire, improved strong point at same locality and improved trenches in front line.	
			1/2 section R.E and 20 Pioneers improved block in front trench and wired it in.	
			103rd Field Company cleared and enlarged 3 dugouts, also erected 3 Calais dugouts and commenced 5 additional ones, also constructed additional Communication trench and Fire Trench about 250 yards in all.	
			104th Field Company connected up advanced posts in front of Right Brigade about 160 yards 4 foot deep. Continued work on dugouts for dressing station and erecting shelters in back area, owing to shortness of Infantry 104th Field Company carried up ammunition and bombs.	
	4th		Fighting continued during the night news received that GUILLEMONT and part of GINCHY captured. Attack on GINCHY renewed in afternoon	
			103rd Field Company ordered by Brigade to build strong point in Front line, but were unable to reach site owing to heavy barrage. Casualties 1 Officer 2 O.R. Infantry attached RE wounded, 3 O.R. RE wounded.	

Army Form C. 2118.

WAR DIARY
or
INTELLIGENCE SUMMARY.
(Erase heading not required.)

Instructions regarding War Diaries and Intelligence Summaries are contained in F. S. Regs., Part II. and the Staff Manual respectively. Title pages will be prepared in manuscript.

Place	Date	Hour	Summary of Events and Information	Remarks and references to Appendices
E 11 Central Sheet 62d.	4th		129th Field Company removed block constructed previous night, and erected another 80 yards further on. Reclaiming and making fire bays in captured trench, as O.C. Battalion said he was unable to hold it. Block re-erected in original site, and new trench wired up.	
			Remainder of Company with Pioneers clearing C.Ts. near front line which had been obliterated by shell fire.	
			1 Company Pioneers repairing roads.	
			104th Field Company continuing dressing station + erecting shelter in back area.	
			Received O.O. 94. Right Sector also relieved by 55th Division	
			Telegram received that RE and Pioneers would remain behind for special work.	
		9.45pm	S.O.S. signal on our front.	
	5th		Operation Order 95 received. Field Companies and 12th Sherwood Foresters under CRE to remain in 15th Corps to work under Chief Engineer. 15th Corps.	
			Received instructions from C.E. to complete and extend two C.Ts. in Right Division Sector of Corps Front, also to repair certain roads and build bridges over trenches to carry heavy artillery, also labour and material for Brigade Headquarters, Tunnelled dug-outs to be erected by 178th Tunnelling Company.	

Instructions regarding War Diaries and Intelligence Summaries are contained in F. S. Regs., Part II. and the Staff Manual respectively. Title pages will be prepared in manuscript.

WAR DIARY
or
INTELLIGENCE SUMMARY.
(Erase heading not required.)

Army Form C. 2118.

Place	Date	Hour	Summary of Events and Information	Remarks and references to Appendices
E 11 central Sheet. 62 d	6th		Companies and Pioneers rested. Got out design for ~~carry~~ bridge to carry heavy artillery, maximum load 19 tons, 9 p.m. Saw C.E. and explained that to carry 19 tons axle load much material would be necessary for bridge and for revetting trench and that it would be simpler to fill in where heavy guns had to be moved as at that time C.Ts were hardly likely to be required as such. C.E. cancelled instruction and ordered bridges to be made for Field guns only.	
			Divisional H.Q. left for AILLY - ~~SUR CLOTCHER~~ LE HAUT CLOCHER 7th. Technical Troops 34th Division attached to 55th Division.	
	7th		Pioneers employed on extending and improving two C.Ts., providing latrines for Brigade H.Q and filling shell holes on roads. Field Companies on bridging, making roads and runners posts at 500 yards intervals along C.Ts. Work hampered owing to difficulty of obtaining Transport and congestion of traffic. Visited all works. One Company of Pioneers placed at disposal of 41st Division.	
	8th		Work continued. Visited Companies. Inspected road to LONGUEVAL and DEVILS LANE.	

2353 Wt. W2541/1454 700,000 5/15 D. D. & L. A.D.S.S./Forms/C. 2118.

Army Form C. 2118.

WAR DIARY
or
INTELLIGENCE SUMMARY.
(*Erase heading not required.*)

Instructions regarding War Diaries and Intelligence Summaries are contained in F. S. Regs., Part II. and the Staff Manual respectively. Title pages will be prepared in manuscript.

Place	Date	Hour	Summary of Events and Information	Remarks and references to Appendices
E 11 Central Sheet 62b	9th		Asked for return of Company of Pioneers from 41st Division, as amount of work to be done, and time available short. Visited work being carried on by 104th Field Company. All working parties ordered by 55th Division to be clear of shelled area by 9 am owing to attack.	
	10th		Work continued but hampered by heavy shelling. Casualties 2/Lieuts CARDEW and ROBIN wounded. O.R. 1 killed, 1 wounded, Pioneers 2 killed 3 wounded. Company of Pioneers from 41st Div. returned and put to work. 2 Companies 1/4th S. Lancs. (Pioneers) from 55th Division placed at CRE's disposal and detailed for work on rear portion of CTs. Visited companies + Pioneers.	
	11th		OO. 15. Attachment of 55th Pioneers cancelled and orders received that 31st Division only responsible for Right trench of Sector, road leading past CRUCIFIX and Brigade H.Q. Remainder handed over to CRE 55th Division. Visited whole of work. Transport promised by XV Corps, (16 G.S. Wagons) only 4 reported at time asked for (6.30 am). 8 more reported 1-30 p.m.	
	12th		Work continued.	

2353 Wt. W2544/1454 700,000 5/15 D. D. & L. A.D.S.S./Forms/C. 2118.

Instructions regarding War Diaries and Intelligence Summaries are contained in F. S. Regs., Part II. and the Staff Manual respectively. Title pages will be prepared in manuscript.

WAR DIARY
or
INTELLIGENCE SUMMARY.
(Erase heading not required.)

Army Form C. 2118.

Place	Date	Hour	Summary of Events and Information	Remarks and references to Appendices
E. 11 Central Sheet 62b.	13th	12 30a	Received orders from CE 15th Corps. that one company of Pioneers was to be placed at disposal of CRE 55th Division for work on DELVILLE LANE.	
			All work allotted to 34th Division completed.	
			Visited CRUCIFIX ALLEY and Tunnelled dugouts for Brigade H.Q.	
		9pm.	Received orders from XV Corps. to move at 8 am. 14th inst to camp near BUIRE. All huts, shelters and tents to be taken and re-erected at new camp.	
		10.30p.	March order No 44 issued.	
	14th	8am	Moved off to new camp.	
			Warned by XV Corps to be ready to move RE to RAINVILLE, Pioneers to CARDONETTE.	
			All huts erected to be handed over to Town Major BUIRE to form nucleus of a rest camp.	
	15th		Warned by XV Corps that mounted portions will move by road to X Corps rest area dismounted by returning supply train to PONT REMY to rejoin Division.	
	16th	8 30. a	Received orders from XV Corps. Transport of Pioneer Battalion + Field Coys will march at 2 p.m. via QUERRIEUX and ALLONVILLE to POULAINVILLE. Continue the march on 17th inst to FLIXEVILLE.	
		9.45	March order No 45 issued.	
		11 30a	Transport to go via QUERRIEU, AMIENS, to ST. SAUVEUR and march on 17th	

2353 Wt. W2544/1454 700,000 5/15 D. D. & L. A.D.S.S./Forms/C. 2118.

Instructions regarding War Diaries and Intelligence Summaries are contained in F. S. Regs., Part II. and the Staff Manual respectively. Title pages will be prepared in manuscript.

WAR DIARY
or
INTELLIGENCE SUMMARY.
(Erase heading not required.)

Army Form C. 2118.

CRE 24th Division

Place	Date	Hour	Summary of Events and Information	Remarks and references to Appendices
			on 17th inst to FLIXEVILLE clearing ST. SAUVEUR by 10 am. Message attached.	
		2 pm	Transport moved as above.	
		11 pm	Orders received from 15th Corps dismounted portion to embus at BUIRE CHURCH 8 am for PONT REMY	
	17th	8 am	Dismounted portion embussed and moved off at 9 am. arriving PONT REMY 2 pm.	
			At 8 am only 32 busses and 6 lorries, later 10 more busses reported.	
			Transport marched from ST SAUVEUR arriving PONT REMY 4. 30 pm.	
			All Divisional Technical Troops billeted PONT REMY	
			Received orders from 24th Division to entrain on 19th inst.	
PONT REMY	18th		GOC visited Field Companies.	
			CRE attended conference of B. G. C. Decided that 1 Officer, 205 O.R. per Inf Battalion, be attached to Field Companies for periods to be decided later.	
			Orders for entrainment issued to Companies attached.	
	19th		Divisional RE entrained. Destination of Division transferred from XI Corps to IV Corps with Headquarters at BRUAY. Consequently some delay in departure of trains.	
	20th		Orders received that Division would take over front from 9th Division in LORETTE SOUCHEZ Sector.	
			Visited CRE 9th Division	
			Divisional Operation Order No 96 received.	

2353 Wt. W2544/1454 700,000 5/15 D. D. & L. A.D.S.S./Forms/C. 2118.

Army Form C. 2118.

Instructions regarding War Diaries and Intelligence Summaries are contained in F. S. Regs., Part II. and the Staff Manual respectively. Title pages will be prepared in manuscript.

WAR DIARY
or
INTELLIGENCE SUMMARY.
(*Erase heading not required.*)

CRE 24th Division

Place	Date	Hour	Summary of Events and Information	Remarks and references to Appendices
BRUAY.	21st		Visited IV Corps. H.Q and COUPIGNY Dump. Arranged for Field Companies to visit sectors of front.	
	22nd		Visited CRE 9th Division and went over line with him. OC. 197th Coy RE also accompanied us to investigate question of water supply from Springs in ZOUAVE VALLEY.	
	23rd		Visited Field Companies in billets	
			Orders received Captain P. F. Whittall RE 129th Field Coy posted to command 157th Coy. RE.	
	24th		Visited IVth Corps dump at SAVY	
	25th		Visited C.R.E. 9th Division and went round front area with him	
			Adjutant went round back area with Adjutant 9th Division	
			Capt. Rivers. Moore. RE. joined 129th Field Company RE.	
CAMBLAIN. L'ABBÉ	26th		Divisional Headquarters moved to CAMBLAIN L'ABBÉ	
			Visited Field Companies in billets.	
			Captain Cheetham RE Adjutant RE to hospital.	
			Lieut Kynnersley. RE. took over duties of Adjutant	

Instructions regarding War Diaries and Intelligence Summaries are contained in F. S. Regs., Part II. and the Staff Manual respectively. Title pages will be prepared in manuscript.

WAR DIARY

or

INTELLIGENCE SUMMARY.

(Erase heading not required.)

Army Form C. 2118.

CRE 24th Division

Place	Date	Hour	Summary of Events and Information	Remarks and references to Appendices
CAMBLAIN L'ABBE'	27th		Routine.	
			Captain E. F. Whitsall RE. left to join 157th Company RE. 16th Division	
	28th		Visited Front Area with G. S. O.2.	
	29th		Visited Corps Dump + 1st Army workshops BETHUNE.	
	30th		60 men Corps Mounted troops commenced work on back portion of CABARET ROAD. Communication Trench.	
			Visited front area with O.C. 104th Field Company	

8 OCT 1916

[signature]

Lt. COL. R.E.
C. R. E. 24th DIV.

2353 Wt. W2544/1454 700,000 5/15 D. D. & L. A.D.S.S./Forms/C. 2118.

S E C R E T

Copy No, 10

Operation Order No, 42

by Lieut Colonel A.J. Craven R.E.

C.R.E. 24th Division.

Reference: Trench Map 1/10,000

2nd September 1916

1. The 24th Division will attack on September 3rd. Zero hour will be 12 noon.

2. The objective allotted to the 24th Division is as follows:-

(a) 72nd Infantry Brigade

To establish a line of posts along BEER TRENCH from T.13.a.8.9. to S.12. central and to join up with the 7th Division at about T.13.a.5.8.

The above line of posts to be subsequently joined up so as to form a continuous trench.

(b) 17th Infantry Brigade

To clear WOOD LANE Northwards from the present block at about S.11.a.4.1. to the right of the objective of the 1st Division about S.11.a.1.3.
To form a strong point at the junction of TEA TRENCH with WOOD LANE about S.11.a.3.3. with a block in TEA TRENCH in front of this strong point.

The plan of attack of the 17th Infantry Brigade to conform to the plan of attack of the 1st Division on WOOD LANE which plan will be notified to the B.G.C. 17th Infantry Brigade.

3. On the night of the 3rd/4th September endeavours will be made to establish a line of posts North of TEA TRENCH from TEA LANE and from WOOD LANE North of its junction with TEA TRENCH.
The object of these posts is to isolate any Germans in TEA TRENCH.

4. The 103rd Field Company R.E. has been placed at the disposal of B.G.C. 72nd I.B. and the 129th Field Company R.E. has been placed at the disposal of the B.G.C. 17th I.B. for work on strong points and to assist in consolidating.

5. The 104th Field Company R.E. will be in Divisional Reserve and will be ready to move at 30 minutes notice.

6. Acknowledge.

G. Cheetham

Issued at 7 p.m.

Captain & AdjutantR.E.

for C.R.E. 24th Division.

Copy No, 1 to Headquarters "G"	No, 6 17th I.B.
2 " "Q"	7 72nd I.B.
3 103rd Field Company R.E.	8 73rd I.B.
4 104th Field Company R.E.	9 Diary
5 129th Field Company R.E.	10 Record

S E C R E T

Copy No. 8.

March order No. 44.

by Lieut Col: A.J. Craven R.E.

C.R.E. 24th Division.

13th September 1918

1. The Field Companies R.E. (at F 10 a, F 4 b and F 8 c) and Pioneer Battalion(at F 9 b.) of 24th Division will march tomorrow, September 14th., to Area B (Sheet 62 c N.E. D 24) as follows.

2.

UNIT	Starting point	Time at which head of column will pass starting point
12th Sherwood For:	Road junction at F 9 a 4.0.	9 a.m.
129th Field Coy	"	9.20 a.m.
103rd Field Co	"	9.30 a.m.
104th Field Coy	"	9.40 a.m.

3. ~~Starting point - Road junction at F 9 a 4.0~~
~~Head of column will pass starting point at 9 a.m.~~
Route - Forward Track just North of the BRIGUEMY - HEADLAM Road - Pontoon Bridges North of VIVIER MILL - Level crossing S 15 b 0.2.

4. Intervals of ¼ of a mile will be maintained between each Field Company and Pioneer Battalion.

5. Units will send representatives to meet the Adjutant R.E. at 8.30 a.m. at the Cross Roads at Sheet 62 c N.E. D 30 c.9.8.

6. Rations tomorrow will be drawn according to present arrangements.

7. Please acknowledge by bearer.

G Cheetham

Issued at 10-30 p.m.

Captain & Adjutant R.E.

For C.R.E. 24th Division.

Copy No. 1 to C.E. XV Corps
2 H.Q. 41st Division
3 H.Q. 24th Division
4 12th Sherwood Fors
5 103rd Fd. Coy.R.E.
No. 6 104th Fd. Coy R.E.
7 129th Fd. Coy R.E.
8 Diary
9 Record.

SECRET

Copy No, 9

Operation Order No, 48

by Lieut Colonel A.J. Craven R.E.

C.R.E. 24th Division.

Reference:
Trench Map
1/10,000

2nd September 1916

1. The 24th Division will attack on September 3rd. Zero hour will be 12 noon.

2. The objective allotted to the 24th Division is as follows:-

(a) 72nd Infantry Brigade

To establish a line of posts along BEER TRENCH from T.13.a.5.8. to S.12. central and to join up with the 7th Division at about T.13.a.5.8.

The above line of posts to be subsequently joined up so as to form a continuous trench.

(b) 17th Infantry Brigade

To clear WOOD LANE Northwards from the present block at about S.11.a.4.1. to the right of the objective of the 1st Division about S.11.a.1.5.
To form a strong point at the junction of TEA TRENCH with WOOD LANE about S.11.a.3.3. with a block in TEA TRENCH in front of this strong point.

The plan of attack of the 17th Infantry Brigade to conform to the plan of attack of the 1st Division on WOOD LANE which plan will be notified to the B.G.C. 17th Infantry Brigade.

3. On the night of the 3rd/4th September endeavours will be made to establish a line of posts North of TEA TRENCH from TEA LANE and from WOOD LANE North of its junction with TEA TRENCH.
The object of these posts is to isolate any Germans in TEA TRENCH.

4. The 103rd Field Company R.E. has been placed at the disposal of B.G.C. 72nd I.B. and the 129th Field Company R.E. has been placed at the disposal of the B.G.C. 17th I.B. for work on strong points and to assist in consolidating.

5. The 104th Field Company R.E. will be in Divisional Reserve and will be ready to move at 30 minutes notice.

6. Acknowledge.

Issued at 7 p.m.

G. Chetham
Captain & AdjutantR.E.

for C.R.E. 24th Division.

Copy No,			No.	
1	to Headquarters "G"		6	17th I.B.
2	" "Q"		7	72nd I.B.
3	103rd Field Company R.E.		8	73rd I.B.
4	104th Field Company R.E.		9	Diary
5	129th Field Company R.E.		10	Record

SECRET

Copy No, 9

Operation Order No, 43

by Lieut Col: A.J. Craven R.E.

C.R.E. 24th Division.

4th September 1916.

1. The 165th Infantry Brigade will take over from the 17th Infantry Brigade the section of the line now held by the latter.

2. The 2/1st West Lancs: Field Company R.E. (T) and the 55th Divisional Pioneers will take over the work in this sector now being done by the 129th Field Company R.E. and the 12th Sherwood Foresters under arrangements being made by the C.R.E. 55th Division.

3. No change of camps is involved.

4. Special instructions have been issued to the 129th Field Company R.E. and the Sherwood Foresters regarding work to be carried out in the front line of the Left Brigade area to-night.

Issued at 4-30 p.m.

Capt: & Adj: R.E.

for C.R.E. 24th Division.

Copy No, 1 to Headquarters "G"
2 " "Q"
3 103rd Field Company R.E.
4 104th Field Company R.E.
5 129th Field Company R.E.
6 12th Sherwood Foresters
7 C.R.E. 55th Division
8 Record
9 Diary

SECRET

Copy No, 9

March order No, 44.

by Lieut Col: A.J. Craven R.E.

C.R.E. 24th Division.

13th September 1916

1. The Field Companies R.E. (at F 10 a, F 4 b and F 2 c) and Pioneer Battalion(at F 9 b,) of 24th Division will march tomorrow, September 14th., to Area B (Sheet 62 d N.E. D 24) as follows.

2.

UNIT	Starting point	Time at which head of column will pass starting point
12th Sherwood For:	Road junction at F 8 a 4.0.	8 a.m.
129th Field Coy	"	8.20 a.m.
103rd Field Coy	"	8.30 a.m.
104th Field Coy	"	8.40 a.m.

3. Route Starting point - Road junction at F 8 a 4.0
Head of column will pass Starting Point at 8 a.m.
Route - Horse Track just North of the FRICOURT - MEAULTE Road - Pontoon Bridges North of VIVIER MILL - Level crossing E 15 b 0.8.

4. Intervals of ¼ of a mile will be maintained between each Field Company and Pioneer Battalion.

5. Units will send representatives to meet the Adjutant R.E. at 8.30 a.m. at the Cross Roads at Sheet 62 D N.E. D 30 a.8.2.

6. Rations tomorrow will be drawn according to present arrangements.

7. Please acknowledge by bearer.

G. Chetham

Issued at 10-30 p.m.

Captain & Adjutant R.E.

For C.R.E. 24th Division.

Copy No, 1 to C.E. XV Corps
2 H.Q. 41st Division
3 H.Q. 24th Division
4 12th Sherwood For:
5 103rd Fd, Coy.R.E.
No,6 104th Fd. Coy R.E.
7 129th Fd. Coy R.E.
8 Diary
9 Record.

S E C R E T Copy No, 9

March Order No, 46

by Lieut Colonel A.J. Craven R.E.

C.R.E. 24th Division.

September 16th 1916.

Reference maps AMIENS 17 LENS 11 Sheet 62 d N.E.

1. The technical Troops of the 24th Division will move to area 6. Transport and Mounted portion (including cyclists) going by road on 16th. The remainder by rail on 17th.

2. Mounted Portion.

Order of march
129th Field Company R.E.
H.Q.R.E.
104th Field Company R.E.
103rd Field Company R.E.
12th Sherwood Foresters (Pioneers)
Starting point :- D 12 d 8.8.
Time Head of column will pass starting point at 2 p.m. and march to POULAINVILLE.
Route QUERRIEU - ALLONVILLE.
Captain P.F. Whittall R.E. will command this column.

3. Intervals of 500 yards will be kept between units. The unit in rear being responsible that the interval is maintained.

4. The march will be continued on 17th to Area six. Column will be clear of POULAINVILLE by 10 a.m.
Route LONGPRE - ~~ARGOEUVRES~~ LACHAUSSEE - FLIXECOURT.

5. Order for train movement on 17th will be issued later.

6. All huts, tents, tent bottoms and tarpaulins will be handed over to the Town Major ~~whose~~ BUIRE whose representative will attend at a time to be notified later. Units will have duplicate lists prepared and will obtain a receipt on one of them.

7. Please acknowledge.

Issued at 9-45 a.m.

E Chetham
Capt & Adjt R.E.
for C.R.E. 24th Division.

Copy No, 1 to XV Corps
2 41st Division
3 24th Division
4 12th Sherwood Foresters
5 103rd Field Company R.E.
6. 104th Field Company R.E.
7. 129th Field Company R.E.
8 Diary
9 Record

<u>SECRET</u> Copy No, 8

March Order No, 48

by Lieut Colonel A.J. Craven R.E.

C.R.E. 24th Division.

Reference maps
AMIENS 17
LENS 11
Sheet 62 d N.E.

1. The Technical Troops of the 24th Division will move to area 6. Transport and Mounted portion (including) cyclists) going by road on 16th. The remainder by rail on 17th.

2. <u>Mounted Portion</u>.

Order of march.

129th Field Company R.E.
H.Q.R.E.
104th Field Company R.E.
103rd Field Company R.E.
12th Sherwood Foresters (Pioneers)

<u>Starting point</u>:- D 12 d 6.8.

<u>Time</u> Head of column will pass starting point at 2 p.m. and march to POULAINVILLE

<u>Route</u> QUERRIEU - ALLONVILLE.

Captain P.F. Whittal R.E. will command this column.

3. Intervals of 500 yards will be kept between units. The unit in rear being responsible that the interval is maintained.

4. The march will be continued on 17th to Area six 6. Column will be clear of POULAINVILLE by 10 a.m.

<u>Route</u> ~~[illegible]~~ LONGPRE - LACHAUSSEE - FLIXECOURT.

5. Order for train movement on 17th will be issued later.

6. All huts, tents, tent bottoms and tarpaulins will be handed over to the Town Major [illegible] whose representative will attend at a time to be notified later. Units will have duplicate lists prepared and will obtain a receipt on one of them.

7. Please acknowledge.

[signature]

Issued at 9-45 a.m. Captain & Adjutant R.E.
for C.R.E. 24th Division.

S E C R E T Copy No, 1

Operation Order No, 46.
by Lieut Colonel A.J. Craven R.E.
C.R.E. 24th Division.

Reference:-
Trench Map 1/10,000
Sheet 36.c.S.W.(VIMY)
Map 1/40,000 Sheet 36.b.

September 22nd 1916.

1. The 24th Division will relieve the 9th Division in the line between the 23rd and 26th September 1916.

2. The front to be taken over extends from LASSALLE AVENUE S.21.d.(exclusive) to the SOUCHEZ RIVER.
The front will be taken over by the 17th Infantry Brigade on the right and by the 73rd Infantry Brigade on the left.
The dividing line between the 17th and 73rd Infantry Brigades will be - GOBRON ALLEY (S.15.a.4.5.) which will be inclusive to the 73rd Infantry Brigade.
The 72nd Infantry Brigade will be in reserve.

3. The 104th Field Company R.E. will take over the R.E. work in the Right Section from the 63rd and 64th Field Companies R.E. and will take over billets from the 63rd Field Company R.E.

4. The 129th Field Company R.E. will take over the R.E. work in the Left Section from the 90th Field Company R.E. and will take over billets from the 64th Fiel d Company R.E.

5. The 103rd Field Company R.E. will take over the work in the back area now being done by the 64th Field Company R.E., and the Divisional Workshops, and will take over billets from the 90th Field Company R.E.

6. The Field Companies of the 24th Division will relieve the Field Companies of the 9th Division according to the attached march table.

7. All defence schemes, maps, trench stores, tables of work in hand and proposed, etc., will be taken over from relieved units of the 9th Division and a list of all articles taken over will be forwarded to 24th Divisional Headquarters.

8. Command of the front and area now held by the 9th Division will pass to G.O.C. 24th Division at 10 a.m. on the 26th September, at which hour 24th Divisional Headquarters will close at BRUAY and re-open at CAMBLAIN L'ABBE.

9. Completion of releifs will be reported to this office.

10. Acknowledge. Done

A J Craven

Issued at 11-30 a.m. Lieut Colonel R.E.

C.R.E. 24th Division.

Copy No, 1 to "G"
2 "Q"
3 103rd Fd. Coy. R.E.

Copy No, 1 to Headquarters "G"
2 " "Q"
3 103rd Field Company R.E.
4 104th Field Company R.E.
5 129th Field Company R.E.
6. 17th Infantry Brigade
7. 72nd Infantry Brigade
8 73rd Infantry Brigade
9 C.R.E. 9th Division
10 Record
11 Diary

Date	UNIT	From	To.	Remarks.
Sept 23rd	129th Field Company R.E.	BRUAY	PETIT SERVINS	
	104th Field Company R.E.	CONTEVILLE	CHATEAU DE LA HAIE	
	64th Field Company R.E.	Concentrate at	VILLERS	
Sept 24th	64th Field Company R.E.	VILLERS	Training Area	With S.A. Brigade.
	129th Field Company R.E.	PETIT SERVINS	VILLERS AU BOIS	Billets of 64th Field Company R.E.
Sept 25th	90th Field Company R.E.	Concentrate	GOUY SERVINS	Relieved by 129th Fd. Coy. R.E.
	63rd Field Company R.E.	"	CHATEAU DE LA HAIE	Relieved by 104th Field Company R.E.
	104th Field Company R.E.	CHATEAU DE LA HAIE	VILLERS	
Sept 26th	90th Field Company R.E.		X Area	With 27th Brigade
	63rd Field Company R.E.		X Area	Independently to join 26th Brigade
	103rd Field Company R.E.	PETIT SERVINS	GOUY SERVINS	Billet of 90th Field Company R.E.

Instructions regarding War Diaries and Intelligence Summaries are contained in F. S. Regs., Part II. and the Staff Manual respectively. Title pages will be prepared in manuscript.

WAR DIARY
or
INTELLIGENCE SUMMARY.
(Erase heading not required.)

Army Form C. 2118.

CRE 24th Division

Place	Date	Hour	Summary of Events and Information	Remarks and references to Appendices
CAMBLAIN L'ABBE.	Oct:. 1st.		Visited Divisional Dump and 103rd Field Company R.E. also Corps Dump at COUPIGNY.	
	2nd		Visited front Line with G.S.O.2.	
	3rd		Visited Chief Engineer IV Corps. Visited 104th, 129th Field Companies R.E. and Pioneers. ½ Company 138th A.T. Company R.E. and 75 men Entrenching Battalion also ½ Company 1/1st Sussex A.T. Company R.E. and 40 P.R. Corps Mounted Troops placed at C.R.E's disposal for work in Trench area.	
	4th		Round Line with Adjutant. Progress on dug-out for Brigade Headquarters very slow. 138th A.T. Company and 1/1st Sussex should work on dug-outs.	
	5th		Making up recommendations for Honours and Rewards. Attended conference of C.R.Es at Chief Engineer IV Corps discussed Winter preparations, electric lighting scheme and standard size for dug-out caves. Recommended 6' X 2'6" in clear.	
	6th		Visited front area with O.C. 104th Field Company R.E.	
	7th		Visited front area with G.S.O. 2.	
	8th		Visited Dump, 103rd and 104th Field Companies. Routine.	
	9th		Round front area with O.C. Pioneers to inspect work done by his companies. 1/1st Sussex A.T. Company R.E. left area. Work on dug-outs they had in hand stopped.	
	10th		Corps Mounted Troops working for this Division ordered away and not replaced. Work on CABARET ROAD stopped. Working out details of scheme. Visited 104th and 129th Field Companies R.E. Visit from C.E. IV Corps. Conference of Brigadiers.	
	11th		Getting out details of labour and materials for scheme. Ordered to send 5 Officers and 150 O.R. of Pioneers to work on Railway for 17th Corps. Instructions issued accordingly.	

2353 Wt. W2544/1454 700,000 5/15 D. D. & L. A.D.S.S./Forms/C. 2118.

Instructions regarding War Diaries and Intelligence Summaries are contained in F. S. Regs., Part II. and the Staff Manual respectively. Title pages will be prepared in manuscript.

WAR DIARY
or
INTELLIGENCE SUMMARY.
(Erase heading not required.)

Army Form C. 2118.

CRE 24th Division

Place	Date	Hour	Summary of Events and Information	Remarks and references to Appendices
CAMBLAIN L'ABBE	12th		5 Officers 150 O.R. Pioneers ordered to work on 17th Corps Light Railway. Company on Railway construction in ZOUAVE VALLEY sent	
	13th		Round Left Sector with O.C. 103rd Field Company R.E. Inspected work of 138th A.T. Company in ZOUAVE VALLEY. Visited 104th Field Company R.E. and Pioneers. 138th A.T. Company R.E. received orders to concentrate to-day and be ready to leave area on 16th. They moved to GOUY. 150 Entrenching Battalion left at C.R.E's disposal.	
	14th		Division came under XVII Corps(from IV Corps) Attended lecture and demonstration at Gas School. Visited Divisional Dump and 103rd Field Company R.E. Captain Cheetham returned from leave.	
	15th		Went along proposed tramway line between CARENCY and ZOUAVE VALLEY with O.C. Light Railways IV Corps and Field Engineer, Canadian Corps (who are taking over from IV Corps). Decided alignment and arranged for supply of rails.	
	16th		To HOUDAIN to see work on incinerator. To COUPIGNY. Received orders that 1st Canadian Division is to relieve 24th Division after 23rd inst:, and that 24th will then relieve 40th Division in line about HULLUCH.	
	17th		To Right Sector with O.C. 104th Field Company R.E. and O.C. Pioneers.	
	18th		Round back area with D.A.Q.M.G. and S.O.R.A.	
	19th		To NOEUX LES MINES to see C.R.E. 40th Division to make enquiries about area etc:.	
	20th		Visited 103rd Field Company, Divisional Dump and shops., Camouflage Officer's shops. Received Operation Orders Nos. 101, 102 + 103	
	21st		Round Right Sections. New Communication Trenches REGGIE and MIKE, Progress impeded by heavy rains, being pumped out. Visited First Corps Park at MINX.	
	22nd		Visited 104th and 129th Field Companies. Trying to get into touch with C.R.E. Canadian Division to arrange reliefs and handing over.	

2353 Wt. W2544/1454 700,000 5/15 D. D. & L. A.D.S.S./Forms/C. 2118.

Instructions regarding War Diaries and Intelligence Summaries are contained in F. S. Regs., Part II. and the Staff Manual respectively. Title pages will be prepared in manuscript.

WAR DIARY
or
INTELLIGENCE SUMMARY.
(Erase heading not required.)

Army Form C. 2118.

Place	Date	Hour	Summary of Events and Information	Remarks and references to Appendices
CAMBLAIN L'ABBE	23rd		Visited 103rd Field Company R.E. to investigate a case of attempted suicide. No, 62050 Sapper. Andrews. Remanded for F.G.C.M. Visited Dump and Workshops. Visited 17th Corps Advanded Park at BOIS DE BRAY.	
	24th		C.R.E. 1st Canadian Division arrived to obtain information and arrange details of transfers. C.E. XVII bCorps came to make enquiries about CARENCY - ZOUAVE VALLEY railway line. Issued Operation Order No, 47.	
	25th		C.R.E. 1st Canadian Division arrived to stay - Took him round portion of Front area. In afternoon took him to Division and Corps Dumps and round Field Company Billets. 103rd Field Company R.E. left area and reached NOUEX LES MINES.	
	26th		Visited new area - went round portion of Right Section, visited billets of Field Companies and Divisional Dump. 103rd Field Company R.E. took over ~~Right~~ Left Sector, 104th Field Company R.E. reached NOUEX LES MINES. Major G.F. Evans appointed C.R.E. 33rd Division. Captain Rivers-Moore took over command of 129th Field Company R.E.	
	27th		Handed over office etc: to C.R.E. 1st Canadian Division. Chief Engineer 1st Army called. 129th Field Company R.E. reached NOUEX LES MINES. 104th Field Company R.E. took over R.E. work in Centre Section.	
	28th		Mover to BRAY. Visited C.E. 1st Corps.	
	29th		To BRAQUEMONT to take over office etc, from C.R.E. 40th Division. Visited Divisional Dump and billet of 104th Field Company R.E. 129th Field Company R.E. reported commenced taking over but not completed.	
	30th		To LOOS with O.C. 194th Field Company R.E. and Adjutant.	
	31st		To 129th Field Company R.E. and Dump.	

F.P. Heath.
Capt RE
a/CRE 24th Division
5/11/16

SECRET

Copy No, 11

Operation Order No, 47
by
Lieut Colonel A.J. Craven R.E.
C.R.E. 24th Division.

Reference
Map 1/10,000
LENS Sheet.

24th October 1918.

1. The 24th Division will relieve the 40th Division in the line.
Reliefs of Field Companies will take place in accordance with attached March Tables.

2. On arrival in the 40th Divisional area Field Companies of the 24th Division will come under the orders of the C.R.E. 40th Division until 10 a.m. on October 30th at which hour the G.O.C. 24th Division will assume command of the new sector.

3. Arrival at destination and completion of reliefs will be reported by wire to 24th and to 40th Divisions.

4. All stores, reports of work in hand, maps etc will be handed over to relieving units and receipts obtained which will be forwarded to 24th Divisional Headquarters.

5. Arrangements for reliefs of Companies of 40th Division will be made direct with O.Cs of Field Companies of 40th Division.

6. The 24th Division Headquarter offices will close at CAMBLAIN L'ABBE at 10 a.m. on 28th inst and re-open at BRUAY. They will close at BRUAY at 10 a.m. on 30th and re-open at BRAQUEMONT at the same date and time.
The Headquarters Divisional Engineers will move with the Divisional Headquarters.

7. Acknowledge.

Issued at 7 p.m.

Captain & Adjutant R.E.
for C.R.E. 24th Division.

Copy No, 1 to Headquarters "G"
2 " "Q"
3 C.R.E. 1st Canadian Division
4 C.R.E. 40th Division
5 17th Infantry Brigade
6 72nd " "
7 73rd " "
8 103rd Field Company R.E.
9 104th Field Company R.E.
10 129th Field Company R.E.
11 Record
12 Diary.

RE
WO 14

Amendment to C.R.E's Operation Order No, 47.

In movement table last line.

For October 28th read October 29th.

Acknowledge.

Captain & Adjutant R.E.

28/10/18.

for C.R.E. 24th Division.

Copy No, 1 to Headquarters "G"
2 " "Q"
3 129th"Field Company R.E.
4 C.R.E. 40th Division.
5 73rd Infantry Brigade.
6 Divisional Train.
7 Diary.
8 Record.

MOVEMENT TABLE TO ACCOMPANY C.R.E. 24th DIVISION OPERATION ORDER No,

Date	103rd Field Company R.E.	104th Field Company R.E.	129th Field Company R.E.	
Oct: 24th	Section in front line to be withdrawn.			
Oct: 25th	Advance party by bus leaving GOUY SERVINS 9-15 a.m. to new area billets. Company to march to NOEUX LES MINES at 9-30 a.m. (1)	Section in front line to be withdrawn. Advance parties by bus leaving VILLERS au BOIS at 9-15 a.m. to new area billets.	Advance parties by bus leaving VILLERS au BOIS at 9-15 a.m. to new area billets.	(1) Town Major at NOEUX LES MINES will indicate billets.
Oct: 26th	Take over billets and work from 231st Field Company (H.Q. at PHILOSOPHE) 2 sections in the line to arrive at H.Q. at 12 noon.	March to NOEUX LES MINES STARTING AT 9-30 a.m.(1)		
Oct 27th		Take over billets and work from 229th Field Company. (H.Q. at LES BREBIS. 2 sections in LOOS) to arrive at H.Q. at 12 noon.	March to NOEUX LES MINES starting at 9-30 a.m.(1)	
Oct 28th			Take over billets and work from 224th Field Company (H.Q. at GRENAY. 2 sections in LOOS.) To arrive at H.Q. at 12 noon	

Instructions regarding War Diaries and Intelligence Summaries are contained in F. S. Regs., Part II. and the Staff Manual respectively. Title pages will be prepared in manuscript.

WAR DIARY
or
~~INTELLIGENCE SUMMARY~~.
(Erase heading not required.)

Army Form C. 2118.

C.R.E. 24th Division

Vol 15

Place	Date	Hour	Summary of Events and Information	Remarks and references to Appendices
BRAQUEMONT	1st	Nov./16	Visited HULLUCH Sector with O.C. 103rd Field Company R.E.	
	2nd		Visited 14 BIS Sector with O.C. 104th Field Company R.E.	
	3rd		Visited LOOS Sector with O.C. 129th Field Company R.E.	
	4th		Conference with C.E. 1st Corps and G.S.O.1., 1 Field Company R.E., 2 Companies Pioneers, and 1 Infantry Battn. from 6th Division to be employed on dug-outs and underground C.Ts. in this area. 2nd Lieut A W PAPWORTH R.E. joined 129 Field Coy	
	5th		C.R.E. went on leave. Capt. Heath R.E. acting C.R.E. Lieut. Kynnersley R.E. acting O.C. 103rd Field Company R.E. Attended Conference to decide on programme of work for dug-outs and underground C.Ts. Parties to arrive on 6th and start work 7th. 1 Battn Infantry underground C.Ts. & 1 Battn. Infantry dug-outs reserve line. 1 Field Company supervise above. 2 Companies Pioneers work on reserve line.	
	6th		Visited 'G' and discussed dug-out scheme. Visited 103rd and 129th Field Companies to discuss details of dug-out work. Work to begin, - LOOS Sector 7th, 14BIS and HULLUCH 8th.	
	7th		Visited 'G' discussedreport called for by First Corps on work being started by 6th Division parties. Visited 104th - 129th Field Companies and 9th Suffolks. Made out reports on work, giving map reference of dug-outs being commenced.	
	8th		In the office - preparing type design on dug-outs - O.C. 104th Field Company R.E. came to office at 11.30 a.m. to discuss dug-outs being constructed in 17th Brigade Area.	
	9th		A/C.R.E. and Adjutant presented to Duke of Connaught at 11.15 a.m.- In the afternoon visited 129th Field Company R.E. and 6th Division Pioneers to discuss work.	
	10th		Went round Reserve Trench with G.S.O.1., from MAROC to RAILWAY ALLEY, looking at TRAVERS KEEP and T.M.Emplacements ENGLISH ALLEY. Went to Conference at C.R.E. 21st Division H.Q. to decide best type of deep dug-out to be adopted as a standard.	
	11th		Went round Reserve Trench 14 BIS Sector and C.Ts. RAILWAY ALLEY- NORTH STREET.	

2353 Wt. W2544/1454 700,000 5/15 D. D. & L. A.D.S.S./Forms/C. 2118.

Instructions regarding War Diaries and Intelligence Summaries are contained in F. S. Regs., Part II. and the Staff Manual respectively. Title pages will be prepared in manuscript.

WAR DIARY
or
INTELLIGENCE SUMMARY.
(Erase heading not required.)

Army Form C. 2118.

C.R.E. 24th Division.

Place	Date	Hour	Summary of Events and Information	Remarks and references to Appendices
BRAQUEMONT	12th		Conference at Divisional Headquarters.	
	13th		Visited HULLUCH Sector, including new dug-outs.	
	14th		Visited C.O. 11th Leicesters(6th Division Pioneers) and 1st Army Workshops, also 103rd Field Company R.E.	
	15th		Visited 129th, 104th and 103rd Field Companies also 12th Field Company at MAZINGARBE.	
	16th		Went via. MAROC-PICCADILLY and NORTH STREET to LOOS to visit Company 12th Sherwood Foresters. Met O.C.104th Field Company at his advanced billet and went round RESERVE LINE and new dug-outs.	
	17th		C.R.E. returned from leave. Visited Special Works Park BOULOGNE.	
	18th		Routine work.	
	19th		Conference of Brigadiers. Visited Divisional Dump, 104th Field Company and 12th Field Company.	
	20th		With O.C. 104th and 12th Field Companies round work in 14 BIS area.	
	21st		To Corps Park MINX and Divisional School.	
	22nd		Round Left Sector with O.C. 103rd Field Company R.E.	
	23rd		Round Right Sector with G.S.O.2.and O.C. 129th Field Company R.E.	
	24th		With A.A.&.Q.M.G. to Divisional School and D.A.C. HOUCHIN.	
	25th		To LOOS with O.C.12th Field Company, arranged with O.C.Divisional Pioneers for him to take over the work of constructing 6 of the 8 deep dug-outs being made by 6th Divn.Infantry and 12th Field Company R.E. The Sappers to be replaced by skilled miners of the Pioneers. Visited LOOS Defences.	
	26th		Divisional Conference.	

2353 Wt. W2544/1454 700,000 5/15 D. D. & L. A.D.S.S./Forms/C. 2118.

Army Form C. 2118.

Instructions regarding War Diaries and Intelligence Summaries are contained in F. S. Regs., Part II. and the Staff Manual respectively. Title pages will be prepared in manuscript.

WAR DIARY
or
INTELLIGENCE SUMMARY.
(Erase heading not required.)

C.R.E. 24th Division

Place	Date	Hour	Summary of Events and Information	Remarks and references to Appendices
BRAQUEMONT	27th		With C.R.E. 3rd Canadians to visit H.T.M.Emplacement in his Sector.	
	28th		With O.C.103rd Field Company R.E. round left sub-section of left section. 2nd Lieut. BENNETT 129th Field Company R.E., killed by a sniper.	
	29th		To Divisional Laundry and First Army Workshops.	
	30th		With O.C.104th Field Company R.E. round centre Section.	

[signature]

Lt. COL. R.E.
C. R. E. 24th DIV.

2353 Wt. W2544/1454 700,000 5/15 D. D. & L. A.D.S.S./Forms/C. 2118.

Instructions regarding War Diaries and Intelligence Summaries are contained in F. S. Regs., Part II. and the Staff Manual respectively. Title pages will be prepared in manuscript.

WAR DIARY
or
INTELLIGENCE SUMMARY.
(Erase heading not required.)

T332 Secret

Army Form C. 2118.

C. R. E. 24th. Division.

Vol 16

Place	Date	Hour	Summary of Events and Information	Remarks and references to Appendices
BRAQUEMONT	Dec. 1st.		To Divisional Dump & Baths at MAZINGARBE. With A.A.& Q.M.G. to LES BREBIS & MAZINGARBE, saw Town Major MAZINGARBE about Pioneers employed on improving billets and O.C. 2nd D.L.I. about Working Parties provided, Although the whole of his Battalion is available for work, he can only promise 250 men & 28 N.C.Os.	
	2nd		Met Capt. Roberts of Pioneers to discuss details of new Battalion H.Q. in Right Section.	
	3rd		Divisional Conference.	
	4th		Round Left Sector with O.C. 129th Field Company R.E.	
	5th		Routine.	
	6th		Round Left Sector with O.C. 103rd Field Company R.E. 1 Platoon Pioneers 6th Division & 1 Battalion Infantry 6th Division, who had been working for the Division left the Area. Lieut. Bradley.G.L.H. joined 104th. Field Co., R.E. from No.4 G.B.D.	
	7th		Routine. Met Inspector of Corps Tramways to discuss details of organization of Divisional Lines. Lieut. M. H. Schwab. joined 104th. Field Co., R.E. from the 98th. Field Co.,R.E.	
	8th		Round 14 BIS Sector with O.C. 104th Field Company R.E.	
	9th		Routine.	
	10th		Meeting of Brigadiers.	
	11th		Visited Corps Workshops MINX, Army Workshops BETHUNE, Army Park LILLERS.	
	12th.		Round LOOS Sector with O.C. 129th Field Company.	
	13th		Visited Reserve Line from MAROC to VENDIN ALLEY. Visited Commandant LOOS.	
	14th		Visited Fosse 3, 103rd Field Company , 104th Field Company, Dump at Fosse 6. Saw R.T.O. about extension of B.L.Line to Church Square LES BREBIS.	

2353 Wt. W2544/1454 700,000 5/15 D. D. & L. A.D.S.S./Forms/C. 2118.

Army Form C. 2118.

Instructions regarding War Diaries and Intelligence Summaries are contained in F. S. Regs., Part II. and the Staff Manual respectively. Title pages will be prepared in manuscript.

WAR DIARY
or
INTELLIGENCE SUMMARY.
(Erase heading not required.)

C. R. E. 24th. Division.

Place	Date	Hour	Summary of Events and Information	Remarks and references to Appendices
BRAQUEMONT	Dec. 15th		Visited LOOS Defences and arranged for work on Platoon dugouts in Reserve with O.C. Pioneers. Visited Divisional Dump, Baths at LES BREBIS and Transport Lines of 103rd Field Company, where harness was not satisfactory. 2nd. Lieut Roberts W.J. joined 129th. Field Co.,R.E. from 104th. Field Co., R.E.	
	16th		Routine. Adjutant trained scratch party from Divisional Headquarters and trained in wiring party composed of servants and grooms.	
	17th		Meeting of Brigadiers. Visited work at LES BREBIS with Hutting Officer. Visited 104th Field Company Billets.	
	18th		Round left half of ~~[illegible]~~ (HULLUCH) section with O.C. 103rd Field Company R.E. Field Company Commanders promoted acting Majors.	
	19th		Inspected special wiring party of servants and A.S.C. wiring near MAROC. Withdrew them as they were being shelled.	
	20th		Round left sub-section of centre (14 BIS) Sector with O.C. 104th Field Company R.E.	
	21st		Round right and centre of LOOS Sector with G.S.O. and O.C. 129th Field Company R.E.	
	22nd		Routine.	
	23rd		Along Reserve Line from LOOS to VENDIN ALLEY with G.S.O., with a view to inspecting state of wire which is good but only about 3 or 4 yards thick. Decided to thicken belt to 12 yards.	
	24th		Conference at Divisional H.Q. Visited all Field Companies.	
	25th		Xmas Day- Office Routine.	
	26th		To Corps Dump MINX.	
	27th		Round HULLUCH Sector with O.C. 103rd Field Company, R.E.	

2353 Wt. W2544/1454 700,000 5/15 D. D. & L. A.D.S.S./Forms/C. 2118.

Army Form C. 2118.

Instructions regarding War Diaries and Intelligence Summaries are contained in F. S. Regs., Part II. and the Staff Manual respectively. Title pages will be prepared in manuscript.

WAR DIARY
or
INTELLIGENCE SUMMARY.
(Erase heading not required.)

C. R. E. 24th. Division.

Place	Date	Hour	Summary of Events and Information	Remarks and references to Appendices
BRAQUEMONT	Dec. 28th		Visited 1st Army T.M.School at CLAQUES. Very little useful information to be obtained about Emplacements.	
	29th		Round 14 BIS North Sub-section with O.C. 104th Field Company and G.S.O. 2.	
	30th		To 103rd, 104th, & 129th Field Companies. Meeting with Tunnelling Officers. Ordered by G.O.C. to take over work on Range at ALLOUAGNE from A.T. Company, who were doing it under Corps.	

[signature]

Lieut. Col. R. E.,

C. R. E. 24th. Division.

2353 Wt. W2544/1454 700,000 5/15 D. D. & L. A.D.S.S./Forms/C. 2118.

Instructions regarding War Diaries and Intelligence Summaries are contained in F. S. Regs., Part II. and the Staff Manual respectively. Title pages will be prepared in manuscript.

WAR DIARY
or
INTELLIGENCE SUMMARY.
(Erase heading not required.)

~~Draft~~ T425 Vol 17

Army Form C. 2118.

C.R.E. 24th. Division.

Place	Date Jan/17.	Hour	Summary of Events and Information	Remarks and references to Appendices
BRAQUEMONT.	1st.		Captain MARVIN took over work at ALLOUAGNE Range from O.C. 1st. Hants Army Troops Co.,R.E. Visited O.C's 103rd. and 104th. Field Co's R.E. and Divisional Dump, LES BREBIS.	
	2nd.		Round portion of LOOS Sector with G.S.O_2 and O.C. 129th. Field Co.,R.E. Visited O.C. Pioneers at LOOS and went round dug-outs E.F.G.H. and Brigade H.Q. in UNION St. with Pioneer Officers in charge.	
	3rd.		Visited Brigadier Generals of each Infantry Brigade to arrange about special wiring parties of 50 each (which have been trained by Adjutant R.E), to start wiring on 5th. Saw O.C. Field Companies to ensure all arrangements being made for wiring of RESERVE LINE.	
	4th.		R.E. Band performed at BRAQUEMONT and LES BREBIS also at Divisional Headquarters in the evening.	
	5th.		To BETHUNE to meet Lieut. Col. LINDSAY whose arrival on tour of instruction had been reported by R.T.O. Rest of party had arrived but not he. Visited MINX, and 129th. Field Co.,R.E. and Divisional Dump. Chief Engineer called.	
	6th.		Round left of HULLUCH Section with O.C. 103rd. Field Co.,R.E., Settled sites of new deep dug-outs in RESERVE Line, explained requirements to Captain MOHR (PIONEERS) on site.	
	7th.		All day on Court of Enquiry on result of enemy raid on left Battalion of 14 BIS Sector. Captain MARVIN injured in motor cycle accident.	
	8th.		All day on Court of Enquiry on result of enemy raid on left Battalion of 14 BIS Sector, report submitted to Divisional Headquarters at 7p.m.	
	9th.		To ALLOUAGNE to inspect work on Range. To LILLERS. Visited 103rd. and 104th. Field Co's ~~R-E-~~	
	10th.		Round left portion of LOOS Sector with O.C. 129th. Field Co.,R.E.	

2353 Wt. W2544/1454 700,000 5/15 D. D. & L. A.D.S.S./Forms/C. 2118.

Instructions regarding War Diaries and Intelligence Summaries are contained in F. S. Regs., Part II. and the Staff Manual respectively. Title pages will be prepared in manuscript.

Army Form C. 2118.

WAR DIARY
or
INTELLIGENCE SUMMARY.
(Erase heading not required.)

C.R.E. 24th. Division.

Place	Date	Hour	Summary of Events and Information	Remarks and references to Appendices
BRAQUEMONT.	Jan/17.			
	11th.		To LES BREBIS where demonstration was given by Tunnelling Officer (detailed by Controller of Mines) of working of hydraulic pushing jack. Visited Range of 73rd. Infantry Brigade and Divisional Dump.	
	12th.		Round left subsection of 14 BIS Section with O.C. 8th. Buffs O.C. 3rd. Australian Tunnelling Co. and O.C. 104th. Field Co.,R.E. re defensive measures at posts.	
	13th.		Routine. Conference with O.C. Tunnelling Companies (173, 253 and 3rd. Australian).	
	14th.		Divisional Conference. Visited Dump and 103, 104 and 129th. Field Co's R.E. Orders received that Captain G.Cheetham has been selected as Instructor to PORTUGUESE Division.	
	15th.		Reported that mobile charges (20lbs each) used by men of 104th. Field Co.,R.E. in raid on enemies trenches last night were very successful. 2 o.r. of 104th. Field Co.,R.E. out of 5 slightly wounded in raid.	
	16th.		Round left of HULLUCH Sector with O.C. 103rd. Field Co.,R.E., also dug-outs in RESERVE Line with Lieut. Lewis (Pioneers). 1 Company Pioneers & Brigade wiring party ordered to work on Pioneer trench urgently required for mining operations.	
	17th.		Visited range at ALLOUAGNE. Received instructions from G.O.C. regarding special new trench in LOOS Sector.	
	18th.		To Corps Park, MINX and BETHUNE. O.C. 1st. Fusiliers submitted recommendations for Sergt. T. TELFORD and Sapper J McCOLE	
	19th.		Round portion of LOOS Sector with O.C. 129th. Field Co.,R.E. and Adjutant R.E. especially inspecting H.T.M. Emplacements and site of proposed new forward trench.	
	20th.		Visited work on huts at LES BREBIS and baths at MAZINGARBE. Went to lecture on tanks at BRUAY. Conference with O.C's Tunnelling Co's, G.O.C. and G.S.O1.	

Instructions regarding War Diaries and Intelligence Summaries are contained in F. S. Regs., Part II. and the Staff Manual respectively. Title pages will be prepared in manuscript.

WAR DIARY
or
INTELLIGENCE SUMMARY.

(*Erase heading not required.*)

Army Form C. 2118.

C.R.E. 24th. Division.

Place	Date	Hour	Summary of Events and Information	Remarks and references to Appendices
BRAQUEMONT.	Jan/17			
	21st.		Successful raid by 8th. Middlesex in which 1N.C.O. and 7 men of 129th. Field Co.,R.E. took part. They blew up one concrete M.G. emplacement and entrances to two dug-outs. Visited Brigadier General Commanding 73rd. Infantry Brigade to arrange about reconnaissance for new trench to be dug in an existing reentrant in our line. Visited 104th. Field Co.,R.E.	
	22nd.		C.R.E. 21st. Division came to arrange taking over our present front. Orders received that Captain G.Cheetham (Adjutant) appointed to Mission with Portuguese Division and Captain J.R.Grant appointed in his place.	
	23rd.		To ALLOUAGNE to see work on range, thence to AIRE . Visited Bridging School where met E. in C. and C.E. 1st. Army. Arranged for instruction of parties of Field Co's during rest period. Operation Order No. 118 received .	
	24th.		To 72nd. Infantry Brigade, Headquarters to see Brigadier. Visited 104th. Field Co.,R.E.	
	25th.		Visit from C.R.E. 21st. Division to discuss handing over. Raid by 9th.East Surrey Regt. 1N.C.O. and 6 Sappers of the 103rd. Field Co.,R.E. took part, carrying mobile charges, they blew up 2 dug-outs. Three Sappers wounded, two seriously by M.G. fire during return.	
	26th.		Issued Operation Order No. 48 (COPY attached). Raid by 12th. Fusiliers and 8th. Buffs 1 N.C.O. and 5 sappers took part the N.C.O. was wounded. Move cancelled.	
	27th.		Major DAVENPORT, R.E.arrived for period of 6 days instruction.	
	28th.		Major DAVENPORT, R.E. attached to 103rd. Field Co.,R.E. for instruction. Visited Divisional Laundry. Orders received for Captain CHEETHAM to report to AIRE forthwith, C.R.E.s Adjt. PORTUGUESE Expeditionary Force having arrived .	

2353 Wt. W2544/1454 700,000 5/15 D. D. & L. A.D.S.S./Forms/C. 2118.

Army Form C. 2118.

Instructions regarding War Diaries and Intelligence Summaries are contained in F. S. Regs., Part II. and the Staff Manual respectively. Title pages will be prepared in manuscript.

WAR DIARY
or
INTELLIGENCE SUMMARY.
(*Erase heading not required.*)

C.R.E. 24th. Division.

Place	Date	Hour	Summary of Events and Information	Remarks and references to Appendices
BRAQUEMONT	Jan/17			
	29th.		To Divisional School, ALLOUAGNE Range and MINX Yard. Captain CHEETHAM handed over and Captain GRANT took over the duties of Adjutant. Captain CHEETHAM joined PORTUGUESE Mission.	
	30th.		Routine.	
	31st.		With Brigadier General Commanding 73rd. Infantry Brigade and also O.C. 173rd. Tunnelling Co., R.E. to arrange details of defence of subways in LOOS Sector.	

[signature]
Lieut. Colonel, R-E
C. R. E. 24th. Division.

2353 Wt. W2544/1454 700,000 5/15 D. D. & L. A.D.S.S./Forms/C. 2118.

Instructions regarding War Diaries and Intelligence Summaries are contained in F. S. Regs., Part II. and the Staff Manual respectively. Title pages will be prepared in manuscript.

Vol 18

Army Form C. 2118.

WAR DIARY
or
~~INTELLIGENCE SUMMARY~~.
(Erase heading not required.)

C.R.E., 24th. Division.

Place	Date 1917.	Hour	Summary of Events and Information	Remarks and references to Appendices
BRAQUEMONT ~~LABEUVRIERE~~.				
	February 1st		With G.S.O2 round Reserve Line.	
	2nd		To 104th. Field Co.,R.E. and Divisional Dump. Visited LES BREBIS (Huts) and PETIT SAINS (Erection of Y.M.C.A. huts).	
	3rd		Round Reserve Line with C.E. 1st. Corps selecting sites for M.G. posts. Meeting of Tunnelling Company Officers at Divisional Headquarters.	
	4th		Attended distribution of decorations by G.O.C. 1st. Corps. Visited 104th. & 129th. Field Companies.	
	5th		Round HULLUCH Sector with O.C. 103rd. Field Co.,R.E. Visited inter alia HULLUCH Subways.	
	6th		Divisional Conference. Visited 129th. & 104th. Field Companies.	
	7th		Visited Range at ALLOUAGNE 1st. Army Workshops and Divisional School. Information received that 24th. Division is to be relieved by 37th. Division.	
	8th		C.R.E. 37th. Division called to discuss details of handing over. Divisional Operation Order No. 121 received. R.E. Operation Order No. 49 issued. Orders received that Lieut. Colonel A.J.CRAVEN is selected to form part of Mission to ITALY, probably assemble at PARIS February 14th.	O.O. 49 attached
	9th		Acting C.R.E. 37th. Division called, visited portion of LOOS Sector with him and O.C's 129th.&153 Field Co's,R.E. Issued amendments to Operation Order No. 49.	Attached
	10th		129th. Field Company moved out - relieved by 153rd. Field Company. Meeting at Headquarters with Tunnelling Officers.	

2353 Wt. W2544/1454 700,000 5/15 D. D. & L. A.D.S.S./Forms/C. 2118.

Army Form C. 2118.

Instructions regarding War Diaries and Intelligence Summaries are contained in F. S. Regs., Part II. and the Staff Manual respectively. Title pages will be prepared in manuscript.

WAR DIARY
or
~~INTELLIGENCE SUMMARY.~~
(Erase heading not required.)

C.R.E. 24th. Division.

Place	Date	Hour	Summary of Events and Information	Remarks and references to Appendices
BRAQUEMONT ~~LABEUVRIERE.~~				
February	11th		C.R.E. 37th. Division (Lieut. Colonel Pollard LOWSLEY) came to obtain information. 103rd. Field Co.,R.E. moved to NOEUX les MINES.	
	12th		Major C.N.RIVERS-MOORE moved to H.Q. to take over duties of C.R.E. C.R.E. left in car to join party proceeding to ITALY. 103rd. Field Co.,R.E. to ALLOUAGNE. 104th. Field Co.,R.E. to NOEUX les MINES.	
LABEUVRIERE	13th		Handed over to C.R.E. 37th. Division. Division moved to LABEUVRIERE.	
	14th		Orders issued for parade of 73rd. Brigade by General NIVILLE on 16th. Visited 129th. Field Co.,R.E. Lieut. Lloyd Davis reported for duty with 129th. Field Co.,R.E.	
	15th		Visited Parade Ground, HESDIGNEUL and arranged for duckboarding for Generals Inspection.	
	16th		Inspection of 73rd. Brigade by General NIVILLE. Major C.N.RIVERS-MOORE Commanded 129th. Field Co.,R.E. on this Parade. Visited Range at ALLOUAGNE, 1st. Corps Workshops and 1st. Army Workshops.	
	17th		Visited Range at ALLOUAGNE and 103rd. Field Co.,R.E. afterwards, 1st. Army Workshops re alterations to target design.	
	18th		Visited Range and 72nd. Brigade Headquarters, also Sherwood Foresters H.Q.	
	19th		Routine. Firing commenced on 6 targets at ALLOUAGNE. Infantry working parties withdrawn.	
	20th		Visited 104th. Field Co.,R.E. and MINX. Arranged for Captain MARVIN to hand over work in Range at ALLOUAGNE to Lieut. Lloyd DAVIES.	

2353 Wt. W2544/1454 700,000 5/15 D. D. & L. A.D.S.S./Forms/C. 2118.

Instructions regarding War Diaries and Intelligence Summaries are contained in F. S. Regs., Part II. and the Staff Manual respectively. Title pages will be prepared in manuscript.

Army Form C. 2118.

WAR DIARY
or
~~INTELLIGENCE SUMMARY.~~
(Erase heading not required.)

C.R.E. 24th. Division.

Place	Date	Hour	Summary of Events and Information	Remarks and references to Appendices
LABEUVRIERE.				
	February 21st.		Visited Divisional School and 129th. Field Co.,R.E. in morning. Received warning order for move to relieve 1st Canadian Division.	
	22nd		Visited Range and 103rd. Field Co.,R.E. ALLOUAGNE.	
	23rd.		Operation Order No. 122 Copy 11 received. 2nd Lieut. D.M.CRISTISON joined 103rd. Field Co.,R.E.	
	24th		Visited C.R.E. 1st. Canadian Division, also COUPIGNY Dump, AIX la NOULETTE and BULLY GRENAY Dumps.	
	25th		Conference at Divisional H.Q. Visited ALLOUAGNE rifle range. Major R.A.B.SMITH rejoined from R.E. School, LE PARCQ. Captain M.H. SCHWAB rejoined from School of Instruction CONDETTE and was admitted to 73rd. Field Ambulance with measles .	
	26th		Visited C.R.E. 1st. Canadian ~~Divisions~~. Issued Operation ~~Raid~~ Order No. 50. Visited 129th. Field Co.,R.E. at night work on strong point. Captain MARVIN returned to 129th. Field Co.,R.E. from ALLOUAGNE.	O.O. 50 attached
	27th		Inspection of turnouts of the 3 Field Companies by Major BLAKENEY at LABUISSIERE. Result 104th. - 1st. 129th. - 2nd. Issued amendment to Operation Order No 50	attached
	28th		Met 104th. Field Co.,R.E. on Route March. Visited Divisional School and inspected Hospital Hut.	

Captain & Adjutant,R.E.,
for C.R.E. 24th. Division.

S E C R E T.

Copy No. 12

OPERATION ORDER No. 49
by

Lieut. Colonel A.J.CRAVEN, R.E.

C.R.E. 24th. Division.

Reference
Map 1/40,000
Sheet 36B. and
Map 1/100,000
HAZEBROUCK 5A.

8th. February 1917.

1. The 24th. Division will be relieved by the 37th. Division. Infantry reliefs being completed by midnight 13/14 Feb. 17.

2. Field Companies will be relieved in accordance with attached Table F.

3. Details of transfer will be arranged direct between Field Companies concerned.

4. All trench stores, defence schemes, tables of work in hand and proposed will be handed over to relieving units of 37th. Division and a list of all articles handed over will be forwarded to C.R.E. for transmission to Divisional H.Qrs.

5. Copies of handing over reports to be sent to C.R.E. 24th.Div

6. Completion of reliefs and arrival at destination will be reported by wire to C.R.E.

7. 24th. Division Headquarters will close at BRAQUEMONT at 4p.m. Feb. 13th. and reopen at a place to be notified later.

8. Acknowledge.

J Stout [signature] Capt. & Adjutant,R.E.,
for C.R.E. 24th. Division.

Issued at 8.0 pm.

Copies to:- No.1 -H.Q.(G).
2 -H.Q.(Q).
3 -A.D.M.S.
4 -O.C.Train.
5.-17th. I.B.
6 -72nd. I.B.
7 -73rd. I.B.
8 -O.C.24th. Divl. Signal Co.
9 -O.C.103rd. Field Co.,R.E.
10 -O.C.104th. Field Co.,R.E.
11 -O.C.129th. Field Co.,R.E.
12 -War Diary.
13 -Record.
14 -C.R.E.37th. Division.

MARCH TABLES DIVISIONAL R.E.

Table F.

Field Co. 24th Div.	Field Co. 37th.Div.	8th.February.	9th.February.	10th.February.	11th.February.	12th.February.	REMARKS.
	153rd.	PETIT SAINS	PETIT SAINS.	GRENAY & LOOS.			In relief of 129th. Field Co.,R.E.
129th.				PETIT SAINS.	*73rd. Brigade area		*Under Brigade arrangements.
	154th.	BETHUNE.	BETHUNE.	"HALTE" at L. 33. B.	PHILOSOPHE.		In relief of 103rd Field Co.,R.E.
103rd.						*72nd. Brigade area.	*Under Brigade arrangements.
	152nd.			BETHUNE.	"HALTE" at L. 33. B.	LES BREBIS & LOOS.	In relief of 104th Field Co.,R.E.
104th.					"HALTE at L. 33. B.	*17th. Brigade area.	*Under Brigade arrangement.

S E C R E T.
****

CORRECTION TO

C.R.E's OPERATION ORDER No.49 of 8/2/17.

Para 2 for "Table F" substitute "Table G" (attached).

Para 7 cancel "a place to be notified later" and substitute "LABEUVRIERE".

Please acknowledge.

J R Grant
Captain & Adj.,R.E.,
for C.R.E. 24th. Division.

Issued at 6-30pm
9/2/1917.

Copies to :-
No.1 - H.Q.(G).
2 - H.Q.(Q).
3 - A.D.M.S.
4 - O.C. Train.
5 - 17th. I.B.
6 - 72nd. I.B.
7 - 73rd. I.B.
8 - O.C. 24th. Div. Signal Co.
9 - O.C. 103rd. Field Co.,R.E.
10 - O.C. 104th. Field Co.,R.E.
11 - O.C. 129th. Field Co.,R.E.
12 - War Diary.
13 - Record.
14 - C.R.E. 37th. Division.

S E C R E T
****

MARCH TABLES DIVISIONAL R.E.
****

TABLE G.

Field Co. 24th Div.	Field Co. 37th.Div.	9th. February.	10th. February.	11th. February.	12th. February.	REMARKS.
	153rd.	PETIT SAINS.	GRENAY & LOOS.			In relief of 129th. Field Co.,R.E.
129th.			PETIT SAINS.	*73rd. Brigade area.		*Under Brigade arrangements.
	154th.	BETHUNE.	"HALTE" at L. 33. B.	PHILOSOPHE.		In relief of 103rd. Field Co.,R.E.
103rd.				NOEUX les MINES.	*72nd. Brigade area.	*Under Brigade arrangements.
	152nd.		BETHUNE.	"HALTE at L. 33. B.	LES BREBIS & LOOS.	In relief of 104th. Field Co.,R.E.
104th.					NOEUX les MINES.	

SECRET

Copy No 12

OPERATION ORDER No. 50.
by
MAJOR C.A.RIVERS MOORE, R.E.

Reference :-
Map 1/40,000
Sheet 36B, &
Map 1/100,000
HAZEBROUCK,5,a.
LENS,11.

28th February,1917.

1. The 24th Division will relieve the 1st Canadian Division on the front SOUCHEZ River to DOUBLE CRASSIER. The relief to be completed by 6th March.

2. Field Companies will relieve in accordance with attached table "C".

3. Details of transfer will be arranged direct between Field Companies concerned.

4. All trench stores,Defence schemes,tables of work in hand and proposed,will be taken over from Field Companies of 1st Canadian Engineers,and a list of all articles (n taken over will be forwarded to the C.R.E.for transmissin to Divisional H.Q.

5. Copies of handing over reports to be sent to C.R.E.24th Division.

6. Units of the 24th Division arriving in 1st Canadian Div--ision area will come under the orders of G.O.C.1st Canadian Division until 12 noon March 6th

7. Command of Brigade Sectors will pass from B.G's.C.1st Canadian Division to B.G's.C.24th Division on completion of relief in the front trenches.

8. Completion of reliefs will be wired by B.A.B.Code to C.R.E.

9. 24th Divisional Headquarters will close at LABEUVRIERE at 12 noon March 6th ,and reopen at BARLIN.at same hour

10. On March 6th O.Cs.Field Companies will each send a guide to H.Q.R.E.to direct C.R.Es orderlies to their Company Headquarters and Horse Lines.

11. Acknowledge.

J.R. Grant
Capt & AdjtR.E.
for C.R.E.24th Divn.

Issued at 10.0 pm
Copies to :-No.1.H.Q."G"
" 2.H.Q."Q"
" 3.A.D.M.S.
" 4.O.C.Train.
" 5.17th I.B.
"6.72nd I.B.
" 7.73rd I.B.
" 8.O.C.24th Div Signal Co.
"9. O.C.103rd Fd Co.R.E.
"10.O.C.104th Fd Co.R.E.
"11.O.C.129th Fd Co.R.E.
"12.War Diary.
"13.Record.
"14.C.R.E.1st Canadian Divn.

MARCH TABLE - TABLE "C"

UNIT		1st	2nd	3rd	4th	5th	6th	Will relieve	REMARKS
103rd Fd COY R. E.	1st Half	FOUQUEREUIL	BULLY GRENAY	LINE				3rd Co. 1st C. E.	Billets at FOUQUEREUIL to be arranged with O.C. 129th Fd Coy
	2nd Half		ALLOUAGNE	FOUQUEREUIL	BULLY GRENAY				
104th Fd COY R. E.	1st Half	NOEUX	BULLY GRENAY	LINE				2nd Co. 1st C. E.	
	2nd Half		NOEUX	BULLY GRENAY					
129th Fd COY R. E.	1st Half			FOUQUEREUIL	AIX NOULETTE*			1st Co. 1st C.E.	* O.C. 1st Co. C.E. will arrange temporary billets for this half Company.
	2nd Half					FOUQUEREUIL	AIX NOULETTE		

(Handwritten above the 1st–6th columns: ← March →)

NOTE:- The 1st Half Company will consist of the two Sections detailed to take over work in the line in each case, and will be accompanied by sufficient transport to meet their requirements.

Headquarters and the remainder of the transport will accompany the second Half Company.

All Mounted Sections will proceed to SAINS EN GOHELLE and be billetted there.

Starting time will be 10.0 a.m. in each case except for 129th Field Coy, which will move off at 8.30. a.m.

<u>T A B L E "D"</u>

<u>ROUTES</u>

1. (a) ALLOUAGNE to FOUQUEREUIL :-

ALLOUAGNE - LAPUGNOY - LABEUVRIERE - FOUQUEREUIL.

(b) FOUQUEREUIL to BULLY GRENAY :-

FOUQUEREUIL - Road Junction R.30.d. - VAUDRICOURT - DROUVIN - NOEUX LES MINES - PT SAINS - BULLY GRENAY.

2. FOUQUEREUIL to AIX NOULETTE :-

FOUQUEREUIL - GOSNAY - HESDIGNEUL - Road Junction K.13.b. - HAILLICOURT - BARLIN - HERSIN - SAINS EN GOHELLE - AIX NOULETTE.

Secret.

AMENDMENT TO C.R.E's OPERATION ORDER No.50.

Paras 6 and 9 of Operation Order No.50, for:- 12 noon March 6th, - read:- 4-0.p.m.March 5th.

J. R. Grant

Capt & Adjt, R.E.

27th Febry, 1917. for C.R.E.24th Divn.

Army Form C. 2118.

Instructions regarding War Diaries and Intelligence Summaries are contained in F. S. Regs., Part II. and the Staff Manual respectively. Title pages will be prepared in manuscript.

WAR DIARY
or
INTELLIGENCE SUMMARY.
(Erase heading not required.)

C.R.E., 24th. Division.

Vol. 19

Place	Date	Hour	Summary of Events and Information	Remarks and references to Appendices
LABEUVRIERE				
	March 1917			
	1st.		Visited Headquarters of 1st. Field Company, 1st. Canadian Engineers, and walked round defences of LORETTE Spur.	
	2nd.		Conferred with G.O.C. in LORETTE Defences. Visited 129th. Field Company.	
	3rd.		Visited Range at ALLOUAGNE and arranged to hand over work to Interpreter to Chief Engineer 1st. Corps.	
	4th.		Visited B.G.C., 73rd. Brigade and 129th. Field Company. R.E. Received handing over notes from C.R.E., 1st. Canadian Division. Lieut Colonel CRAVEN returned from duty with Mission to ITALIAN Front. Major RIVERS-MOORE returned to 129th. Field Company. R.E.	
	5th.		Divisional Headquarters moved to BARLIN, in relief of 1st. Canadian Division.	
BARLIN.	6th.		Visited COUPIGNY Park, billets of 129, 104 & 103 Field Companies R.E., also Divisional Dump at BULLY GRENAY. Major HEATH rejoined from sick leave.	
	7th.		Visited portion of ANGRE Sector with O.C. 104th. Field Company. Visited C.E. 1st. Corps. Captain SCHWAB returned from sick leave.	
	8th.		Visited 129th. Field Co., R.E. 104th. Field Co., R.E. and Divisional Dump.	
	9th.		Inspected MAISTRE Line with G.O.C.	
	10th.		Visited Right Sub-Sector of CALONNE Sector with O.C. 103rd. Field Co., R.E.	
	11th.		Divisional Conference. Visited R.E. Wharf, BETHUNE, MINX Yard.	
	12th.		To MARQUEFFLES Farm and inspected Roads in Divisional Area To lecture on Sound Ranging .	

2353 Wt. W2544/1454 700,000 5/15 D. D. & L. A.D.S.S./Forms/C. 2118.

Army Form C. 2118.

WAR DIARY
or
INTELLIGENCE SUMMARY.
(Erase heading not required.)

Instructions regarding War Diaries and Intelligence Summaries are contained in F. S. Regs., Part II. and the Staff Manual respectively. Title pages will be prepared in manuscript.

C.R.E., 24th. Division.

Place	Date	Hour	Summary of Events and Information	Remarks and references to Appendices
BARLIN.	March 1917			
	13th.		Round SOUCHEZ Sector with O.C. 129th. Field Company R.E.	
	14th.		To Divisional School regarding Huts &c, 1st. Army Workshops and MINX.	
	15th.		Round ANGRES Sector with O.C. 104th. Field Co.,R.E.	
	16th.		To Divisional Dump and 1st. Army Park, LILLERS.	
	17th.		Round CALONNE Sector with O.C. 103rd. Field Co.,R.E.	
	18th.		Divisional Conference at BULLY GRENAY. To Headquarters 129th. Field Co.,R.E., Divisional Dump and SAVY.	
	19th.		Visited 104th. and 129th. Field Co.,R.E. Routine.	
	20th. "		Round sites of proposed Water Supply for additional horses with D.A.Q.M.G. To Chief Engineer, 1st. Corps.	
	21st.		Round Right Subsector of SOUCHEZ Section with O.C. 129th. Field Co.,R.E.	
	22nd.		Round CALONNE Sector with O.C. 103rd. Field Co.,R.E.	
	23rd.		To FOSSE No.10. Visited Pioneer Battalion and Divisional Dump. Water Supply for 1,000 horses urgently required at FOSSE 10.	
	24th.		Visited ANGRES Sector with O.C. 104th. Field Co., R.E.	
	25th.		Divisional Conference.	
	26th.		Visited C.R.E., 4th. Canadian Division to arrange transfer of portion of line to 24th Division.	
	27th		Visited Left of CALONNE Section with O.C. 103rd Field Company R.E., specially inspected defences of MAROC.	

Army Form C. 2118.

Instructions regarding War Diaries and Intelligence Summaries are contained in F. S. Regs., Part II. and the Staff Manual respectively. Title pages will be prepared in manuscript.

WAR DIARY
or
INTELLIGENCE SUMMARY.

(Erase heading not required.)

C.R.E. 24th Division.

Place	Date	Hour	Summary of Events and Information	Remarks and references to Appendices
BARLIN.	March 1917.			
	28th		To FOSSE 10 and SAINS EN GOHELLE in connection with move of Divisional Headquarters. Notification received 150 O.R. Entrenching Battalion with Officers will be attached for work on MAISTRE Line.	
	29th		Round part of MAISTRE Line with G.S.O.3. To lecture at BRAQUEMONT with G.O.C.	
	30th		With G.S.O.3. to meet O.C. 191. M.G. Company re M.G. positions in and about MAISTRE Line. Orders received posting Brevet Lieut: Colonel, A.J. Craven. R.E. (C.R.E. 24th Division) to V Corps as Chief Engineer.	
	31st		To BETHUNE with Adjutant. Conference with G.O.C., G.S.O.1., and Tunnelling Officer.	

J.R. Grant

Captain & Adj: R.E.

for C.R.E. 24th Division.

2353 Wt. W2544/1454 700,000 5/15 D. D. & L. A.D.S.S./Forms/C. 2118.

= = = = = = =

S E C R E T

= = = = = = =

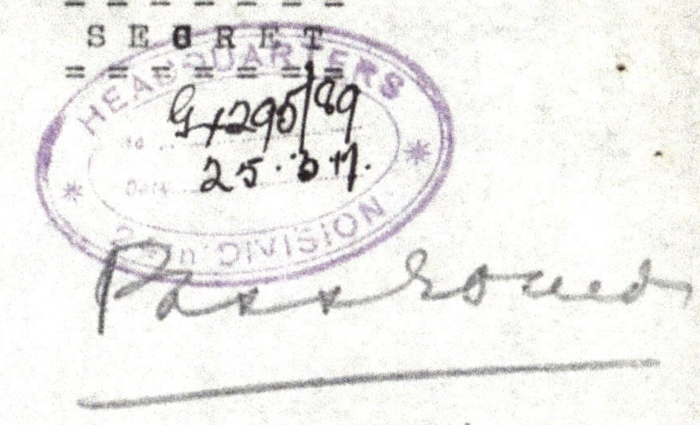

To. 24TH DIVISION.

REPORT

on

OPERATIONS NOS. 1 & 2. Night 22/23 March 1917.

"B" Special Company, R.E.

OPERATION NO. 1.

Bombardment of Enemy Works with 2" T.M. Lethal Bombs.

(a) FRONT. 72nd. Infantry Brigade., 24th Division. CALONNE Sector.

(b) TARGET. Enemy T.Ms. and Dug-outs in ruined houses. Map Ref. Sheet 36C S.W.1. 1:10,000. M.20.b.40.35. to M.20.b.95.35.

CITE DES CORNAILLES T.M. Emplacements at M.20.b.6.3. and M.20.b.95.30.

(c) PROGRAMME.

Zero Time, 8 p.m. 22:3:17. Thursday.

4 Guns of Y24 T.M.B. firing 2" T.M. Lethal Bombs, 8.p.m. - 8.30 p.m.

Artillery Barrage in Co-operation on the Left. M.10.c. 8 p.m. - 8.30 p.m.

Artillery Shrapnel over M.20.b., i.e., area bombarded with gas bombs. 9 p.m. - 9.15 p.m.

(d) PERSONNEL.

Lt. A. FOWLER, "B" Special Coy. i/c Operation assisted by 6 Other Ranks who prepared bombs for firing and who were attached to Gun Teams of Y24 T.M.B.

****

OPERATION NO. 2.

Bombardment of Enemy Works with 2" T.M. Lethal Bombs.

(a) FRONT. 17th. Infantry Brigade. ANGRES Sector.

(b) TARGET. Enemy Dump at head of Trench Railway, Trench Mortar and Machine Gun Emplacements and Dug-outs at and near M.26.a.65.70. Map Sheet 36^c S.W.1.

(c) PROGRAMME.

Zero Time, 8 p.m., 22:3:17. Thursday.

3 Guns, Z24 T.M.B. Firing 2" T.M. Lethal Bombs, 8 p.m. - 8.30 p.m.

Artillery Barrage in Co-operation on M.26.d., 8 p.m. - 8.30 p.m.

Artillery Shrapnel on M.26.a., i.e., area bombarded with gas bombs, 9 p.m. - 9.15 p.m.

(d) PERSONNEL.

2/Lieut. W.M.COOKSEY, "B" Special Coy. i/c Operation, assisted by 6 Other Ranks.

****

BATTLE REPORT.

Both these operations took place on the day and at the times stated, the wind then being W.N.W., 3 - 4 Miles per hour.

The following observations made by the officers in charge of these operations are shown in tabular form for the sake of comparison.

OPERATION NO. 1.		OPERATION NO. 2.	
CALONNE SECTOR.		ANGRES SECTOR.	
Enemy Regt. Opposite - 10th.Res. Regt.		Enemy Regt. Opposite - 14th.Bav. Regt.	
47 2" T.M. Lethal Bombs fired on Enemy Works, 8 p.m. 22:3:17.		30 2" T.M. Lethal Bombs fired on Enemy Works, 8 p.m., 22:3:17.	
Time.	**Enemy Action.**	**Time.**	**Enemy Action.**
Zero.	- - - - - -	Zero.	- - - - - - - - -
0.2 Min.	1 Light (rocket) bursting into Golden Rain.	0.1.	1 Light bursting into a shower of Golden Rain.
0.12.	White flare bursting into Two Green Stars.	0.2.	1 Single Red Light.
0.12.	1 Light bursting into 1 Red and 1 Green Star.	0.8.	1 Single light bursting into 2 Green Stars.
		0.9.	1 Single light bursting into 1 Red and 1 Green Star.
		0.9.	The same again immediately afterwards.
No apparent action was taken by the Enemy on any of these Light signals.		No apparent action was taken by the Enemy on any of these Light signals.	

Our Artillery and Machine Gun fire in Co-operation with the bombardment with Lethal Bombs, was heavy.

In Operation No. 2, the Rifle Mechanism breaking in each of the 3 Guns employed, prevented more than 30 Bombs out of 50 being fired.

Our Casualties were NIL.

(signed) G. P. CROWDEN. Lieut.
Comdg; "B" Special Company, R. E.

S.31.
23:3:1917.

C. R. E.

24th DIVISION

APRIL I917

Instructions regarding War Diaries and Intelligence Summaries are contained in F. S. Regs., Part II. and the Staff Manual respectively. Title pages will be prepared in manuscript.

WAR DIARY
or
INTELLIGENCE SUMMARY.

(Erase heading not required.)

Vol 20

Army Form C. 2118.

C.R.E., 24th. Division.

Place	Date 1917	Hour	Summary of Events and Information	Remarks and references to Appendices
	APRIL			
BARLIN.	2nd		Lieut: Col: CRAVEN ordered to V Corps as C.E. Handed over to Major F.P. HEATH.	
BARLIN &	3rd		Office moved from BARLIN to SAINS EN GOHELLE.	
SAINS EN GOHELLE.	4th.		Lieut: Col: T.T.BEHRENS, R.E. joins and takes over from Major F.P. HEATH.	
	11th		Arranged with O.C. 12th. Sherwood Foresters (Pioneers) to send me an officer to train as C.R.E's stores officer.	
	12th.		Discussed roads for an advance with C.E. 1st. Corps, Brig: Gen: ATKINSON.	
	13th.		Enemy retire in the night and we advance all along the line about 800 yards forward. The preparation for rapid repair of roads for an advance have not been foreseen and made in time. 3 Field Companies and Pioneers (4 Co'ys) occupied in opening up a temporary passage over "no man's land" for horsed transport and guns as rapidly as possible. Each Brigade being provided with one road. The weather is cold,wet, with sleet and the mud is considerable. The making of a passage over the badly shell shattered stretches without any previously collected timber is very slow. Had timber been collected the work could have been rapidly organized.	
	14th.		One Field Company and one Company of Pioneers (total working strength 230 men) upon each road except the COLONELS HOUSE - ANGRES track where a second Pioneer Company was added (total 370 men) One R.E. Officer told offfrom each Field Company for Reconnaissance of Roads and Bridges etc. Note :- This afterwards proved of no use as the officers were not sufficiently trained to make useful reports. Their view point was untrained: the reports therefore without an intelligent grasp of the situation.	
	15th. "		The rain and sleet are making all but corduroy and planked roadways useless. The 129th. Field Company R.E. on ANGRES Road now has 120 men (M.G. Coy & R.A) added, making 490 men on the work.	
	16th.		Conference all O.C. Field Companies, explained at length the requirements of good Reconnaissance necessity for prompt transmission of information.	

P.T.O.

2353 Wt. W2544/1454 700,000 5/15 D. D. & L. A.D.S.S./Forms/C. 2118.

Army Form C. 2118.

WAR DIARY
or
INTELLIGENCE SUMMARY.
(Erase heading not required.)

Instructions regarding War Diaries and Intelligence Summaries are contained in F. S. Regs., Part II. and the Staff Manual respectively. Title pages will be prepared in manuscript.

C.R.E., 24th. Division.

Place	Date	Hour	Summary of Events and Information	Remarks and references to Appendices
SAINS EN GOHELLE.	16th contd.		O.C. 104th. Field Company R.E. had rapidly laid and reconnoitred 800 yards of 60 c.m. tramline between our own and enemy's rail. This line was fit today only for daylight man pushed trucks.	
	17th.		Progress of the work by 129th. Field Company R.E. on the ANGRES Road poor. The organization appears poor.	
	18th.		104th. Field Company R.E. relieved by 466 Field Company R.E. of 46th. Division relieving 24th. Division. Visited this Companies tramline and found that nothing effectual had beer done on 17th. to improve the line, though the Company had laid some new line very well further forward. Concentrated 3 Pioneer Companies and 14 D.A.C. waggons on this reconstruction of track.	
	20th.		C.R.E., 46th. Division B.G. WINGFIELD-STRATFORD takes over at 10 a.m. Office moves ~~from~~ to NORRENT FONTES to rest. 104th. Field Company to ECURIE to work under C.E. 1st. Army.	
	22nd.		Arranged with O.C. Divisional Train for attachment of officers for training in horse management. The horse management and mounted turnout of the Field Companies is very poor. The Divisional Commander has remarked upon it. Visited C.E. II Corps at AIRE with reference to provision of baths etc. for Division while in rest.	
	24th.		Division moved to BOMY. C.R.E. remains behind as there is no accommodation for his H.Q. there.	
	25th.		Visited 104th. Field Company R.E. at MAISON BLANCHE near ARRAS.	
	26th.		Was to have moved to BOMY. 17th. & 73rd. Brigades withdrawn to Corps reserve Eastwards. Cancel my move.	
	27th.		On orders being received ~~from~~ for Left Brigade Groups to move and upon instructions from ~~xxx~~ "G" that each Group should include one Field Company, I issued the necessary orders to attach 129th. Field Co., R.E. to 73rd. Brigade -- 103rd. Field Company R.E. to 17th. Brigade, and to Brigades to give necessary orders for movement; "G" then cancelled orders for move of 103rd. Field Company R.E. This is a recurrence of the trouble caused by the indefinite position occupied by the C.R.E. with reference to the Staff. In my opinion the C.R.E. not the Staff should give orders to the individual Companies.	

2353 Wt. W2544/1454 700,000 5/15 D. D. & L. A.D.S.S./Forms/C. 2118.

Instructions regarding War Diaries and Intelligence Summaries are contained in F. S. Regs., Part II. and the Staff Manual respectively. Title pages will be prepared in manuscript.

WAR DIARY
or
INTELLIGENCE SUMMARY.
(Erase heading not required.)

Army Form C. 2118.

C.R.E., 24th. Division.

Place	Date	Hour	Summary of Events and Information	Remarks and references to Appendices
	1917 April.			
SAINS EN GOHELLE	28th.		Move from NORRENT-FONTES to BOMY.	
BOMY.	29th.		Visited Divisional Train Company with O.C. Train. Saw a portable sheet iron cooker for 200 men original cart from a firm in BEXHILL, SUSSEX, cost £17. This cooker folds up (except the cooking containers) into 2 wooden boxes for transport. Some such cooker or the Infantry Travelling Kitchen Mark II is really as essential for R.E. Companies as for the Infantry.	
	30th.		"Q" has been asked today to find an officer suitable for training as C.R.E's stores officer. The Pioneer officer who left me when the Division was relieved was not likely to prove suitable. The most important point that has emerged during this month is the paramount necessity of collecting material and making preparations of an exact kind for the immediate repair of roads by Divisions for an advance. The advance of 24th. Division was so well timed, the ~~relieving~~ retiring enemy so taken by surprise, that during the first part of the advance strong positions were abandoned to us without opposition. For 48 hours no guns could be got across the old lines to support the Infantry, and this allowed the enemy time to begin to hold in strength the position in front of LENS. Had the roads been made passable before the night of the 14th. and had they been corduroyed completely by the night of the 15th. as they might have been by careful preparation beforehand, the Division might have been able to push on through LENS before it was relieved.	

[signature] Lt. Col.

~~Captain & Adjutant, R.E.,~~

~~for~~ C.R.E. 24th. DIVISION.

2353 Wt. W2544/1454 700,000 5/15 D. D. & L. A.D.S.S./Forms/C. 2118.

SECRET

Copy No. 12

OPERATION ORDER No. 51.
by
Lieut Colonel T.T. Behrens. R.E.
C.R.E. 24th Division.

References:-
Map 1/40,000
Sheet 36B & 36C.
Map 1/100,000
Sheet HAZEBROUCK 5A.

(1) The 24th Division will be relieved by the 46th Division.
Infantry reliefs will be completed by the night of the 19th/20th April, 1917.

(2) The Field Companies will be relieved as follows:-
103rd Field Company R.E. by 468th Field Company R.E. on 20/4/17.
104th Field Company R.E. by 466th Field Company R.E. on 19/4/17.
129th Field Company R.E. by 465th Field Company R.E. on 20/4/17.
In accordance with March table "A" attached.

(3) The 104th Field Company R.E. when relieved will proceed to GOUY SERVINS in relief of the 466th Field Company R.E. They will be employed on water duties under the C.E. 1st Army whom they will inform direct of their arrival by telegram.

(4) Details of transfer will be arranged direct between the Field Companies concerned.

(5) Restrictions as to movement are as follows:-
(a) All movement East of NOEUX LES MINES will be by parties not larger than Companies, and forward of the AIX NOULETTE - BULLY GRENAY - MAROC road will be by parties not larger than platoons.
(b) There will be no movement from East to West of troops on relief West of the old German front line until after dark. (This in order that all movement seen by the enemy shall be movement in a forward direction only and so induce him to think that reinforcements are being sent up).

(6) All trench stores, Defence Schemes, and tables of work in hand or proposed will be handed over to the relieving units of the 46th Division, and a list of all articles handed over will be forwarded to this office for transmission to Divisional Headquarters.

(7) Copies of handing over reports to be sent to this office.

(8) Completion of reliefs and arrival at destination to be reported to this office by wire.

(9) 24th Divisional Headquarters will close at SAINS EN GOHELLE at 10 a.m. on April 20th and re-open at a place to be notified later, at the same hour.

(10) Acknowledge.

Issued at

on 18th April 1917.

Capt: & Adj: R.E.

for C.R.E. 24th Division.

Copy No. 1. to Headquarters "G"
2 Headquarters "Q"
3 A.D.M.S.
4 O.C. Divisional Train.
5 17th Infantry Brigade.
6 72nd Infantry Brigade.
7. 73rd Infantry Brigade
8 O.C. 103rd Field Company R.E.
9 O.C. 104th Field Company R.E.
10 O.C. 129th Field Company R.E.
11 O.C. 24th Divisional Signal Company
12 War Diary
13 Record.
14 C.R.E. 48th Division.

S E C R E T
===========

M A R C H   T A B L E

TABLE "A"

24th Divisional R.E.

Date. 18th April 1917.

Field Company 24th Div:	Field Company 46th Div:	18/4.	19/4.	20/4.	21/4.	22/4.	REMARKS.
	466th	LES BREBIS	BULLY GRENAY				
104th		BULLY GRENAY	GOUY SERVINS				
	468th	LES BREBIS	LES BREBIS	MAROC			
103rd		MAROC	MAROC	To be notified later	72nd Brigade area under Brigade arrangements		
	465th	~~goup~~ GOUY SERVINS	AIX NOULETTE	ANGRES			
129th		ANGRES	ANGRES	AIX NOULETTE	To be notified later.	73rd Brigade area under Brigade arrangements.	

SEE CLAUSE 5 AS TO RESTRICTIONS TO MOVEMENT.

S E C R E T.

CORRECTION TO

C.R.E's OPERATION ORDER NO. 51 of 18/4/17.

Para 2 line 3.
For Table "A" substitute Table "B" attached.

Para 9 lines 2 & 3.
Cancel "a place to be notified later" and substitute "NORRENT-FONTES".

ACKNOWLEDGE.

Issued at 1-15 a.m.

on 19/4/1917.

Captain & Adjutant, R.E

for C.R.E. 24th. Division.

Copy No. 1 to Headquarters "G"
2 Headquarters "Q"
3 A.D.M.S.
4 O.C. Divisional Train.
5 17th. Infantry Brigade.
6 72nd Infantry Brigade.
7 73rd Infantry Brigade.
8 O.C. 103rd. Field Company R.E.
9 O.C. 104th. Field Company R.E.
10 O.C. 129th. Field Company R.E.
11 O.C. 24th. Divisional Signal Company.
12 War Diary.
13 Record.
14 C.R.E. 46th. Division.

SECRET.

Table "B"

MARCH TABLE.

24th. DIVISIONAL R.E.

Field Company, 24th. Division.	Field Company 46th. Division.	18/4.	19/4.	20/4.	21/4.	22/4.	Remarks.
	466th.	LES BREBIS	BULLY GRENAY				
104th.		BULLY GRENAY	GOUY SERVINS.				
	468th.	LES BREBIS	LES BREBIS	MAROC			
103rd.		MAROC	MAROC	AUCHEL	AUCHY AU BOIS		
	465th.	GOUY SERVINS	AIX NOULETTE	ANGRES			
129th.		ANGRES	ANGRES	AIX NOULETTE	AUCHEL	FLECHINELLE	

SEE CLAUSE 5 AS TO RESTRICTIONS TO MOVEMENT.

S E C R E T

Operation Order No, 52. by Lieut Colonel T.T. Behrens R.E. C.R.E. 24th Division.

Copy No. 5

1. The 24th Division less Artillery and 73rd Infantry Brigade group will move to the HOMY area on the 24th April.

2. Divisional Headquarters will close at NORRENT FONTES at 10 a.m. on 24th and re-open at the same hour at HOMY.

3. The 103rd Field Company R.E. will be billeted in the 72nd Infantry Brigade area at

4. Application has been made for the 73rd Infantry Brigade to remain in its present area, but this Brigade will be prepared to move at short notice.

5. Maps showing the Army Training area for Tactical Training have been sent to 103rd and 129th Field Companies R.E.

6. Acknowledge.

Issued at

23/4/1917.

Capt: & Adj: R.E.
for C.R.E. 24th Division.

Copy No, 1 to 103rd Field Company R.E.
2 104th Field Company R.E.
3 129th Field Company R.E.
4 Record.
5 War Diary.

S E C R E T

Copy No, 9

Operation Order No, 53.
by
Lieut Colonel T.T. Behrens. R.E.
C.R.E. 24th Division.

Reference
map 1/100,000
Hazebrouck & Lens.
sheets.

1. The 17th and 73rd Infantry Brigade Groups will move to the BETHUNE and NOEUX LES MINES areas respectively.

#. The Brigade at BETHUNE will be available to support the XI Corps and the Brigade at NOEUX LES MINES the I Corps on application by those Corps to Advanced Army H.Q.

2. The 103rd Field Company R.E. will for part of the 17th Infantry Brigade Group and the 129th Field Company R.E. will form part of the 73rd Infanfry Brigade Group.

They will move, each under orders of its own Brigade.

3. All surplus kit will be collected and left under charge of a small guard per Company until arrangements can be made to carry this kit.

4. Acknowledge.

Issued at 5.30 p.m.
26/4/17.

J.R. Grant
Capt: & Adj: R.E.
for C.R.E. 24th Division.

Copy No, 1 to "G" 24th Division Headquarters
2 "Q" 24th Division Headquarters
3 17th Infantry Brigade.
4 73rd Infantry Brigade
5 103rd Field Company R.E.
6 129th Field Company R.E.
7 24th Divisional Train
8 Record
9 War Diary.

Instructions regarding War Diaries and Intelligence Summaries are contained in F. S. Regs., Part II. and the Staff Manual respectively. Title pages will be prepared in manuscript.

WAR DIARY
or
INTELLIGENCE SUMMARY.
(Erase heading not required.)

Army Form C. 2118.

HQ RE 24 D
Vol 21

Place	Date	Hour	Summary of Events and Information	Remarks and references to Appendices
	1917. May 1st.		Division is in rest. CAPTAIN SHARPE R.E. No.20 A.T.Coy.reported at Divisional R.E.Headquartersfor attachment.	
	2nd.		2nd.Corps Commander saw all Officers of the Divisional Headquarters,72nd.Infantry Brigade and 103rd.FieldCompany personally.	
	4th.		Divisional Commander (General Capper) inspected the 129th.Field Company R.E. at VERQUIN - Parade in Marching Order.	
	8th.		Much greater effort is necessary to institute a high standard of horsemastership in the Field Companies. There is not one of the Companies where horsemanagement is understood and practised with any success at present.	
	9th.		Divisional R.E.Headquarters moved from BOMY to NORRENT-FONTES. C.E. 2nd.Corps inspected Field Companies on the march. Turnout and march discipline indifferent.	
	11th.		C.R.E. inspected mounted portions of all 3 Field Companies. The turn out of the animals and horses is still indifferent but has improved. All the Officers shewed ignorance of the Field Service Manual, the mobilization equipment and how it should be carried. ¾ Hrs.with each Company was enough to shew many but not nearly all defects.	
	12th.		Divisional R.E.Headquarters to STEENVOORDE. Divisional Headquarters at WINNEZEELE. Visited C.R.E. 23rd. Division. (Lt.Col.Rooke).	
	14th.		Visited portion of the line to be taken over by this Division. C.R.E. 23rd.Divisionhanding over took me round the HOOGE Sector, going up through YPRES.	
	15th.		Divisional R.E.Headquarters to BRANDHOEK Camp. Relief in the line took place last night.	

Army Form C. 2118.

Instructions regarding War Diaries and Intelligence Summaries are contained in F. S. Regs., Part II. and the Staff Manual respectively. Title pages will be prepared in manuscript.

WAR DIARY
or
INTELLIGENCE SUMMARY.
(Erase heading not required.)

Place	Date	Hour	Summary of Events and Information	Remarks and references to Appendices
	1917. May 18th.		Visited Right sector of Brigade front with B.G.Stone 17th.Infantry Brigade & G.S.O.	
	21st.		C.E. 2nd.Corps called to get information about 24th.Divisional area prior to taking over from 24th. Division.	
	22nd.		Visited 23rd.Divisional Sector with all O.C.Field Companies, 24th. Division.	
	23rd.		" 47th. " " " " " " " " "	
	24th.		" 41st. " " " " " " " " "	
			The light Railway has been tried for bringing up Stores to the end of theDivisional Tramline at KRUISTRAAT. This has had to be abandoned, on account of the unreliability of this service and the local subordinate staff of the A.D.L.R.R. It is impossible to have unloading parties waiting about for hours at night for trains that may never arrive.	
	26th		Lt.E.Y.Collison-Morley, 8th.Buffs, joined today to be attached to me as Stores Officer (learner).	
	28th		Relief of R.E's from the line 28/29.	
	30th.		Divisional R.E.Head Quarters moved to Reninghelst. C.R.E. visited 41st. Divisional area with C.R.E. 41st. Division.	
	31st.		Discussed with B.G.G.S. and C.E. Xth. Corps the preparations for road making as far as the work of 24th. Divisional R.E's and Pioneers was concerned.	

[signature]
Lt.Col.
C.R.E. 24th. Division.

2353 Wt. W2544/1454 700,000 5/15 D. D. & L. A.D.S.S./Forms/C. 2118.

CONFIDE[illegible]

24th Division No. C/

D. A. G.,
3rd Echelon,
Base.

Herewith Operation Orders relating to War Diary of the Royal Engineers for the month of MAY 1917.

July 7th 1917.

Major General,
Commanding 24th Division.

R.E. 1011.

"Q"
24th. Divisional Headquarters.

WAR DIARY-HEADQUARTERS R.E.-MAY 1917.

Herewith Operation Orders relating to the above.

J. R. Grant
Capt. & Adjt. R.E.
for C.R.E. 24th. Division.

5.7.1917.

S.E.C.R.E.T.

Copy No 12

Operation Order No. 84
by
Lieut Colonel T.T. BEHRENS, R.E.

C.R.E. 24th. Division.

Reference
Map 1/100,000
Sheet
HAZEBROUCK 5.A.

1. The 24th. Division, accompanied by Divisional Supply Column, Ammunition Sub-Park, Cable Section, and sub section Army Wireless Co'y, is ~~to~~ be transferred from First Army. (2nd Corps) to 2nd Army (10th. Corps) and will no longer be held in G.H.Q. reserve.

2. ~~The moves to take place on May 9th. and 10th. are given in the attached March Table.~~

The Division will be concentrated in the STEENBECQUE area by the evening of May 10th.

The Division will move on the 11th. & 12th May to the STEENVOORDE area, the Div. Arty. moving on the 11th. and the remainder of the Division on the 12th. May.

~~3. The 12th. Bn. Sherwood Foresters (Pioneers) will move to the STEENBECQUE area on the 9th. May by bus.~~

3. The Field Companies R.E. will move to the new area in accordance with march table "A" attached

4. Billets in the STEENVOORDE area will be allotted by the Area Commandant ~~STEENVOORDE.~~ STEENVOORDE

5. Supplies will be drawn at WIPPENHOEK on the 12th. May for consumption on the 13th. May.

6. 24th. Divisional Headquarters will close at BOHY at 4 p.m. on the 9th. May and reopen at the same time at ~~XXX~~ NORRENT FONTES. 24th. Divl. Headquarters will move on the 10th. May to STEENBECQUE the time that Headquarters will ~~xx~~open at this place will be notified later.

7. Acknowledge.

J. R. Grant

Captain & Adjt R.E.,

for C.R.E. 24th. Division.

Issued at 11.0 pm

9/5/1917.

Copy No. XX 1 "G" 24th. Division Headquarters.
2 "Q" 24th. Division Headquarters.
3 A.D.M.S.
4 O.C. Divisional Train.
5 17th. Inf. Bde.
6. 72nd. Inf. Bde.
7. 73rd. Inf. Bde.
8. O.C. 103rd. Field Co. R.E.
9. O.C. 104th. Field Co. R.E.
10. O.C. 129th. Field Co. R.E.
11 24th. Divisional Signal Co. R.E.
12 War Diary.
13 Record.

M A R C H T A B L E S "B" F O R F I E L D C O M P A N I E S, R. E.

Issued with O.O. 84 dated 8/5/17.

DATE.	UNITS.	FROM.	TO.	ROUTE & TIMES.		REMARKS.
9th. May	103rd. Field Co: R.E.	CAPELLE SUR LA LYS	ESTREE BLANCHE	CAPELLE SUR LA LYS	10 a.m.	
				COYECQUE.	10-30 a.m.	
				ENQUIN LES MINES.	12-30 p.m.	
				ESTREE BLANCHE	1 p.m.	
9th. May	104th. Field Co.R.E.	DENNEBROEUCQ	ESTREE BLANCHE	DENNEBROEUCQ	10 a.m.	
				COYECQUE	11 a.m.	
				ENQUIN LES MINES	1 p.m.	
				ESTREE BLANCHE.	1-30 p.m.	
10th. May	103rd. Field Co.R.E. 104th. Field Co.R.E. 129th. Field Co.R.E.	ESTREE BLANCHE	DESTINATION TO BE NOTIFIED LATER.			

SECRET

COPY No 12

OPERATION ORDER No. 55
BY
Lieut: Col: T. T. BEHRENS R.E.
C.R.E. 24TH DIVISION.

Reference
1/100,000 Map
Sheet
HAZEBROUCK 5A

(1) The Field Companies R.E. of the 24th Division will move from ESTREE BLANCHE to MORBECQUE on the 10th May 1917 in acco ance with the following table :-

LEAVE	ESTREE BLANCHE	7.0 AM.
	LIETTRES	7.30 AM.
	WITTERNESSE	8.0 AM.
	AIRE	9.0 A.M.
	BOESEGHEM.	10.0. A.M.
	STEENBECQUE	10.45 A.M.
ARRIVE	MORBECQUE	12. 0 NOON.

(2) Order of march will be 103rd, 104th & 129th Field Company

(3) Major I. W. LAMONBY, O.C. 103 Field Co. RE will be in Command and will arrange other details.

(4) All troops & transport must be clear of Railway Crossing N.E. of AIRE by 9-45 AM.

(5) The C.R.A., 24th Division will arrange for billets to be allotted to the R.E in the MORBEQUE

S E C R E T.

OPERATION ORDER NO. 56 Copy No. 13

BY

Lieut: Colonel T.T. BEHRENS, R.E.

C.R.E., 24th. DIVISION.

Reference
1/100,000 Map
Sheet HAZEBROUCK 5.A.

(1) The 24th. Division will move to the STEENVOORDE Area on the 12th May 1917.

(2) The Field Companies R.E. of the 24th. Division will move from MORBECQUE and the 12th Sherwood Foresters (Pioneers) from PAPOTE to the STEENVOORDE Area.

Details of this move are given on the attached March Table "A"

(3) The 72nd Infantry Brigade will relieve the 70th Infantry Brigade (23rd Division) in the OBSERVATORY RIDGE - HOOGE SECTORS on the 14th May and the night of 14th/15th May.

(4) The details regarding the relief of R.E. and Pioneers will be notified later.

(5) The 73rd Infantry Brigade, one Field Company R.E. and one Company of the 12th Sherwood Foresters (Pioneers) are detailed for work under the C.E. X Corps.

One Company of the 12th Sherwood Foresters (Pioneers) is detailed for work under the G.O.C. X Corps H.A.

(6) Headquarters 24th. Divisional R.E. will move from NORRENT FONTES to STEENVOORDE on the 12th May.

(7) Each unit will send a billeting party in advance to the Area Commandants Office, STEENVOORDE (opposite the Mairie) to ascertain the location of their billets.

(8) Acknowledge.

J. R. Grant

Issued at 11-10 p.m.
11/5/1917.

Captain & Adjutant, R.E.,
for C.R.E. 24th. Division.

/P.T.O.

Copies to :-

1 "G" 24th Division
2 "Q" 24th Division
3 A.D.M.S.
4 24th Divl Train
5 17th I.B.
6 72nd I.B.
7 73rd I.B.
8 12th Sherwood Foresters (Pioneers)
9 103rd Field Company R.E.
10 104th Field Company R.E.
11 129th Field Company R.E.
12 24th Divisional Signal Company
13 War Diary
14 Record
15 C.R.E 23rd Division

MARCH TABLE "A"
For
Field Companys R.E. and 12th Sherwood Foresters (Pioneers).

issued with O.O. 56 dated 11/5/1917.

Date	Unit	From	To	Route	REMARKS.
12/5/17	103rd Field Company R.E. 104th Field Company R.E. 129th Field Company R.E.	MORBECQUE	STEENVOORDE Area	HAZEBROUCK STEENVOORDE	Starting Point Cross Roads 120 yards S.E. of the last E in LA CUNEWELE. Head of column will pass at 7-40 a.m. Distance between Companies will be 100 yards only.
	12th Sherwood Foresters (Pioneers)	PAPOTE	STEENVOORDE Area	HAZEBROUCK STEENVOORDE	To follow in rear of 3 Field Companies.

Secret Copy No 13

Operation Order No [illegible]

by

Lieut Col. T.T. BEHRENS, R.E.

C.R.E., 23rd Division

Reference

[illegible] Sheet 28 [illegible]

(1) All movements East of VLAMERTINGHE [illegible] [illegible] on the [illegible] [illegible] with intervals of 100 yards between each.

(2) One Company of the 9th Sherwood Foresters (Pioneers) will move to BRANDHOEK on the [illegible] day. They will [illegible] [illegible] [illegible] BRANDHOEK area [illegible] available.

The Company [illegible] allotted for work [illegible] C.E., X Corps H.Q. [illegible] accommodation [illegible] RAMPARTS [illegible] as stated in para 8 of the 24th Division O.O. 150. The accommodation for this Company will be notified later.

(3) The 102nd Field Co R.E. [illegible] [illegible] C.E. X Corps. The details for this move (probably on the [illegible] night) will be issued later.

(4) The [illegible] R.E. [illegible] move [illegible] May from STEENVOORDE to BRANDHOEK.

(5) The [illegible] [illegible] [illegible] 72 [illegible] [illegible] [illegible] [illegible] Co, R.E. be pre- pared to [illegible] the area from the 14th/15th May.

(6) Officers of the 72nd [illegible] on the [illegible] and [illegible] to the area [illegible] should if possible be [illegible] of their [illegible].

(7) Details for the move of the 127th Field Coy [illegible] issued later.

(8) Details for the move of the 12th Sherwood Foresters (Pioneers) less one Company will be issued later.

(9) 24th Divisional R.E. H.Q. will close at STEENVOORDE at 9 a.m. on the 15th May and will reopen at BRANDHOEK on the same day.

(10) Acknowledge.

Issued at 7 pm.
12/5/17

[illegible]
Capt & Adjt R.E.
for C.R.E. 24th Div.

Copies issued to

1 G. 24th DIV.

2 Q. 24th DIV.

3 A.D.M.S.

4 24th. DIV. Train

5. 17th. Inf. Bde.

6 72nd Inf Bde.

7 73rd. Inf. Bde.

12th Sherwood Foresters (Pioneers)

103rd. Field Co. R.E.

104th. Field Co. R.E.

[illegible] Field Co. R.E.

24th Div. Signal Co.

[illegible]

[illegible]

G.R.A., 23rd Div.

SECRET.

Copy No. 4

Operation Order No. 58
by
Lieut: Colonel T.T. BEHRENS, R.E.

C.R.E., 24th. Division.

Reference
1/20,000 Sheet 28 N.W.
1/100,000 HAZEBROUCK 5.A.

1. Headquarters R.E., 24th Division and the 104th. Field Company R.E. will move on the 15th. inst. from STEENVOORDE to BRANDHOEK Area.

2. The head of the column will pass the cross roads 300 yards S.E. of the last E in BEAUVOORDE at 10 a.m., and the route will be ABEELE, POPERINGHE, BRANDHOEK.

3. The O.C. 104th. Field Company R.E. will be in Command.

4. The 104th. Field Company R.E. will move into billets vacated by the 1st. North Staffs in the BRANDHOEK Area.

5. Acknowledge.

J. L. Grant
Captain & Adjutant, R.E.,
for C.R.E., 24th. Division.

Issued at 8 p.m.
14th. May 1917.

Copy No. 1 - 103rd. Field Company R.E.
2 - 104th. Field Company R.E.
3 - 129th. Field Company R.E.
4 - War Diary.
5 - Record.

Secret.

COPY No. 12.

Operation Order No. 59.
By
Lieut Colonel T. T. Behrens. R.E.
C.R.E. 24th Division.

Reference:
1/40000 Sheet 28.

(1) The 24th Division is to be relieved by the 30th Division. The relief will commence on the night of the 28th/29th May and the Infantry reliefs will be completed on the night of 29th/30th May.

(2) On relief the 24th Division will be in Corps reserve.

(3) Details of the relief of Field Companies R.E. and 12th Sherwood Foresters (Pioneers) will be notified later.

(4) All maps, aeroplane photos, defence schemes, trench stores etc. will be handed over to the relieving units of the 30th Division and receipts for same forwarded to this Office.

(5) Copies of handing over reports to be sent to this office.

(6) Restrictions as to movement are as follows:-

All movement East of ~~Vlamertinghe~~ VLAMERTINGHE will be by platoons or sections, with an interval of at least 100 yards between each.

(7) Completion of reliefs and arrival at destination to be reported to this Office.

(8) The 24th Divisional Headquarters will close at BRANDHOEK ~~Brandhoek~~ at 9 a.m. on 30th May and reopen at RENINGHELST ~~Reninghelst~~ at the same hour.

(9) Acknowledge.

Issued at 11.0 pm
May 25th 1917.

R. Grant
Capt. and Adjt. R.E.
for C.R.E. 24th Division.

Copies to. - 1. Headquarters "G."
2. Headquarters "Q."
3. A.D.M.S.
4. O.C. Divisional Train.
5. 17th Infantry Brigade.
6. 72nd Infantry Brigade.
7. 73rd Infantry Brigade.
8. O.C. 103rd Field Company R.E.
9. O.C. 104th Field Company R.E.
10. O.C. 129th Field Company R.E.
11. O.C. 24th Divisional Signal Company.
12. War Diary.
13. Record.
14. C.R.E. 30th Division.

Secret.

Copy No: 13.

Operation Order No. 10

by

Lieut. Colonel [illegible] R.E.

C.R.E. 24th Division.

Reference:
1/40000 Sheet 28.

Move. Details of relief of Field Companies see O.O. 59. para: 3 of 26.5.17

1. 104th Field Company R.E. will move to bivouac at H.20.c.b.1.
on 29.5.17 on which date its present lines will be taken over by
201st Field Company R.E. 30th Division.
Arrangements will be made direct between O.C. Companies for
handing over the lines.
An advanced party will be sent as soon as possible to occupy the
new bivouac at H.20.c.b.1.

2. 129th Field Company R.E. will move to bivouac at (Sheet 28)
M.6.a.8.2. on 29.5.17 on which date it will be relieved by
200th Field Company R.E. 30th Division, who will take over 129th
present billets and horse lines.
Arrangements will be made direct between O.C. Companies
for the relief in the line and for handing over billets and horse lines.

3. Acknowledge.

Issued at 3.30 p.m.

May 28th 1917.

R. Grant
Capt. & Adjt. R.E.
for C.R.E. 24th Division.

Copies to:-

1. Headquarters G.
2. do Q.
3. A.D.M.S.
4. O.C. Divisional Train.
5. 17th Infantry Brigade.
6. 72nd do. do.
7. 73rd do. do.
8. O.C. 103rd Field Coy. R.E.
9. O.C. 104th do. do. R.E.
10. O.C. 129th do. do. R.E.
11. O.C. 24th Divisional Signal Coy.
12. War Diary.
13. Record.
14. C.R.E. 30th Division.

R.E. 1010.

"Q"

24th. Divisional Headquarters.

Herewith War Diaries for the month of June 1917.

Kindly acknowledge receipt.

Done

5.7.1917.

J R Grant
Capt. & Adjt. R.E.
for C.R.E. 24th. Division.

Instructions regarding War Diaries and Intelligence Summaries are contained in F. S. Regs., Part II. and the Staff Manual respectively. Title pages will be prepared in manuscript.

WAR DIARY
or
INTELLIGENCE SUMMARY.
(Erase heading not required.)

C.R.E. 24 Div

Vol 22

Army Form C. 2118.

Place	Date	Hour	Summary of Events and Information	Remarks and references to Appendices
	1917. June 1st.		Mobile charges for destruction of enemy guns in forthcoming operation are required. It has not been possible to ascertain the chamber or cartridge dimensions of the German guns. 2nd. Army Workshop have arranged to make a few special charges in tin cylinders - for 3" bore 6lbs. for 5.9" bore 20lbs.	
	2nd.		Testing improvised pack loads for R.E. material. A special addition to the service packsaddle should be devised to enable R.E. material generally to be easily carried. Improvised packing in bundles, specially tied up first, is too long a process, although in an emergency it has proved to answer.	
	3rd.		Camp shelled by H.V. gun. One shell only landed in Camp and destroyed a hut. C.R.E. and Adjutant attended Lecture on VIMY operations 2nd. Army School.	
	7th.		Zero at 3.10 a.m. summer time. Saw mines go up from ZEVETCOTEN Windmill. Divisional H.Q. still at RENINGHELST. Inspected work on opening up communication past ST. ELOI craters at 1 p.m.	
	8th-11th.		Work continued by Pioneers on the opening of road to DOME HOUSE from ST. ELOI. The Xth. Corps taking over from them with Corps labour as fast as possible.	
	12th.		Fixed approximate alignment of SHELLEY FARM-PHEASANT WOOD 9lb. tram line with Capt. HINE., 12th. Sherwood Foresters (Pioneers). This line satisfactorily completed by Pioneers by 15th. inst.	
	13th.		Xth. Corps required to give up Dump and Workshops to 2nd. Corps. 24th. Division therefore have no source from which to commence building up a Dump. No existing dump of material falls in the new 24th. Divisional area. The building up of supply of material anew is therefore very difficult. The assistance of the new Stores Officer, Lt. COLLISON-MORLEY, 8th. Buffs, whose services I have just acquired is invaluable. He has been accompanying the Lorries and actually collecting the material. Collection has been greatly expedited in this way and the training afforded is the best possible.	

2353 Wt. W2544/1454 700,000 5/15 D. D. & L. A.D.S.S./Forms/C. 2118.

CONTINUED.

Instructions regarding War Diaries and Intelligence Summaries are contained in F. S. Regs., Part II. and the Staff Manual respectively. Title pages will be prepared in manuscript.

WAR DIARY
or
INTELLIGENCE SUMMARY.
(Erase heading not required.)

Army Form C. 2118.

Place	Date	Hour	Summary of Events and Information	Remarks and references to Appendices
	14th.		R.E. H.Q. moved to MICMAC CAMP.	
	16th.		C.E's conference of C.R.E"s at Xth. Corps H.Q. C.R.E. takes over duties with 24th. Division again, C.R.E. 23rd. Division was left with 23rd. Division R.E. in the line taken over by 24th Division while 24th. Divisional R.E. completed work and assisted 41st. Division in their Sector (in which 24th. Division operation of 7th. inst. had taken place) from 10th. to 16th. inst.	
	17th.		Pushing forward work on the entirely new communications required by readjustment of Divisional and Corps Boundaries much hindered by shell fire.	
	22nd.		Work continues to be shelled both on 161b. Light Railway and on road from CHESTER Farm. Work on advanced sections entirely prevented from progressing.	
	23rd.		Composite Company, equal to one third of the actual strength of the 3 Companies, is organized (dismounted only) and first section proceeds to Rest Camp AMBLETEUSE.	
	24th.		C.R.E. chooses site in training area for model of area embraced by forthcoming 24th. Divisional operation.	
	25th.		Adjutant (Capt. Grant) returned from leave.	
	26th.		Lt. Gameson and 20 special men of 103rd. Field Company proceed to SENINGHEM to make model.	
	28th.		Light Railway broken in 8 places by direct hits on the VORMEZEELE-LOCK 8 Section.	
	29th.		Transport of all Companies marches to rest area on relief by 23rd. Division.	
	30th.		Dismounted proceed by Bus to BARLINGHEM where transport arrives in afternoon. R.E. H.Q. move to BARLINGHEM.	

[signature]
Lt. Col.
C.R.E. 24th. Division.

2353 Wt. W2544/1454 700,000 5/15 D. D. & L. A.D.S.S./Forms/C. 2118.

OPERATION ORDER NO. 62.

by

LIEUT COLONEL T.T.BEHRENS R.E.

C.R.E. 24th. Division.

****

1. The R.E. Field Companies and Pioneers, 24th. Division, will be relieved by units of 23rd. Division as under:-

   12th. Sherwood Foresters (Pioneers) will be relieved by 9th. South Staffs (Pioneers) on 28.6.1917.

   129th. Field Company will be relieved by the 128th. Field Company in Left Brigade Area on 29.6.1917.

   104th. Field Company will be relieved by the 102nd. Field Company in Right Brigade Area on 29.6.1917.

   103rd. Field Company will be relieved by 101st. Field Company in Back Area on 29.6.1917.

   Advanced parties will proceed to take over from units on the previous day in each case.

2. Reliefs will be arranged direct between units.

3. The Divisional Dump at VOORMEZEELE I.31.a.4.2. will be handed over to the R.S.M. 23rd. Division on the afternoon of 29th. instant.

4. 24th. Division units will return to their Transport lines. Orders for move to Rest Area will be issued as soon as this area is known.

5. The Infantry attached to Field Companies (except 2nd.Leinsters and 3rd. Rifle Brigade) will cease to be attached to the R.E. Companies at 6 a.m. on the 29th. instant.
   The attached men of the 2nd. Battalion Leinster Regiment and 3rd. Rifle Brigade will rejoin their units on the 27th. June.

6. ACKNOWLEDGE.

J C Grant
Capt & Adjt R.E.
~~Lt. Col.~~
for C.R.E. 24th. Division.

26.6.1917. 11 a.m.

COPIES TO -

1. 103rd.Field Coy.R.E.
2. 104th. " " "
3. 129th. " " "
4. 12th.Sherwood Foresters. (Pioneers)
5. C.R.E. 23rd. Division.
6. "G"
7. "Q"
8. File.
9. War Diary.

* ******** *

Copy No. 14.

Operation Order No. [illegible]

by

Lieut. Col. T. T. BEHRENS. R.E.

C.R.E. 24th Division

Reference maps

$\frac{1}{20000}$ Sheet 28

$\frac{1}{100000}$ Sheet HAZEBROUCK 5A.

1. Headquarters Divisional Engineers and 3 Field Companies R.E. will move to the BLARINGHEM Area on the 30th June 917.

2. The transport and cyclists will start on the 29th inst.
The Head of the Column will pass the starting point i.e. junction of road at H.33. [illegible] near DICKEBUSCH Church at 2 p.m. Order of march

103rd Field Company R.E.
104th " " R.E.
129th " " R.E.

250 yards interval will be kept between companies until the first hourly halt is reached when the interval will be closed up. Headquarters transport will reach MILLE KRUIS in time to follow on the rear of the 104 Field Company R.E.

They will bivouac for the night of the 29th/30th June at a point to be notified later.

3. An Officer from each Company will be in charge of the company transport and cyclists and Captain J. M. GREATHEAD will be in charge of the whole convoy.

4. The dismounted portion of the companies less the cyclists will proceed by bus on the 30th inst at 9 a.m.

5. The interpreter from Headquarters R.E. will proceed to BLARINGHEM on the 29th inst to arrange for billets with the area Commandant.

6. The cyclists will start on the 30th inst so as to reach the area Commandants Office near the Railway Station BLARINGHEM in time to be able to return and meet the convoy when it reaches WALLON CAPPEL so as to direct the transport to the billets.

7. ACKNOWLEDGE.

Issued at 9 a.m.
June 28th 1917.

J. C. Grant
Capt. [illegible] Adjt R.E.
for C.R.E. 24th Division.

Copies to:—

1. G. 24th D.H.Q.
2. Q. — —
3. G.O.C. 17th Inf. Bdge.
4. " " 72nd "
5. " " 73rd "
6. C.R.E. 23rd Division
7. C.R.A.
8. O.C. Div. Train
9. O.C. [illegible]
10. O.C. 104th Field Coy. R.E.
11. O.C. 103rd Field Coy. R.E.
12. O.C. 129th " " "
13. O.C. 24th Div. Signal Coy.
14. War Diary.
15. Records.

D.506.

SECOND ARMY OFFENSIVE.

C.R.E's INSTRUCTIONS NO.2.

TASKS ALLOTTED TO R.E. COMPANIES FOR THIS OPERATION.

1. Each Field Company will have received a permanent attached working party of 100 men on June 4th. Special attention will be paid by O.C.Companies to the preservation of discipline in these parties during their attachment.

2. 104th. Field Company will operate with the 17th.Infantry Brigade.
129th. Field Company will operate with the 73rd.Infantry Brigade.
103rd. Field Company will be in reserve.

3. The Field Companies will not have to vacate their present lines.

4. a. The role of the 104th. and 129th. Field Companies will be to make strong and supporting points after having made a careful reconnaissance of the ground on which suitable sites may be expected to exist. Not more than one section of each Company will be sent forward for this.

The greatest care should be taken to so arrange the subsequent advance of the remainder of the Company that it arrives fresh on the work without having been worn out by a slow continuous advance lasting all day and without its ranks being depleted owing to an unnecessarily early advance.

It is probable that work can only be carried out after dusk and in any case their advance should be so timed as to get the men no sooner to the site than the time at which work can be carried on without risking the annihilation of the working parties.

b. The O.C.Company will arrange to make the reconnaissance of the Brigade Area in which he is working a very thorough one in respect of 1. State of roads.
2. State of trenches.
3. State of Tram lines.
4. State of Water Supply.

These are likely to be the more important R.E. matters in the area.

The reconnaissance should be carried out with a view to making constructive proposals which should accord with the general plan and course of the operations.

O.C.Companies will see that those who they send out understand the situation sufficiently to do this.

c. The O.C.Company will keep the C.R.E. closely in touch with the progress of events; but in sending in his reports on the results of the reconnaissance from time to time he will see that his report forms an intelligible précis of what he has himself received and that at suitable stages, his own constructive proposals are included.

It is the duty of the O.C.Company to make out the reports from those sent in to him, as he alone with his knowledge on the spot can be expected rightly to interpret the latter.

d. Information should as far as possible be put in map (or graphic) form. Tracings on the 1/10,000 scale (shewing map squares) will be suitable.

e. The O.C. Field Company will receive orders direct from the Brigade concerned as to when and where he should join Brigade Head Quarters.

The Company transport except as otherwise ordered will remain in the present Company Lines.

5. 103rd. Field Company will continue energetically to push forward the construction of the SHELLEY Farm light railway and will endeavour on Z day to join up railhead with the enemy tramline which after examination offers the chance of getting supplies forward with least delay.

O.C.103rd.Field Company will also 1. Administer the Mobile Reserve of R.E. Stores and Pack train so formed. 2. Take over the management of the

Divisional Dump at 29 Central, and provide the necessary loading and unloading parties for it.

Lieut. Col.

4.6.1917. C.R.E. 24th. Division.

Copy to - 1. Office.
1. War Diary.
1. 103rd.Field Company R.E.
1. 104th. Field Company R.E.
1. 129th. Field Company R.E.
1. O.C. 12th. Sherwood Foresters (Pioneers)
1. 17th. Infantry Brigade.
1. 72nd. Infantry Brigade.
1. 73rd. Infantry Brigade.
1. G.
1. Q.
2. Spare.

SECOND ARMY OFFENSIVE.

C.R.E's INSTRUCTIONS NO.3.

FORMATION OF MOBILE RESERVE OF R.E.STORES & PACK TRAIN OF R.E. MATERIAL.

1. A Mobile Reserve of R.E.Stores consisting of -

6 Pontoon Waggons.	2 from each Field Company.
3 Trestle "	1 " " " "
8 G.S. "	From 12th.Sherwood Foresters (Pioneers)

loaded with miscellaneous R.E.Material will be formed at the 104th. Field Company Lines H.20.d.3.2.(where room exists for the formation)on the morning of Y day.

2. Two pack trains of 15 animals each with the necessary pack equipment (See Instructions No.1) will also be formed as follows:-

20 animals from 103rd. Field Company.
5 " " 104th. " "
5 " " 129th. " "

3. Both the mobile reserve and the two pack trains will be commanded by Capt. R.E. He will be assisted by an Officer to be nominated by O.C. 103rd. Field Company.

4. The whole will be administered by 103rd.Field Company.

5. Each unit concerned will send in the waggons, and the pack animals as detailed above to reach H.20.d.3.2. at 8 a.m. on "Y" day.

The waggon contingent from each unit will be complete with teams, drivers, brakemen and a mounted or transport N.C.O. in charge.

The Pack contingent will be complete with pack saddles (or improvised arrangements) and ropes, each animal with its driver, one loader to every 4 animals and one N.C.O. with each Company contingent.

Each loader will carry a shovel.

6. Each pack train of 15 animals will be thus formed and similarly organized, (10 animals from 103rd.Field Company plus 5 animals

from 104th. or 129th. Field Companies).
Each train will then have 2 responsible N.C.O's and 4 loaders besides a driver to each animal.
The extra loaders will be found by 103rd Field Company.
Each loader will be provided with a shovel, a pair of wire cutters attached by a string to his person, and a hand axe.
One N.C.O. and the loaders will march at the head of the column to prepare a passable track and cut away all wire etc. which could possibly damage the animals legs. One N.C.O. will bring up the rear
A small number of light pickets with pieces of bunting attached will be taken to mark out any unmarked route traversed when going up.

7. The materials to be carried by the Pontoon and G.S.Waggons and by the pack animals are shown on the attached list.

8. O.C.103rd.Field Company R.E. will arrange to collect the necessary stores (for loading the waggons once and the pack animals twice) in a suitable place adjacent to a metalled road for loading up on "Y" day.

9. Capt. R.E. will take executive charge of all the arrangements upon the arrival of vehicles and animals at 8 a.m. on "Y" day. He will immediately get into touch with 17th. and 73rd. Brigade Head Quarters (who should inform him of their positions) and arrange the time and place at which these two pack trains should join the Brigade supply trains on "Z" and succeeding days.

10. The pack trains will return atonce to the Mobile Reserve Park after dumping the material at Brigade forward dump. They will, however, be under the orders of the Brigade Transport Officer daily from the time of reporting to him till ordered by him to leave his train on the return of the column from out of the shelled area.
The pack train will be thus packed and go up daily with the Brigade supply train while the forward road is unable to take wheeled transport. This will probably last 2 days at the most.

11.a. The Mobile Reserve will remain at the Park until ordered forward.

b. The Pontoon and Trestle Waggon loads are for the formation of an advanced Divisional Dump as soon as ever the road forward is passable for wheeled transport.

They will be ordered forward by the C.R.E.

c. The 8 G.S.Waggons are for the use of the Pioneer Battalion working on the St. ELOI - DOME House road and these will be ordered forward by the Pioneer Officer i/c of the work as soon as he considers that the material is wanted and that the Waggons can get up.

After delivering their material he will give orders as to what material for the road is to be brought up next and when.

d. As soon as the DOME House road has a temporary surface completed for wheeled traffic as far as it is safe to go the G.S.Waggons will return to the Mobile Park and will be available as necessary to feed the Divisional forward Dump with material.

12.The 15 pack animals prepared by 104th and 129th. Field Companies as part of the 20 animals ordered in C.R.E's Instructions No.1 will be loaded with such standard loads as the O.C.Company in each case may decide.

Each of these Field Companies will then have a train of 15 of their own animals to take up the Stores required for its own use on "Z"day. These Field Company trains will in other respects be formed as detailed in paras 5 & 6 above.

[signature]
Lieut.Col.
4.6.1917. C.R.E. 24th. Division.

Copy to -

1. Office.
1. War Diary.
1. 103rd.Field Co.R.E.
1. 104th. " " "
1. 129th. " " "
2. O.C.12th.Sherwood Foresters (Pioneers)
1. 17th.Infantry Brigade.
1. 72nd. " "
1. 73rd. " "
1. G.
1. Q.
2. O.i/c.Mobile Reserve.
2. Spare.

LIST OF LOADS.

(to accompany C.R.E's instructions No.3.)

1. Each Pontoon or trestle Waggon will carry -

20 Coils Barbed Wire.

20 Coils French Wire.

80 Medium Screw posts.

2,000 Sandbags.

50 G.S.Shovels.

10 Picks.

2. Each G.S.Waggon will carry -

At first 8 "Roadmats" each.

3. Each Packtrain of 15 animals will consist of -

8 Medium screw picket loads. Type 2. (C.R.E's Instructions No.1)

7 French wire loads. Type 3. (C.R.E's Instructions No.1)

SECOND ARMY OFFENSIVE.

C.R.E's INSTRUCTIONS No.4.

PIONEERS.

1. The 12th. Sherwood Foresters (Pioneers) (less 1½ companies) will complete a temporary roadway fit for wheeled traffic by as early an hour as possible on "Z" day, from a point exactly 200 yards S.E. of our present front line trench at ST. ELOI to DOME House (O.8.d.9.6).
The former point is about where road junction on the old road from ST. ELOI is shown upon the map at O.z.d.3.7.
One Company of the 41st. Divisional Pioneers is clearing a track between this point and St.ELOI Cross roads and the roads behind that are being repaired on "Z" day under the X Corps Forward Roads Officer.

2. From the point (paced off) 200 yards S.E. from our Front line, as nearly on the alignment of the old road as practicable, a centre line giving the prospect of getting the quickest temporary vehicle track through, will be pegged out by the Pioneer Officer in charge of the work.
After this the working parties will be got on to this work as soon as practicable; The 2½ Companies will work at full strength (not in reliefs) until the track is cleared.

3. The C.R.E. will be informed by O.C.12th.Sherwood Foresters (Pioneers) of the orders given by him for the organization of the work.

4. The Officer i/c of the work will send a special orderly to report to C.R.E. on "Z" day so that orders may be able to reach the O i/c from C.R.E. by orderly at any time.
The C.R.E. will then keep him informed of the situation and will
XX send him orders when to move up from Camp towards the work.

5. The Officer i/c. of the work will inform the C.R.E., at Divisional H. Q. with as little delay as possible of the hour at which the working parties commenced to be all employed at once.

He will keep him constantly informed of the progress of this work.

6. A level and roughly graded track, minimum width 13' 6" wide will be cleared as quickly as possible.

All holes which have to be filled in doing this are to be filled with well filled sandbags carefully packed together to avoid interstices.

Great stress is to be laid upon this procedure.

The track when cleared will be covered with Wooden road Mats made of rough timber.

Each mat measures about 3' 3" x 6'. Four of these laid abreast, with the longitudinal bearers underneath lying in the direction of the road, make a carriage surface 13 feet wide.

Four mats thus make 2 yards run of roadway.

These mats will be at first brought up in G.S. Waggons and will be used in the softest places first.

The local conditions on "Z" day must decide the Officer i/c of the work where to make use of the mats as they arrive so as to enable guns and ammunition through as soon as possibly can be done.

7. The 14 pack mules of the Battalion will take up sandbags for the work, accompanying the working party.

2 bales of sandbags (500) should be carried by each animal.

These can be conveniently steadied when slung over a service pack saddle (or universal saddle) by the use of the same rope and the hitch which is used with the sack-packs for packing rations.

If this offers any difficulty ~~you can see~~ how it has been done with other loads of R.E. material can be seen.

8. The necessary cordage and sandbags should be indented for atonce, as well as any tools you may require.

9. This pack train will be used to go on bringing up sandbags from the

XX 24th. Divisional Dump - Map reference to be given later.

10. In addition to this the 8 G.S. Waggons parked with the mobile reserve at H.20.d.3.2. will be used to bring up the road mats.

The second and further loads will be fetched from the Divisional

Dump as in 9.

Lieut. Col.
C.R.E. 24th. Division.

4.6.1917.

Copy to - 1. Office.
1. War Diary.
1. 103rd. Field Co.R.E.
1. 104th. " " "
1. 129th. " " "
1. Officer i/c. Mobile Reserve.
10. 12th. Sherwood Foresters (Oioneers).
1. G.
1. Q.
2. Spare.

O.O. for
MAY

Army Form C. 2118.

CRE 24 DV Vol 23

Instructions regarding War Diaries and Intelligence Summaries are contained in F. S. Regs., Part II. and the Staff Manual respectively. Title pages will be prepared in manuscript.

WAR DIARY
or
INTELLIGENCE SUMMARY.
(Erase heading not required.)

Place	Date	Hour	Summary of Events and Information	Remarks and references to Appendices
	1917. July 1st.		C.R.E. went to Xth. Corps on 30.6.1917 as A/C.E. Today the Division is transferred to II Corps. C.R.E. therefore returns to Division and to Rest billet at BLARINGHEM. Arrangements made with 2nd. Field Survey Company, CASSEL, to photograph the relief-map model of ground for 24th. Divisional operation. The photographs are to be stereo-pairs.	
	2nd.		C.R.E. visited the 3 detachments from the Field Companies in rest camp at AMBLETEUSE. These men are employed on erecting huts for Portuguese Hospital.	
	5th.		C.R.E. visited Special Works Park, WIMEREUX.	
	6th.		M.G.C. (GEN: BOLS) visited R.E. H.Q. rest Billets BLARINGHEM and saw 104th. and 129th. Field Companies' billets and men at instruction.	
	7th.		R.E. Companies Horse Show. MAJOR HERBERT D.S.O. R.A., Xth. Corps Adviser on Horsemastership, and MAJOR A.C. JOHNS, A.S.C. judges. Divisional Commander inspected the turn-out. About 50% of each Company transport shewn. Prizes for best Company, for best Section Transport, for best Bridging Section, and 9 individual prizes given. The Winning Sections Drivers were given a medal.	
	8th.		MAJOR PRIOR R.E. in relief of MAJOR LAMONBY, O.C. 103rd Field Company, reported.	
	10th.		The Model was photographed stereoscopically (6 pairs being taken) by setting up the camera in each case 3 inches to one side of the first picture and with the axis parallel. A special camera should be available for this purpose.	
	11th.		C.R.E. visited 23rd. Division to see C.R.E. who is doing the work in the line preparatory to the operation.	
	14th.		R.E.H.Q. move to LUMBRES where Divisional H.Q. is. This leaves 103rd. Field Company alone at BLARINGHEM now that 104th. Field Company is with 23rd.	

2353 Wt. W2544/1454 700,000 5/15 D. D. & L. A.D.S.S./Forms/C. 2118.

Instructions regarding War Diaries and Intelligence Summaries are contained in F. S. Regs., Part II. and the Staff Manual respectively. Title pages will be prepared in manuscript.

Army Form C. 2118.

WAR DIARY
or
INTELLIGENCE SUMMARY.
(Erase heading not required.)

Place	Date	Hour	Summary of Events and Information	Remarks and references to Appendices
	14th. contd.		Division in the line and 129th. Field Company is at VIII Corps School, MILLAM.	
	15th.		Lieut. GAMESON rejoined R.E. H.Q. on completion of Divisional Model.	
	16th.		C.R.E. visited Heavy Bridging School, AIRE, and saw 103rd. Field Company practicing with Inglis Bridge-heavy and light types.	
	19th.		R.E.H.Q. move to STEENVOORDE.	
	20th.		C.R.E. inspected Advanced D.H.Q. Camp which has been prepared by II Corps, and visited C.E. II Corps.	
	21st.		C.R.E. and Stores Officer (LIEUT. COLLISON-MORLEY) to 23rd. Divisional H.Q. to stay with C.R.E. (LIEUT. COL. ROOKE)	
	22nd.		Visited forward system of reclaimed trenches etc. with C.R.E. 23rd. Division.	
	23rd.		R.E.H.Q. moves to ZEVECOTEN in relief of 23rd. Division R.E.	
	29th.		A party of 200 D.A.C. collected to work on forward KNOLL road clearing a temporary track as far forward as possible prior to the operation. The labour available never permits of any preparations for clearing roads during an advance being made by C.R.E. beforehand. In this case C.R.A. offered his own labour and none other was made available. Of course this labour will not be at disposal on zero or after. There are two Reserve Infantry Battalions whose employment is purely dependant on the operations. C.R.E. visited E. Surreys, one of the above, and spoke to all the Officers on the organization of working parties.	
	30th.		C.R.E. visited 9th. Royal Sussex and spoke to the Officers about the organization of working parties. R.E.H.Q. move to Advanced D.H.Q. Camp.	
	31st.		Z day Zero 3-50 a.m. Enemy fire and situation prevent the construction of S.P's by R.E. parties.	

Instructions regarding War Diaries and Intelligence Summaries are contained in F. S. Regs., Part II. and the Staff Manual respectively. Title pages will be prepared in manuscript.

WAR DIARY
or
INTELLIGENCE SUMMARY.

(*Erase heading not required.*)

Army Form C. 2118.

Place	Date	Hour	Summary of Events and Information	Remarks and references to Appendices
	31st. contd.		The situation in front was very vague and R.E.'s were employed in reconnaissance. No work possible on the forward part of KNOLL Road under these conditions.	
			[signature] Lieut. Col. C.R.E. 24th. Division.	
			6.8.1917.	
			ENCLOSURES.	
			Operation Order No. 64.	
			" " " 65.	
			" " " 66.	
			C.R.E's. Order No.H.Q.4.	
			C.R.E's. " No.H.Q.5.	
			FIFTH ARMY OFFENSIVE.	
			C.R.E's. Instructions No.1.	
			C.R.E's. " No.2.	
			C.R.E's. " No.3.	

No. 12.

OPERATION ORDER No. 64.

by

Lieut. Col. T.T.BEHRENS. R.E.

C.R.E. 24th. Division.

Reference Map.
1/100,000 Sheet HAZEBROUCK 5A.

1. The 104th. Field Company R.E. will move to the 23rd. Divisional Area for work under the C.R.E. 23rd. Division. They will start from BLARINGHEM on the 9th. inst. as per attached March Table A.

2. The 129th. Field Company R.E. will move to the Corps School near MILLAIN for work under C.E. 8th. Corps. They will start from BLARINGHEM on the 9th. inst. as per attached March Table A.

3. ACKNOWLEDGE.

J.K. Grant
Capt. & Adjt. R.E.
for C.R.E. 24th. Division.

Issued at 2.45 p.m.
8th. July 1917.

Copy No. 1 to G. 24th. Division.
" " 2 to Q. 24th. Division.
" " 3 to C.E. 8th. Corps.
" " 4 to C.R.E. 23rd. Division.
" " 5 to A.D.M.S. 24th. Division.
" " 6 to O.C. 24th. Divisional Train.
" " 7 to O.C. 12th. Sherwood Foresters.
" " 8 to O.C. 103rd. Field Company R.E.
" " 9 to O.C. 104th. Field Company R.E.
" " 10 to O.C. 129th. Field Company R.E.
" " 11 to O.C. 24th. Divisional Signal Company.
" " 12 War Diary.
" " 13 Record.

MARCH TABLE A.

To accompany C.R.E. Operation Order No. 64. Issued 8th. July 1917.

Reference Map.
1/100,000 Sheet HAZEBROUCK 5A.

Date.	Unit.	From.	To.	Report for Billets to.	Remarks.
9th. July.	104th. Field Company R.E.	BLARINGHEM.	RENESCURE AREA.	Area Commandant.	
	129th. Field Company R.E.	BLARINGHEM.	FOG DU HAUT PONT.	Area Commdt. ST.MOMELIN on 8th.inst.	
10th. July.	104th. Field Company R.E.	RENESCURE AREA.	EECKE AREA.	Area Commandant.	Route via LES SIX RUES, STAPLE, HONDEGHEM or any roads N. of this.
	129th. Field Company R.E.	FOG DU HAUT PONT.	CORPS SCHOOL near MILLAIN.	Commandant Corps School on 9th.inst.	
11th. July.	104th. Field Company R.E.	EECKE AREA.	23rd.DIVISIONAL AREA.	23rd.Division.	

All roads are available except as noted.

Route supplies will be drawn from present railhead until change of railhead is notified.

****

Copy No. 13

OPERATION ORDER No. 65.

by

COL:

LIEUT. T.T. BEHRENS R.E.

C.R.E. 24th. Division.

Reference Maps.

$\frac{1}{100,000}$ Sheet HAZEBROUCK 5 A.

$\frac{1}{40,000}$ Sheet 27.

(1). The 103rd. Field Company R.E. will move to the 2nd. Corps Area, Fifth Army. leaving BLARINGHEM on the 19th. July 1917.

(2). For the move they will form part of the 73rd. Infantry Brigade Group known as No.2. Group.

They will join the column at its starting point at Road Junction U.7.b.0.3. following the 7th. Northamptons. at 7-40 a.m. on 19th. July 1917 and march by way of STAPLE-HONDEGHEM to the CAESTRE Area.

On the 20th. July they will march to the EECKE Area. They will follow the 73rd. M.G.Company and pass the starting point at Road Junction Q.26.d.2.6. at 8-55 a.m. The CASSEL-ST SYLVESTRE and ST SYLVESTRE-STEENVOORDE Roads are not to be used.

(3). All marches will be completed by 10 a.m.

(4). Packs will be carried by lorries. See 24th.Div.C.238/15.

(5). Instructions re billets will be issued by the 73rd. Infantry Brigade.

(6). ACKNOWLEDGE.

Issued at 7.15 p.m.

July 16th.1917.

J. L. Grant

Capt. & Adjt. R.E.
for C.R.E. 24th. Division.

Copy No.1.to "G" 24th.Division.
" " 2.to "Q" 24th. "
" " 3.to 17th.Infantry Bde.
" " 4.to 72nd. " "
" " 5.to 73rd. " "
" " 6.to A.D.M.S.24th.Divn.
" " 7.to O.C.24th.Div:Train.
Copy No.8.to O.C.12th. Sherwood Foresters.
" " 9.to O.C.103rd.Field Company R.E.
" " 10.to O.C.104th.Field Company R.E.
" " 11.to O.C.129th.Field Company R.E.
" " 12.to O.C.24th.Div.Signal Coy.
" " 13. War Diary.
" " 14. Record.

****

Copy No. 14.

OPERATION ORDER No. 26.

by

LIEUT: COL: I.T. BEHRENS R.E.

C.R.E. 24th. Division.

Reference Map.
1/40,000 Sheet 28.

The 24th. Division R.E. and Pioneers will relieve the 23rd. Division in the line as under -

1. The 104th. Field Company and 103rd. Field Company will relieve the 128th. and 102nd. Field Companies respectively, on the 21st. inst.
The 129th. Field Company will relieve the 101st. Field Company on the 22nd. inst.
The relief will take place by direct arrangement between the Companies.

2. Three sections from each of 104th. and 103rd. Field Companies will take over the forward billets of 128th. and 102nd. Field Companies respectively on the 21st. inst. Advanced parties should be sent up if possible on the 20th. inst.

3. 103rd. and 129th. Field Companies will bivouac at H.28.d.9.6. (The Brewery near Divisional Baths, Nr. DICKEBUSCH.) under arrangements made by Q. 24th. Division Liason at 23rd. Division Headquarters.

4. Map references of 23rd. Division Units are as follows:-

101st. Field Company. H.33.b.9.5.
102nd. Field Company. (I.29.c.5.3.
(H.34.a.8.1. Horse Lines.
128th. Field Company. (I.29.c.5.3.
(H.33.d.8.7. Horse Lines.
9th. South Staffs. (Pnrs.)H.35.c.3.6.
102nd. and 128th. Field Companies Forward billets in LARCHWOOD Tunnels.

5. 12th. Sherwood Foresters (Pioneers) will relieve the 9th. South Staffs (Pioneers) by direct arrangement betw units after day work on the 21st. inst.

6. 24th. Divisional R.E. Headquarters will relieve

Divisional R.E. Headquarters at ZEVECOTEN on 23rd. inst.

7. ACKNOWLEDGE.

Issued at 9.15 p.m.

July 19th. 1917.

Capt. & Adjt. R.E.
for C.R.E. 24th. Division.

Copy No. 1. to "G" 24th. Division.
" " 2. to "Q" 24th. "
" " 3. to 17th. Infantry Brigade.
" " 4. to 72nd. " "
" " 5. to 73rd. " "
" " 6. to C.R.E. 23rd. Division.
" " 7. to A.D.M.S. 24th. Division.
" " 8. to O.C. 24th. Divisional Train.
" " 9. to O.C. 12th. Sherwood Foresters (Pioneers).
" " 10. to O.C. 103rd. Field Company R.E.
" " 11. to O.C. 104th. Field Company R.E.
" " 12. to O.C. 129th. Field Company R.E.
" " 13. to O.C. 24th. Divisional Signal Coy.
" " 14. War Diary.
" " 15. Record.

****

Copy No. 10

C.R.E's. ORDER No. H.Q. 4.

MOVE OF HEADQUARTERS R.E. 24th. DIVISION.

Reference Map.
1/100,000 Sheet HAZEBROUCK 5 A.

1. Headquarters R.E. 24th. Division, less the M.O. i/c. R.E's. with his Staff, The Adjutant, and the horsed transport will move to LUMBRES at 10 a.m. on the 14th. July 1917 by Lorry and Cycle.
2. The Adjutant will move to the 23rd. Divisional H.Q. on the 13th. inst. as Liason Officer.
3. The M.O. i/c. R.E. and Lieut. Mitchell with their Staffs and the Horsed transport will be attached to the 103rd. Field Company R.E. Ration strength of party is 15 Officers and men, and 4 Heavy draft and 6 Riding or Light draft horses.
4. Acknowledge.

Issued at 11 p.m.
13th. July 1917.

J. Grant
Capt. & Adjt. R.E.
for C.R.E. 24th. Division.

Copy No.1. to G. 24th. Division.
" No.2. to Q. 24th. Division.
" No.3. to A.D.M.S. 24th. Division.
" No.4. to O.C. 24th. Divisional Train.
" No.5. to C.O. 12th. Sherwood Foresters.
" No.6. to O.C. 103rd. Field Company R.E.
" No.7. to O.C. 104th. Field Company R.E.
" No.8. to O.C. 129th. Field Company R.E.
" No.9. to O.C. 24th. Divisional Signal Company.
" No.10. War Diary.
" No.11. Record.

Copy No. 9

C.R.E's ORDER NO. H.Q. 5.

MOVE OF HEADQUARTERS R.E. 24TH. DIVISION.

Reference Map.

$\frac{1}{100,000}$ Sheet HAZEBROUCK 5A.

$\frac{1}{40,000}$ Sheet 27.

1). Headquarters R.E. 24th. Division will move to STEENVOORDE on 19th. July 1917, leaving LUMBRES AT 9 a.m.

2). The orderlies and Draughtsman will move by cycle and the remainder of H.Q. by Lorry.

xxx The mens cooking gear, office stores and furniture and Officers Kit to be loaded by 8-40 a.m. and the Officers xxx Mess gear ready to load by 8-45 a.m.

3). The lorry will collect the rations for the 20th. July at T.14.c.8.5. near RENESCURE before proceeding to STEENVOORDE.

4). The M.O. i/c. R.E. and the Horsed transport of H.Q. R.E. will join Headquarters R.E. at STEENVOORDE on the 20th. July. They will bring rations for that day and the supply limber will collect the rations for the 21st. July at [illegible].31.a.[illegible].9. before proceeding to STEENVOORDE.

5). ACKNOWLEDGE.

Issued at p.m.

July 17th. 1917.

Capt. & Adjt. R.E.
for C.R.E. 24th. Division.

Copy No.1. to "G" 24th. Division.
" " 2. to "Q" 24th. "
" " 3. to O.C. 24th. Divisional Train.
" " 4. to C.O. 12th. Sherwood Foresters (Pnrs).
" " 5. to O.C. 103rd. Field Company R.E.
" " 6. to O.C. 104th. Field Company R.E.
" " 7. to O.C. 129th. Field Company R.E.
" " 8. to O.C. 24th. Divisional Signal Coy.
" " 9. xx War Diary.
" " 10. Record.

FIFTH ARMY OFFENSIVE.

C.R.E's. INSTRUCTIONS No. 1.

TASKS ALLOTTED TO R.E. COMPANIES FOR THIS OPERATION.

1). The Companies will be employed in the Brigade Sectors as under -

103rd. Field Company (less 2 Sections) in 72nd. Infantry Brigade Sector.

104th. Field Company in 17th. Infantry Brigade Sector.

129th. Field Company (less 2 Sections) in 73rd. Infantry Brigade Sector.

A map has already been issued to each Company shewing the Divisional and Brigade Boundaries, assembly areas and objectives.

2). One hundred attached Infantry will have joined each Field Company by July 24th.

3). On "Y" day one Section with its attached Infantry from each Field Company will join the Infantry Brigade in whose Sector the Company is working by direct arrangement between O.C. Company and the Brigade H.Q.

This Section will be employed on making Strong Points, the approximate positions of which have been laid down as under -

J.31.a.0.0.
J.31.a.45.90.
J.25.d.60.40.
J.25.b.70.50.
J.20.c.80.40.
J.20.d.85.40.

The Section will not be moved up to work before the Infantry Brigade Commander considers that the situation permits.

4). The O.C. of each Field Company will keep in close touch with the B.G.C. the Infantry Brigade and he will also arrange that the R.E. reconnaissance, and especially that for the final siting of the S.P's., is thoroughly carried out.

5). Instructions as to reconnaissance. See C.R.E's Instructions No.2. dated 4.6.1917. paras. 4b: 4c: 4d:

6). 2 Sections 103rd. Field Company and 2 Sections 129th. Field Company R.E. will be in reserve. Captain MARVIN will be in command.
He will have two Waggons (G.S. or Pontoon) and teams with an N.C.O. detailed by each of these two Field Companies for his use.

7). The remainder of the Field Companies will be employed on preparing and marking the following pack-tracks as rapidly as possible for the use of their respective Brigade Sectors.
The line will be chosen after careful reconnaissance and while it is important that it should be as far as possible under cover from enemy ground observation, it should also be a line fit to be very quickly and easily improved into an overland track for Horsed Vehicles.
The line will be marked every 50 feet with a small picket and white flag or with white painted metal plates and with notice boards about every 250 yards as necessary shewing at first clearly the way to the Front line and the sector which the track serves (Right, Centre, Left). These will afterwards have place names added to them as required.
The clearing of the track will include -

1). Removal of all iron or wire which could damage an animals legs.

2). Making gaps in all obstacles wide enough to allow animals and their drivers in single file to easily clear their packs.

3). The bridging or drifting of other obstacles in such a way that pack animals are not required to jump nor in danger of being bogged.

The probably suitable lines may be looked for as follows:-

Right Sector. 72nd. Infantry Brigade. Starting from the end of "P" track (that is from the end of the old pack-track) at about I.30.c.2.7. then in a south easterly direction to KLEIN ZILLEBEKE road at about I.36.b.1.3. and thence taking advantage of the valley running N.E. towards point J.31.a.3.7. near GRAVEYARD Cottage.

Left Sector. 17th. Infantry Brigade. Leaving the ZILLEBEKE - OBSERVATORY RIDGE road at about I.24.d.3.3, then in an easterly direction to CLONMEL Copse and thence following the water-course running eastwards along the South side of BODMIN Copse to the BASSEVILLE BEEK about J.20.c.10.2. up the valley N. Eastwards towards J.20.d.3.5.

If the situation is not sufficiently favourable this line may have to be deflected northwards from some point about J.20.c.6.2.

Centre Sector. 73rd. Infantry Brigade. From some point on the Left Sector track about I.24.d.9.3. in a South Easterly direction following the general direction of the road shewn on the Map to LOWER STARPOST.

8). Each Company will arrange to pack the stores its own sections may require.

Each Company will be prepared to use 16 pack animals with R.E. Stores besides what it requires for rations and water all of which will be sent up by pack transport.

The loads will be arranged as detailed in the list attached to C.R.E's Instructions No.1. of 2.6.1917.

9). The positions of Companies on and after Y night will be given later.

10. A Map at a scale of 1/5,000 shewing all Infantry and pack tracks, tram lines, roads etc. will be issued later.

Lieut. Col.

21.7.1917. C.R.E. 24th. Division.

COPIES TO -

"G" 24th. Division.
"Q" 24th. Division.
C.R.E. 41st. Division.
C.R.E. 30th. Division.
O.C. 103rd. Field Company R.E.
O.C. 104th. Field Company R.E.
O.C. 129th. Field Company R.E.
C.O. 12th. Sherwood Foresters (Pioneers)
17th. Infantry Brigade.
72nd. Infantry Brigade.
73rd. Infantry Brigade.
War Diary.
Record.

****

FIFTH ARMY OFFENSIVE.

C.R.E's. INSTRUCTIONS No. 2.

PIONEERS.

1.) One Pioneer Company will be attached to the 17th. Infantry Brigade and half a Company each to 72nd. and 73rd. Infantry Brigades for work on communication trenches as detailed in para. 9. of 24th. Divisional Instructions No. 8. (a). of 18.7.1917.

These Companies will go forward on Z day by direct arrangement between B.G's.C. Infantry Brigades and C.C. 12th. Sherwood Foresters (Pioneers).

2.) One Company will be specially detailed for work under A.D.L.R.

3.) The remaining Company will be employed as follows -

2 Platoons on the maintenance of tramway communication from ARMAGH WOOD and LARCHWOOD railheads to VORMEZEELE. These parties will be organized in 3 or 4 shifts who will patrol the line throughout its length at frequent intervals throughout the 24 hours and who will have repair parties constantly ready to make repairs at once with materials already stacked at convenient places.

2 Platoons will be occupied upon the maintenance of the cross country tracks for horsed transport and on the roads. (details to be issued later).

4.) Positions of Companies on Y night will be detailed later.

Lieut: Col:
C.R.E. 24th. Division.

21.7.1917.

COPIES TO -

"G" 24th. Division.
"Q" 24th. Division.
C.R.E. 41st. Division.
C.R.E. 30th. Division.
O.C. 103rd. Field Company R.E.
O.C. 104th. Field Company R.E.
O.C. 129th. Field Company R.E.
C.O. 12th. Sherwood Foresters (Pioneers).
17th. Infantry Brigade.
72nd. Infantry Brigade.
73rd. Infantry Brigade.
War Diary.
Record.

########

FIFTH ARMY OFFENSIVE.

C.R.E's. INSTRUCTIONS No. 3.

ROYAL ENGINEERS & PIONEERS.

1). In accordance with 24th. Divisional Instructions No. 8. G.Y.350/8 of 18.7.1917 and G.Y.309/276 of 24.7.1917, all R.E. Companies and Pioneers will return to their back billets on X/Y night. After this, no work in the forward area other than maintenance of Tramlines and Tracks will be done before zero.

2). The Section R.E. for each Infantry Brigade will be attached from "Y" day, on and after which each Infantry Brigade will make the necessary arrangements.

3). The reserve 4 Sections R.E. will be billeted in the 129th. Field Company lines.

4). The Pioneer Company detailed for work under A.D.L.R. if not ordered to go to Light Railways will be in Reserve.

5). This reserve Company Pioneers will be prepared to work on the repair of the KNOLL Road and VERBRANDEN MOLEN road, and the necessary reconnaissance of these roads within the Divisional Area will be made atonce.

6). Further orders for the Reserve R.E. and Pioneers will be issued direct.

Lieut: Col:
C.R.E. 24th. Division.

25.7.1917.

Distribution the same as C.R.E's Instructions No. 1 & 2.

Instructions regarding War Diaries and Intelligence Summaries are contained in F. S. Regs., Part II. and the Staff Manual respectively. Title pages will be prepared in manuscript.

WAR DIARY of C.R.E 24th Division

or

~~INTELLIGENCE SUMMARY~~.

(Erase heading not required.)

Army Form C. 2118.

Vol 24

Place	Date	Hour	Summary of Events and Information	Remarks and references to Appendices
	1 5/17		C.R.E went up line and visited 72nd Brigade	
	2 5/17		C.R.E visited II Corps and Xth Corps. C.R.E. visited II Corps Park, Corps Workshops, A.D.L.R & C.E II Corps to complete arrangements for a section of a Field Coy to work at Corps Shops making duckboards & mule track	
	3 5/17		C.R.E reported to "Q" damage to tramway track giving names of offenders.	
	4 5/17		Divisional Head Quarters return to ZEVECOTEN.	
	5 5/17		C.R.E. visited C.E II Corps and met C.E 5th Army One Section of a Field Coy goes to II Corps Shops.	
	6 5/17		C.R.E visited 103, 104 & 129 Field Coy	
	7 5/17		C.R.E visited II Corps Workshops to inspect section of Field Coy at Work	

2353 Wt. W2544/1454 700,000 5/15 D. D. & L. A.D.S.S./Forms/C. 2118.

Instructions regarding War Diaries and Intelligence Summaries are contained in F. S. Regs., Part II, and the Staff Manual respectively. Title pages will be prepared in manuscript.

WAR DIARY
or
INTELLIGENCE SUMMARY.
(Erase heading not required.)

Army Form C. 2118.

Place	Date	Hour	Summary of Events and Information	Remarks and references to Appendices
	8/5/17		Major Rivers Moore, O.C 129 Field Coy sent sick to a rest Station.	
			C.R.E. visited Controller of Mines 5th Army H.Q.	
	9/5/17		C.R.E visited C.R.E 41st Div re taking over dump.	
	10/5/17		C.R.E visited 2nd Army Workshops.	
	11/5/17		C.R.E visited 103 Coy.	
	12/5/17		Major Smith. O.C. 104 Field Coy leaves 104 Coy to take over Command of 29th Advanced Park Coy	
			Controller of Mines called & talked over programme of tunnelled accommodation.	
	13/5/17		C.R.E's Conference for O.C's Field Coys.	

2353 Wt. W2544/1454 700,000 5/15 D. D. & L. A.D.S.S./Forms/C. 2118.

Army Form C. 2118.

WAR DIARY
or
~~INTELLIGENCE~~ SUMMARY.

(Erase heading not required.)

Instructions regarding War Diaries and Intelligence Summaries are contained in F. S. Regs., Part II. and the Staff Manual respectively. Title pages will be prepared in manuscript.

Place	Date	Hour	Summary of Events and Information	Remarks and references to Appendices
	14/5/17		C.R.E visits Sherwood Foresters Pioneers.	
	15/5/17		Section of 104 Field Coy returns to Company from II Corps Shops.	
	16/5/17		C.R.E Visited Xth Corps, 104 Field Coy, 175 Tunnelling Coy and Screening factory.	
	17/5/17		C.R.E Visited KLEIN ZILLEBEKE.	
	18/5/17		C.R.E Visited 73 Infantry Brigade.	
	19/5/17		C.R.E Visited 72 Infantry Brigade, 129 Field Coy and 175 Tunnelling Coy.	
	20/5/17		C.R.E Visited II Corps.	

2353 Wt. W2544/1454 700,000 5/15 D. D. & L. A.D.S.S./Forms/C. 2118.

Army Form C. 2118.

WAR DIARY
or
~~INTELLIGENCE SUMMARY~~.
(Erase heading not required.)

Instructions regarding War Diaries and Intelligence Summaries are contained in F. S. Regs., Part II. and the Staff Manual respectively. Title pages will be prepared in manuscript.

Place	Date	Hour	Summary of Events and Information	Remarks and references to Appendices
	21 8/17		C.R.E Visited A.P. & S.S and 2nd Army Workshops.	
	22 8/17		C.R.E Visited 17th Infantry Bde, 129 Field Coy & Pioneers.	
	23 8/17		C.R.E Visited C.E II Corps, 175 Tunnelling Coy & Pioneers.	
	24 8/17		Major Prior took over duties of acting C.R.E 24th Division during the period Lieut Col Behrens on leave of absence. Act C.R.E visited C.R.E 14th Div re extension of Divisional Boundary. Acting C.R.E Went to LARCH WOOD with D.A.D.M.S to examine a Well.	
	25 8/17		Act C.R.E Went to a Conference at IInd Corps H.Q on Winter accommodation etc.	

2353 Wt. W2544/1454 700,000 5/15 D. D. & L. A.D.S.S./Forms/C. 2118.

Army Form C. 2118.

Instructions regarding War Diaries and Intelligence Summaries are contained in F. S. Regs., Part II. and the Staff Manual respectively. Title pages will be prepared in manuscript.

WAR DIARY
or
~~INTELLIGENCE SUMMARY.~~
(Erase heading not required.)

Place	Date	Hour	Summary of Events and Information	Remarks and references to Appendices
	26/5/17		A/C.R.E visited A.P. & S.S, 2nd Army Workshops and Australian E & M. Coy	
	27/5/17		A/C.R.E Visited LOCKE to inspect with a view to its being made into a brigade headquarters.	
	28/5/17		24th Divn & divisional area taken over by Xth Corps from II Corps.	
			A/C.R.E. went up line with G.S.3 to fix position of Camouflage to screen Work on assembly trenches.	
	29/5/17		A/C.R.E attended conference at Office of C.E Xth Corps re Scheme for tramways.	
	30/5/17		C.E Xth Corps visited 24th Div. H.Q.	
			A/C.R.E Visited 103, 104 & 129 Field Coys & Pioneers	

2353 Wt. W2544/1454 700,000 5/15 D. D. & L. A.D.S.S./Forms/C. 2118.

Army Form C. 2118.

Instructions regarding War Diaries and Intelligence Summaries are contained in F. S. Regs., Part II. and the Staff Manual respectively. Title pages will be prepared in manuscript.

WAR DIARY
or
~~INTELLIGENCE SUMMARY~~.
(Erase heading not required.)

Place	Date	Hour	Summary of Events and Information	Remarks and references to Appendices
	31/8/17		a/C.R.E visited C.E X[th] Corps, also A.P & S.S.	
			J. H. Prior Major acting C.R.E 24th Division	

2353 Wt. W2544/1454 700,000 5/15 D. D. & L. A.D.S.S./Forms/C. 2118.

Instructions regarding War Diaries and Intelligence Summaries are contained in F. S. Regs., Part II. and the Staff Manual respectively. Title Pages will be prepared in manuscript.

WAR DIARY
or
INTELLIGENCE SUMMARY
(Erase heading not required.)

Army Form C. 2118.

Vol 25

Place	Date	Hour	Summary of Events and Information	Remarks and references to Appendices
			24 Div. R.E.	
			H.Q.	
			September 1917.	

2449 Wt. W14957/M90 750,000 1/16 J.B.C. & A. Forms/C.2118/12.

Instructions regarding War Diaries and Intelligence Summaries are contained in F. S. Regs., Part II. and the Staff Manual respectively. Title pages will be prepared in manuscript.

WAR DIARY
or
INTELLIGENCE SUMMARY.
(Erase heading not required.)

Army Form C. 2118.

Place	Date	Hour	Summary of Events and Information	Remarks and references to Appendices
1917.	1917. Sept:			
	1st.		C.R.E. 39th. Division visited A/C.R.E. re change of front and handing over.	
			A/C.R.E. visited C.R.E. 23rd. Division re change of front.	
			Instructions received as to handing over of area.	
	2nd.		A/C.R.E. went with G.O.C. and G.S.O. 1 to see G.O.C., G.S.O. 1m and C.R.E. of 23rd. Division in morning.	
			In afternoon went to see C.E. Xth. Corps and afterwards to 103rd. 104th. and 129th. Field Companies R.E. and 12th. Sherwood Foresters (Pioneers).	
	3rd.		Went round new Line with O.C. 103rd. Field Company.	
			Saw A.D.L.R. re transport of working parties.	
	4th.		104th. and 129th. Field Companies took over from 128th. and 101st. Field Companies.	
			Col. Walker joined as C.R.E.	
			Visited C.E. Xth. Corps in afternoon with Major Prior.	
	5th.		Visited Infantry Tracks and Mule Tracks. Also accommodation south of ZILLEBEKE LAKE. (morning)	
			Visited 12th. Sherwood Foresters (Pioneers), 103rd. 104th. and 129th. Field Companies R.E.	
	6th.		Visited tracks and proposed medical arrangements in forward area. (morning)	
			C.R.E. 41st. Division and O.C. 12th. Sherwood Foresters (Pioneers) called. (afternoon)	
			Visited MICMAC Camp and OUDERDOM Dump. (evening)	
	7th.		Visited 103rd. 104th. and 129th. Field Companies.	
			C.R.E. 23rd. Division called and discussed preparations.	
	8th.		Visited works ZILLEBEKE - DICKEBUSCH.	
			Reported personally to G.O.C. re state of preparations.	
	9th.		C.R.E. 23rd. Division arrived as a Liason Officer for preparation work. Visited Workshops and R.E. Units & Pioneers.	
	10th.		Went with C.R.E. 23rd. Division to visit work in advanced area.	
			Visited Sherwood Foresters (Pioneers), 103rd. Field Company R.E. and "C" Company, 9th. South Staffs to arrange work in back area.	
	11th.		Went with C.R.E. 23rd. Division, to visit Units and arrange details of transfer of work and billets.	
	12th.		Went with C.R.E. 23rd. Division to BURGOMASTER'S FARM.	
			Saw 103rd. Field Company R.E. and 12th. Sherwood Foresters (Pioneers).	
	13th.		Went with C.R.E. 23rd. Division to BURGOMASTER'S FARM and Mule Tracks.	
			Handed over Sector at 6 p.m. to C.R.E. 23rd. Division.	

CONTINUED.

Instructions regarding War Diaries and Intelligence Summaries are contained in F. S. Regs., Part II. and the Staff Manual respectively. Title pages will be prepared in manuscript.

WAR DIARY
or
INTELLIGENCE SUMMARY.
(Erase heading not required.)

Army Form C. 2118.

Place	Date	Hour	Summary of Events and Information	Remarks and references to Appendices
	1917 Sept. 14th.		Still at ZEVECOTEN.	
			Settled account of Engine at Workshop up to 13th. September with Owner at STEENVOORDE.	
			103rd. Field Company R.E. moved to MERRIS AREA.	
			129th. Field Company R.E. moved to WESTOUTRE.	
	15th.		C.R.E. moves with Division to MERRIS.	
			129th. Field Company R.E. moved to DOULIEU.	
	16th.		C.R.E. visited 103rd. and 129th. Field Companies, also 72nd. and 73rd. Infantry Brigades.	
			104th. Field Company R.E. moved to near Meteren.	
	17th.		C.R.E. visited 104th. Field Company R.E.	
	18th.		C.R.E. " 129th. " " "	
	19th.		C.R.E. attended Conference at Divisional H.Q. at 3 p.m.	
	20th.		C.R.E. went to new Divisional Headquarters, 4 miles east of BAPAUME.	
	21st.		C.R.E. visited Field Companies in their new Billets, also C.R.E. 4th. Corps Troops with whom revisited Company and arranged details of work on horse lines.	
	22nd.		Visited C.R.E. 34th. Division to arrange details of relief.	
	23rd.		Visited C.R.E. 34th. Division with Adjutant, O.C. 129th. Field Company, and Hutting Officer.	
			Went on to Left Sector of Front Line.	
	24th.		Visited 103rd. 104th. and 129th. Field Companies and 12th. Sherwood Foresters (Pioneers).	
			To 34th. Divisional Headquarters with G.S.O. 1 at 6 p.m.	
	25th.		Went round Left and Centre Sectors new area front and Support Lines.	
	26th.		Went with G.S.O. 1. to Right Sector of new area.	
			H.Q. moved to FLAMICOURT.	
			Went with Adjutant to 104th. Field Company and 12th. Sherwood Foresters (Pioneers).	
	27th.		Routine.	
	28th.		Divisional Headquarters moved to NOBESCOURT Farm.	
			Visited 12th. Sherwood Foresters (Pioneers), 104th. and 129th. Field Companies R.E.	
	29th.		Went with C.R.E. 34th. Division to inspect new Support Line.	
	30th.		Visited Centre Sector.	

ENCLOSURES.
Operation Orders No. 68, 69 & 70.

[signature]
Lieut. Col.
C.R.E. 24th. Division.

2353 Wt. W2544/1454 700,000 5/15 D. D. & L. A.D.S.S./Forms/C. 2118.

14

SECRET.

OPERATION ORDER No. 68.

by

Major J.H.PRIOR R.E.

A/C.R.E. 24th Division.

****

(1) The 104th and 129th Field Companies will take over work in forward area from 128th and 101st Field Companies R.E. respectively tomorrow the 4th inst. The 104th Field Company will work in the Right Sector and 129th Field Company in the Left sector.

(2) Acknowledge.

J.H.Prior

Major.

3rd September 1917. A/C.R.E 24th Division

Copy No.1. to "G" 24th Division
" " 2. " "Q" " "
" " 3. " 17th Infantry Brigade
" " 4. " 72nd " "
" " 5. " 73rd " "
" " 6. " C.R.E. 23rd Division
" " 7. " A.D.M.S. 24th Division
" " 8. " O.C. 24th Divisional Train
" " 9. " O.C. 12th Sherwood Foresters (Pioneers)
" "10. " O.C.103rd Field Company R.E.
" "11. " O.C.104th Field Company R.E.
" "12. " O.C.129th Field Company R.E.
" "13. " O.c. 24th Divisional Signal Co.
" "14. " War Diary.
" "15. " Records.

****

No. 11.

OPERATION ORDER NO. 69.

BY LIEUT. COL. A. D. WALKER, C.R.E. 24TH. DIVISION.

1. Field Companies move out of this area as under:-

Date. Sept.1917.	Unit.	Under orders of.	To.	By.
14th.	103rd.Field Coy.	72nd. Inf. Bde.	MERRIS area.	Bus.
do.	129th.Field Coy.	73rd. Inf. Bde.	WESTOUTRE N.E.Camp.	March route.
16th.	104th.Field Coy.	17th. Inf. Bde.	MERRIS area.	Bus.

Transport of 103rd. and 104th. Field Companies proceeds by march route.

2. Field Companies will get into touch with Brigades and ascertain hours of start, billeting party arrangements, etc.

3. 24th. Divisional Headquarters will close at ZEVECOTEN at 10 a.m. on the 15th. inst. and will open at MERRIS at the same hour.

4. ACKNOWLEDGE.

J. R. Grant
Capt. & Adjt. R.E.
for C.R.E. 24th. Division.

12. 9. 1917.

COPIES TO -

1. O.C. 103rd. Field Company R.E.
2. O.C. 104th. Field Company R.E.
3. O.C. 129th. Field Company R.E.
4. 17th. Infantry Brigade.)
5. 72nd. Infantry Brigade.)
6. 73rd. Infantry Brigade.)
7. "G" 24th. Division.) For
8. "Q" 24th. Division.) information.
9. O.C. 24th. Divisional Train.)
10. C.R.E. 23rd. Division.)
11. War Diary.
12. Office copy.

Secret Copy No: 12.

C.R.E. 24th Division. Operation Order No: 70.

Reference.
1/40,000.
Sheets 57c. and 62 c:

1. Field Companies R.E. 24th Division will relieve the Field Companies R.E. 34th Division in accordance with the attached programme.

2. Field Companies on arrival at MILIEU COPSE will come under the command of the C.R.E. 34th Division until 10 a.m. on the 29th September, at which time the command of the front passes to the 24th Division.

3. Field Company Commanders will arrange direct with the Commanders of the Companies whom they relieve regarding taking over maps work and billets, attachment of advanced parties etc.

4. (a.) 24th Divisional Headquarters will close at I.34.a.3.7. and reopen at PERONNE at 12 noon on 27th September.

(b.) 24th Divisional Headquarters will close at PERONNE and will reopen at NOBESCOURT FARM (K.32.b.) at 10 a.m on 29th September.

5. ACKNOWLEDGE.

J.L. Grant
Capt. & Adjt. R.E.
for Lieut. Col. R.E.
C.R.E. 24th Division.

Issued at 10.30 am
23. 9. 1917.

Copies to:–

1. O.C. 103rd Field Company R.E.
2. O.C. 104th Field Company R.E.
3. O.C. 129th Field Company R.E.
4. 17th Infantry Brigade.
5. 72nd Infantry Brigade.
6. 73rd Infantry Brigade.
7. "G" 24th Division.
8. "Q" 24th Division.
9. S.S.O. 24th Division.
10. O.C. 24th Divisional Train.
11. C.R.E. 34th Division.
} For information.

12&13. War Diary (2)
14 ADMS
15 O.C. 24th Div. Signal Co.
} do.

∞ Programme of Reliefs R.E. – 24th Division. Operation Order No: 70. ∞

Unit.	Date.	From.	To.	Remarks.
129th Field Coy:	24. 9. 17.	BARASTRE.	HAUT ALLAINES (or MOISLAINS)	Under orders of 73rd I.B.
	25. 9. 17.	HAUT ALLAINES (or MOISLAINS)	MILIEU COPSE Q.1.a. 8.8.	Partly by bus under orders of 73rd I.B: take over billets from 207th Field Company who return to PERONNE in buses which have brought up 129th Field Coy:
	26. 9. 17.	MILIEU COPSE Q.1.a. 8.8.	ROISEL & TEMPLEUX	In relief of 208th Field Company R.E. at times to be arranged between Company Commanders.
103rd Field Coy:	25. 9. 17.	BEAULENCOURT	HAUT ALLAINES (or MOISLAINS)	Under orders of 72nd I.B.
	27. 9. 17.	HAUT ALLAINES (or MOISLAINS)	MILIEU COPSE Q.1. a. 8. 8.	Partly by bus under orders of 72nd I.B: take over billets from 208th Field Company who return to PERONNE in buses which have brought up 103rd Field Coy:
	28. 9. 17.	MILIEU COPSE. Q.1. a.8.8.	H.Q. & 1 Section MONTIGNY FARM. 1 Section each TEMPLEUX, JEANCOURT, HESBECOURT.	In relief of 209th Field Coy R.E. at times to be arranged between Company Commanders.
104th Field Coy:	27. 9. 17.	YTRES	HAUT ALLAINES (or MOISLAINS)	Under orders of 17th I.B.
	29. 9. 17.	HAUT ALLAINES (or MOISLAINS)	MILIEU COPSE. Q.1. a. 8. 8.	Partly by bus under orders of 17th I.B: take over billets from 209th Field Company who return to PERONNE in buses which have brought up 104th Field Company.
do. 1 Section.	30. 9. 17.	MILIEU COPSE Q.1.a. 8.8.	VADENCOURT.	Under orders of O.C. 104th Field Company.

Note. 1 Section R.E. includes 1 Officer 25 O.R. attached Infantry in every case.

Confidential

16

Vol 26

War Diary

Oct 1917

C-R-E 24th Div

Instructions regarding War Diaries and Intelligence Summaries are contained in F. S. Regs., Part II. and the Staff Manual respectively. Title pages will be prepared in manuscript.

WAR DIARY
or
INTELLIGENCE SUMMARY.
(Erase heading not required.)

Army Form C. 2118.

Place	Date 1917.	Hour	Summary of Events and Information	Remarks and references to Appendices
	Oct.			
	1st.		Visited Left Sector.	
	2nd.		Visited 12th. Sherwood Foresters (Pioneers), 104th. and 129th. Field Companies.	
	3rd.		" " " " " and 129th. Field Company R.E.	
	4th.		Selected sites of Dugouts and went round Line with Brigade Major, 72nd. Infantry Brigade and Tunnelling Officer.	
	5th.		In evening visited new Support Trench with O.C. 12th. Sherwood Foresters (Pioneers).	
	6th.		Saw O.C. 180th. Tunnelling Company re progress on dugouts.	
	7th.		Routine.	
	8th.		With C.E. to visit Left Sector.	
	9th.		Visited Centre and Right Brigades in connection with Hutting arrangements.	
	10th.		Visited 12th. Sherwood Foresters (Pioneers) and 129th. Field Company R.E.	
	11th.		Inspected new Divisional Support Line and attended Divisional Conference.	
	12th.		With G.O.C. to inspect new Support Line.	
	13th.		Routine.	
	14th.		Visited 73rd. Infantry Brigade, 12th. Sherwood Foresters (Pioneers) and 103rd. Field Company R.E.	
	15th.		Visited 3rd. Army Park.	
	16th.		Visited Cologne Position, Front Line and Support Trench.	
	17th.		Visited C.E. Corps.	
	18th.		With C.Es. 111 and V11 Corps to Cologne position. V11 Corps relieved 111 Corps 12 noon.	
	19th.		To Cologne Position with G.S.O. and B.G.C. 72nd. Infantry Brigade.	
	20th.		C.E. V11 Corps visited Divisional H.Q. C.R.E. went to FINS R.E. Park.	
	21st.		Visited Support Line with G.O.C., 72nd. Infantry Brigade, M.G.O. and Capt. LAYCOCK, Tunnelling Officer, sites of dugouts selected.	
	22nd.		Visited 104th. Field Company R.E.	
	23rd.		Routine.	
	24th.		Visited 12th. Sherwood Foresters (Pioneers), 103 and 129th. Field Companies R.E.	
	25th.		With O.C. 129th. Field Company R.E. to SUGAR, MALAKOFF, Front Line, Support Line etc.	
	26th.		Routine.	
	27th.		With O.C. 104th. Field Company R.E. round COLOGNE position.	
	28th.		Morning-To see C.E. V11 Corps and Controller of Mines. With O.C. 12th. Sherwood Foresters (Pioneers) at night to visit RUBY LANE.	
	29th.			

CONTINUED.

Instructions regarding War Diaries and Intelligence Summaries are contained in F. S. Regs., Part II. and the Staff Manual respectively. Title pages will be prepared in manuscript.

WAR DIARY
or
INTELLIGENCE SUMMARY.

(Erase heading not required.)

Army Form C. 2118.

Place	Date	Hour	Summary of Events and Information	Remarks and references to Appendices
	1917. Oct.			
	29th.		To 17th. Brigade H.Q. and LE VERGUIER.- TWIN CRATER Road.	
	30th.		Routine.	
	31st.		Visited C.E. Vll Corps.	
			A. D. Walker. Lieut. Col. C.R.E. 24th. Division.	
			6.11.1917.	

2353 Wt. W2544/1454 700,000 5/15 D. D. & L. A.D.S.S./Forms/C. 2118.

SECRET

Vol 27.

WAR. DIARY.

C.R.E. 24th DIVISION.

From Nov 1st To Nov 30th.

1917.

Army Form C. 2118.

Instructions regarding War Diaries and Intelligence Summaries are contained in F. S. Regs., Part II. and the Staff Manual respectively. Title pages will be prepared in manuscript.

WAR DIARY
or
INTELLIGENCE SUMMARY.
(Erase heading not required.)

Place	Date	Hour	Summary of Events and Information	Remarks and references to Appendices
	1917. Novr.			
	1st.		Visited TEMPLEUX Quarries with Controller of Mines.	
	2nd.		Visited 3 Brigades, Northants, 12th. Sherwood Foresters (Pioneers), 129th. Field Company R.E.	
	3rd.		Visited 129th. Field Company R.E.	
	4th.		Visited COLOGNE Position.	
	5th.		Routine.	
	6th.		With A.D.M.S. to see new A.D.S. E.of HARGICOURT, and with O.C. 129th. Field Company R.E. to COLOGNE trenches.	
	7th.		With C.E. 3rd. Army and C.E. V11 Corps to COLOGNE Position.	
	8th.		With G.O.C. to TEMPLEUX Quarries.	
	9th.		Routine.	
	10th.		Visited COLOGNE Position.	
	11th.		Went to TEMPLEUX Quarries.	
	12th.		Went to LA FLAQUE and AMIENS in connection with R.E.Stores.	
	13th.		Visited 73rd. Infantry Brigade, 12th. Sherwood Foresters (Pioneers), TEMPLEUX Quarry: at latter place met Water Officer V11th. Corps.	
	14th.		Visited COLOGNE front line etc. with O.C. 103rd. Field Company R.E.	
	15th.		Visited 73rd. Infantry Brigade, MONTIGNY Dump, 12th. Sherwood Foresters (Pioneers) and 103rd. Field Company R.E.	
	16th.		Inspected COLOGNE Position.	
	17th.		Went to TEMPLEUX Quarries.	
	18th.		Saw work in back area at MONTIGNY, BERNES, VENDELLES.	
	19th.		Inspected COLOGNE Position.	
	20th.		Routine.	
	21st.		Visited C.E. V11 Corps, 12th. Sherwood Foresters (Pioneers), 129th. Field Company R.E.	
	22nd.		Attended Conference at Div.H.Q. Went in afternoon to LE VERGUIER & TEMPLEUX QUARRIES.	
	23rd.		Visited Forward Roads with Divisional Roads Officer.	
	24th.		Visited C.R.E. Corps Troops re Targets. Also 180th. Tunnelling Company. C.R.E. proceeded on leave.	
	26th.		Visited Front Line 72nd. Brigade Area.	
	27th.		Went round with Hutting Officer.	
	28th.		Went round with A.A.&.Q.M.G. Hutting at ROISEL Officers Club, MONTIGNY, HERVILLY.	
	29th.		C.R.E. Cavalry Corps came re taking over.	
	30th.		Went with G.S.O.1 to 72nd. and 73rd. Brigades and 129th. Field Company R.E.	

2353 Wt. W2544/1454 700,000 5/15 D. D. & L. A.D.S.S./Forms/C. 2118_7_

Instructions regarding War Diaries and Intelligence Summaries are contained in F. S. Regs., Part II. and the Staff Manual respectively. Title pages will be prepared in manuscript.

WAR DIARY
or
INTELLIGENCE SUMMARY.

(Erase heading not required.)

Army Form C. 2118.

Place	Date	Hour	Summary of Events and Information	Remarks and references to Appendices
	1917 Nov. 30th. contd.		Arranged for 12th. Sherwood Foresters (Pioneers) to dig trench near Hussar Road.	
			J. H. Prior Major R.E. A/C.R.E. 24th. Division. 4th. December 1917.	

2353 Wt. W2544/1454 700,000 5/15 D. D. & L. A.D.S.S./Forms/C. 2118.

Confidential.

24th Divisional Headquarters R.E.

WR 28

War Diary for month of
December 1917.

9

Army Form C. 2118.

WAR DIARY
or
INTELLIGENCE SUMMARY.
(*Erase heading not required.*)

Instructions regarding War Diaries and Intelligence Summaries are contained in F. S. Regs., Part II. and the Staff Manual respectively. Title pages will be prepared in manuscript.

Place	Date	Hour	Summary of Events and Information	Remarks and references to Appendices
	1917. Decr. 1st.		Went with G.S.O. to 73rd. Infantry Brigade and to probable site for wire switch.	
	2nd.		Laid out site for Wire Switch which was commenced in the evening by Pioneers and 129th. Fld.Coy.	
	3rd.		Visited Brigadier General 73rd. Infantry Brigade and discussed defence works required on Left Battalion front. Afterwards saw O.C. Left Battalion on same subject.	
	4th.		Visited various Works in hand on 73rd. Infantry Brigade front.	
	5th.		Conference at Divisional Headquarters.	
			Arranged for strengthening wire W. entrance of HARGICOURT. Work to commence same night.	
			With O.C. 12th. Sherwood Foresters (Pioneers) selected position for trenches to defend TEMPLEUX QUARRIES and afterwards obtained concurrence of B.G.C. 73rd. Infantry Brigade.	
	6th.		Visited B.G.C. 72nd. Infantry Brigade and B.G.C. 73rd. Infantry Brigade.	
			Visited forward work in 73rd. Infantry Brigade area.	
	7th.		Went with B.G.C. 72nd. Infantry Brigade to VILLERET rex making some posts. Saw G.O.C. afterwards and he approved.	
	8th.		With B.G.C. 73rd. Infantry Brigade. re strengthening of defences immediately behind front line by severalx small posts. Submitted scheme to G.O.C. who approved.	

D. D. & L., London, E.C. (A7883) Wt. W809/M1672 350,000 4/17 Sch. 52a Forms/C/2118/14

Instructions regarding War Diaries and Intelligence Summaries are contained in F. S. Regs., Part II. and the Staff Manual respectively. Title pages will be prepared in manuscript.

WAR DIARY
or
INTELLIGENCE SUMMARY.
(Erase heading not required.)

Army Form C. 2118.

Place	Date	Hour	Summary of Events and Information	Remarks and references to Appendices
	9th.		With O.C's 103rd. and 129th. Field Companies pointing out fresh defence works to be done in their areas.	
	10th.		Went with G. to reconnoitre Intermediate Line in vicinity of FERVAQUE FARM,	
	11th.		Further reconnaissance of FERVAQUE FARM District going through Major CHEETHAMS proposals for improving Intermediate Line.	
	12th.		Reconnaissance of FERVAQUE FARM position with C.R.E. Cavalry Corps.	
	13th.		To TEMPLEUX QUARRIES to visit defences of quarries and left flank defence.	
	14th.		With G.S.O.2. to O.C. 103rd. Field Company R.E. to visit BOBBY FARM.	
	15th.		To VRAIGNES, BOUVINCOURT and HANCOURT to visit Camps.	
	16th.		To Forward Area with O.C. 129th. Field Company R.E.	
	17th.		To VRAIGNES, BOUVINCOURT and HANCOURT to visit Camps.	
	18th.		To Forward Area with O.C. 103rd. Field Company R.E.	
	19th.		With O.C's 103rd. and 129th. Field Companies R.E. to visit Brigade in line.	
	20th.		With G.S.O.1. to O.C. 104th. Field Company R.E. to reconnoitre Support Line to Intermediate Line.	
	21st.		To ROISEL to see 129th. Field Company R.E. and 12th. Sherwood Foresters (Pioneers).	
	22nd.		To VRAIGNES, HANCOURT and BOUVINCOURT to see camps in construction.	

D. D. & L., London, E.C. (A7883) Wt. W809/M1672 350,000 4/17 Sch. 52a Forms/C/2118/14

Instructions regarding War Diaries and Intelligence Summaries are contained in F. S. Regs., Part II. and the Staff Manual respectively. Title pages will be prepared in manuscript.

WAR DIARY
or
INTELLIGENCE SUMMARY.
(Erase heading not required.)

Army Form C. 2118.

Place	Date	Hour	Summary of Events and Information	Remarks and references to Appendices
	22nd.		To ROISEL to see 129th. Field Company R.E. re Wiring Support Line with Cavalry.	
	23rd.		To ROISEL to see 129th. Field Company R.E. and 12th. Sherwood Foresters (Pioneers) and TEMPLEUX	
			QUARRY to see O.C. 3rd. Rifle Brigade and Town Major.	
	24th.		To 18th. Division with G.S.O.1.	
	25th.		To front area. saw B.G.C. 49th. Brigade at RONSSOY.	
	26th.		To COLOGNE position with G.S.O.1. and G.O.C.	
	27th.		To 103rd. Field Company R.E. and 12th. Sherwood Foresters (Pioneers).	
	28th.		To 73rd. Infantry Brigade, 12th. Sherwood Foresters (Pioneers), and 129th. Field Company R.E.	
	29th.		To COLOGNE Position.	
	30th.		To TEMPLEUX QUARRIES.	
	31st.		To 73rd. Infantry Brigade. (Brigade in line).	

A. Walther [signature] Lieut. Col.
C.R.E. 24th. Division.

3.1.1918.

D. D. & L., London, E.C. (A7883) Wt W809/M1672 350,000 4/17 Sch. 52a Forms/C/2118/14

Confidential.

C.R.E. 24th Division.

War Diary for month of January 1918.

Army Form C. 2118.

WAR DIARY
or
INTELLIGENCE SUMMARY.
(Erase heading not required.)

Instructions regarding War Diaries and Intelligence Summaries are contained in F. S. Regs., Part II. and the Staff Manual respectively. Title pages will be prepared in manuscript.

Place	Date	Hour	Summary of Events and Information	Remarks and references to Appendices
	1918. Jan.			
In the	1		To COLOGNE position.	
field.	2		Visited 12th. Sherwood Foresters (Pioneers) and 104th. Field Company R.E.	
	3		To TEMPLEUX Quarries and Intermediate Line.	
	4		Visited 103rd. and 104th. Field Companies R.E. and 12th. Sherwood Foresters (Pioneers).	
	5		To ROISEL Dump with C.R.E. Cavalry Corps.	
	6		Went with G.O.C., G.S.O.1., and Major PRIOR to TEMPLEUX QUARRIES and BOLSOVER.	
	7		Major PRIOR, A/C.R.E., went to TEMPLEUX QUARRIES and BOLSOVER to settle details re defences.	
			Lieut. Col. WALKER went to take over duties of C.R.E. Cavalry Corps.	
	8		Reconnoitred HUSSAR ROAD, PIMPLE POST and SHERWOOD TRENCH for improvements.	
	9		Went with G.O.C. 24th. Division and G.S.O.1, to see improvements suggested by Acting C.R.E. as result of previous day's reconnaissance.	
	10		Went with O.C. 12th. Sherwood Foresters (Pioneers) and Capt. GREATHEAD to point out fresh work to be done by them in Battle Zone.	
	11		Went with Capt. FRANCIS, 104th. Field Company R.E. to point out line of new trench from HUSSAR ROAD to connect up with BENJAMIN SWITCH.	
	12		Visited night Working Parties with G.S.O.1.	

D. D. & L., London, E.C.
(A7883) Wt W809/M1672 350,000 4/17 Sch. 52a Forms/C/2118/14

Instructions regarding War Diaries and Intelligence Summaries are contained in F. S. Regs., Part II. and the Staff Manual respectively. Title pages will be prepared in manuscript.

WAR DIARY
or
INTELLIGENCE SUMMARY.
(*Erase heading not required.*)

Army Form C. 2118.

Place	Date	Hour	Summary of Events and Information	Remarks and references to Appendices
.... CONTINUED.				
	16		Went with G.S.O.2 round Defence System.	
	17		Went up the Line revising Battle Zone Scheme.	
	18		do.	
	19		do.	
	20		Army.Commander came to see revised Battle Defence Scheme and went up the line.	
	21		With O.C. "A" Defence Zone shewing him the works in his area.	
	22		With "G" meeting Representatives of 16th. Division on ground fixing junction of defences.	
			Met Corps Hutting Officer at ROISEL re labour for Hutting.	
	23		Visited VERMAND and arranged with O.C. 288th. ~~Tunnelling~~ A.T.Coy. to take over Hutting on following day.	
	24		Visited Officer's Mess Huts to investigate improvements asked for.	
	25		Visited TEMPLEUX Quarry Defences with Corps Commander.	
	26		Went over TEMPLEUX Village defences with O.C. 104th. Field Coy. & Capt. HARRIS.	
			Plans for 24th. Division Defences distributed to all R.E. Officers interested and to Zone Commanders.	

D. D. & L., London, E.C.
(A7883) Wt W809/M1672 350,000 4/17 Sch. 52a Forms/C/2118/14

Instructions regarding War Diaries and Intelligence Summaries are contained in F. S. Regs., Part II. and the Staff Manual respectively. Title pages will be prepared in manuscript.

WAR DIARY
or
INTELLIGENCE SUMMARY.
(Erase heading not required.)

Army Form C. 2118.

Place	Date	Hour	Summary of Events and Information	Remarks and references to Appendices
CONTINUED.				
	27		Saw 104th. Field Company R.E. Also Hutting work, ROISEL, VERMAND, etc.	
			Afternoon_Saw C.R.E. Cavalry Corps re Dugout Programme.	
	28		Visited TEMPLEUX QUARRIES and Centre Sector of front system.	
	29		Visited TEMPLEUX.	
	30.		Visited VRAIGNES, PERONNE, and TEMPLEUX Quarries with Officer of 353 Electrical & Mechanical Coy.	
	31		Saw O.C. 103rd. Field Company R.E.	
			A. D. Walker Lieut.Col.R.E.	
			4.2.1918. C.R.E.. 24th. Division.	

D. D. & L., London, E.C.
(A7883) Wt. W809/M1672 350,000 4/17 Sch. 52a Forms/C/2118/14

Confidential.

Vol 30

H. Q. R. E.

War Diary for month of

February 1918.

Instructions regarding War Diaries and Intelligence Summaries are contained in F. S. Regs., Part II. and the Staff Manual respectively. Title pages will be prepared in manuscript.

WAR DIARY
or
INTELLIGENCE SUMMARY.
(*Erase heading not required.*)

Army Form C. 2118.

Place	Date	Hour	Summary of Events and Information	Remarks and references to Appendices
	1918. February			
In the	1st.		With O.C. 103rd. Field Company R.E. and G.S.O. 1. to Left Front of Blue Zone.	
field.	3rd.		Saw 12th. Sherwood Foresters (Pioneers), TEMPLEUX QUARRIES, and O.C. 103rd. Field Company R.E.	
	4th.		With C.R.E. Cavalry Corps to ROISEL, TEMPLEUX QUARRIES and BOLSOVER.	
	5th.		C.R.E. on leave. Major PRIOR takes over Acting C.R.E. Controller of Mines visited C.R.E.	
	6th.		Visited MONTIGNY, 104th. Field Company R.E., TEMPLEUX.	
			O.C. 258th. Tunnelling Company R.E. came and went through Tunnelling programme with G.O.C.	
	7th.		Up the Line inspecting progress of work in Red Line.	
	8th.		Inspecting Hutting. With G.O.C. settling site for Adrian Hut for Officers Mess at MONTIGNY.	
	9th.		French Interpreter (Commandant MASSON) Cavalry Corps, came with copies of some plans of workings TEMPLEUX QUARRIES.	
	10th.		Visited Red Line. Went down BOLSOVER TUNNEL and saw part opened up.	
	11th.		M.FLEMY, foreman, TEMPLEUX, came from Armies and pointed out and gave information on Workings in neighbourhood of TEMPLEUX.	
	13th.		Went round with, and took over Red Line, Centre Sector, from C.R.E. Dismounted Divisions. G.S.O.1 24th. Division accompanying us.	
	14th.		Visited TEMPLEUX QUARRIES.	

D. D. & L., London, E.C. (A7883) Wt. W809/M1672 350,000 4/17 Sch. 52a Forms/C/2118/14

Instructions regarding War Diaries and Intelligence Summaries are contained in F. S. Regs., Part II. and the Staff Manual respectively. Title pages will be prepared in manuscript.

Army Form C. 2118.

WAR DIARY
or
INTELLIGENCE SUMMARY.
(Erase heading not required.)

Place	Date	Hour	Summary of Events and Information	Remarks and references to Appendices
			CONTINUED.	
	15th.		Visited Red Line throughout with O.C. 103rd. Field Company R.E. and Representative of "G".	
	16th.		With "Q" to MONTIGNY, ROISEL and HERVILLY.	
	17th.		With G.S.O.1 and G.O.C. to visit Red Line - TEMPLEUX to LE VERGUIER.	
	18th.		Visited proposed training area.	
	19th.		With Corps Commander to see TEMPLEUX DEFENCES.	
	20th.		Saw C.R.E. 66th. Division re reliefs and C.R.E. 5th. Army Troops re stores for back area.	
	21st.		With C.R.E. 66th. Division to Front Line.	
	22nd.		Routine.	
	23rd.		With G.O.C. to visit Back Line work HERVILLY, MONTIGNY, VENDELLES and BERNES.	
	24th.		Visited Forward Area.	
	25th.		Visited Brown Line (Left).	
	26th.		Visited Back Area.	
	27th.		With Corps Commander and G.O.C. to visit L.15.a. BROSSE WOODS and JEAN COURT.	
			103rd. Field Company R.E. started for LAMOTTE BREBIERE.	
	28th.		Handing over work to C.R.E. 66th. Division.	

D. D. & L., London, E.C. (A7883) Wt. W809/M1672 350,000 4/17 Sch. 52a Forms/C/2118/14

Instructions regarding War Diaries and Intelligence Summaries are contained in F. S. Regs., Part II, and the Staff Manual respectively. Title pages will be prepared in manuscript.

Army Form C. 2118.

WAR DIARY
or
INTELLIGENCE SUMMARY.
(Erase heading not required.)

Place	Date	Hour	Summary of Events and Information	Remarks and references to Appendices
			CONTINUED.	
	28th.		103rd. Field Company R.E. recalled.	
			[signature] Lieut. Col. R.E.	
			6.3.1918. C.R.E. 24th. Division.	

D. D. & L., London, E.C. (A7883) Wt W809/M1672 350,000 4/17 Sch. 52a Forms/C/2118/14

Confidential.

WO 95/31 [illegible]

24th H.Q. R.E.

War Diary for month of
March 1918

21

Army Form C. 2118.

Instructions regarding War Diaries and Intelligence Summaries are contained in F. S. Regs., Part II. and the Staff Manual respectively. Title pages will be prepared in manuscript.

WAR DIARY
or
INTELLIGENCE SUMMARY.
(Erase heading not required.)

Place	Date	Hour	Summary of Events and Information	Remarks and references to Appendices
	1918. March			
~~In the field~~,	1st.		To new Area. 103rd. and 104th. Field Companies R.E. arrived in new area.	
MERAUCOURT.	2nd.		103rd. and 104th. Field Companies R.E. improving billets in new Area.	
	3rd.		ditto.	
			129th. Field Company R.E. moved to VRAIGNES.	
	4th.		Field Companies settling in.	
	5th.		103rd. and 104th. Field Companies improving billets. 129th. Field Company R.E. partly training, partly Hutting.	
	6th.		ditto.	
	7th.		104th. Field Company R.E. Hutting. 103rd. and 129th. Field Companies R.E. partly Hutting, partly training.	
	8th.		ditto.	
	9th.		ditto.	
	10th.		To BOUVINCOURT to see C.R.E., Dismounted Divisions re relief.	
	11th.		Reconnoitred Left Sector with C.R.E. Dismounted Divisions and O.C. 104th. Field Company R.E.	
	12th.		Took over from C.R.E. Dismounted Divisions.	
BOUVINCOURT.	13th.		Moved to BOUVINCOURT with Division. (Operation Order attached).	

D. D. & L., London, E.C. (A7883) Wt. W809/M1672 350,000 4/17 Sch. 52a Forms/C/2118/14

Instructions regarding War Diaries and Intelligence Summaries are contained in F. S. Regs., Part II. and the Staff Manual respectively. Title pages will be prepared in manuscript.

WAR DIARY
or
INTELLIGENCE SUMMARY.
(Erase heading not required.)

Army Form C. 2118.

Place	Date	Hour	Summary of Events and Information	Remarks and references to Appendices
CONTINUED.	14th.		With G.O.C. and G.S.O. 1 to ESSLING REDOUBT.	
	15th.		Saw new Divisional Headquarters, 17th. Infantry Brigade, O.C. 12th. Sherwood Foresters (Pioneers) and 103rd. ~~Field Company~~ R.E.O.C. 258th. Tunnelling Company R.E.	
	16th.		To right front area with O.C's. 12th. Sherwood Foresters (Pioneers), and O.C. 103rd. Field Company R.E.	
	17th.		Saw O.C. 258th. Tunnelling Company R.E. and O.C. Northants.	
	18th.		Inspected Workshops, LA FLAQUE.	
	19th.		Inspected defences VADENCOURT & MAISSEMY with G.S.O.1.	
	20th.		Arranged with G.S.O.1, Pioneers, and 104th. Field Company R.E. for forward defences of MAISSEMY (finished same night).	
	21st.		To 66th. Division Headquarters, C.E. XIX Corps, 129th. Field Company, 258th. Tunnelling Company R.E.	
			German attack on Battle Zone started.	
			Bridges and Culvert at VADENCOURT and BIHECOURT demolished.	

D. D. & L., London, E.C.
(A7883) Wt. W809/M1672 350,000 4/17 Sch. 52a Forms/C/2118/14

Army Form C. 2118.

Instructions regarding War Diaries and Intelligence Summaries are contained in F. S. Regs., Part II. and the Staff Manual respectively. Title pages will be prepared in manuscript.

WAR DIARY
or
INTELLIGENCE SUMMARY.
(*Erase heading not required.*)

Place	Date	Hour	Summary of Events and Information	Remarks and references to Appendices
	22nd.		Enemy attack continued. Bridges at VERMAND demolished. 104th. Field Company R.E.	
			suffered heavy casualties holding switch line LE VERGUIER. H.Q.R.E. and 129th. Field Company	
			move to BRIE and 103rd. and 104th. Field Companies R.E. to MONCHY LAGACHE.	
BRIE.	23rd.		Headquarters and Field Companies R.E. concentrate at MARCHELEPOT.	
MARCHELEPOT.	24th.		Headquarters and Field Companies R.E. move to HALLU and Sappers of three Companies put in line	
			of defence under Bde. of the Division. Transport of Field Companies move to MEHARICOURT and	
			H.Q.R.E. with Divisional Headquarters to ROSIERES	
ROSIERES.	25th.		Field Company transport moved to CAIX and H.Q.R.E. with Divisional H.Q. to DEMUIN. Company	
			Sappers in line CHAULNES - HALLU - FRESNOY.	
DEMUIN.	26th.		C.R.E. (Lieut. Col. A.D. WALKER) missing, believed killed, near HALLU. Sappers with	
			Brigades retire to WARVILLERS. Field Company transport moves to CAYEUX.	
	27th.		Major PRIOR, O.C. 103rd. Field Company R.E. reports at Divisional Headquarters as acting C.R.E.	
			Heavy transport of Field Companies move to BOVES. 1st. Line Transport to DEMUIN.	
	28th.		H.Q.R.E. and Field Companies move with Division to CASTEL. Heavy Transport to NAMPTY.	
CASTEL.	29th.		Bridge over AVRE at CASTEL prepared for demolition. H.Q.R.E. move to COTTENCHY. 103rd.	
			and 129th. Field Companies R.E. to THEZY and 104th. Company and 1st. Line Transport to COTTENCHY.	

D. D. & L., London, E.C.
(A7883) Wt. W809/M1672 350,000 4/17 Sch. 52a Forms/C/2118/14

Instructions regarding War Diaries and Intelligence Summaries are contained in F. S. Regs., Part II. and the Staff Manual respectively. Title pages will be prepared in manuscript.

WAR DIARY
or
INTELLIGENCE SUMMARY.
(Erase heading not required.)

Army Form C. 2118.

Place	Date	Hour	Summary of Events and Information	Remarks and references to Appendices
COTTENCHY.	30th.		A/C.R.E. visited C.E. 19th. Corps re R.E. material.	
	31st.		A/C.R.E. went around line with G.S.O.1. 103rd. Field Company R.E. moves to join 1st. Line	
			Transport at COTTENCHY.	
			Handed over charge under CASTEL Bridge to French.	
			[signature] Lieut. Col. R.E.	
			C.R.E. 24th. Division.	

D. D. & L., London, E.C.
(A7883) Wt. W809/M1672 350,000 4/17 Sch. 52a Forms/C/2118/14

SECRET. Copy No. 15.

OPERATION ORDER NO. 72.

by

LIEUT. COL. A.D. WALKER R.E.

C.R.E. 24th. Division.

10th. March 1918.

Reference 1/40,000 Maps.
Sheets 62 c. & 62 b.

(1) The 24th. Division, less Artillery, will relieve the Dismounted Divisions in the line.

(2) The Divisional and inter-Brigade boundaries are :-

(a) Southern Divisional boundary :
M.16.c.90.15 - M.20.b.60.65 - R.24.c.2.4. - R.27.c.35.40 - thence along OMIGNON River.

(b) Northern Divisional Boundary :
L.18.c.9.0 - L.23.central - L.23.c.0.0 - L.28.a.0.0 - L.27.d.0.0 - L.32.d.0.0 - R.2.b.0.7.

(c) Inter-Brigade boundary :

WATLING Street - VADENCOURT - R.15.c.central - R.25.central - all inclusive to the Right Brigade.

(3) The 103rd. and 104th. Field Companies R.E. will relieve the 2nd. and 1st. Field Squadrons respectively in accordance with the attached Table "A".

(4) The 129th. Field Company R.E. will remain at their present billet at VRAIGNES.

(5) The relief of the 2nd. Dismounted Divisions by 72nd. Infantry Brigade will be completed by 6 a.m. on 12th. March.

The relief of 1st. Dismounted Division by 17th. Infantry Brigade will be completed by 6 a.m. 14th. March.

72nd. Infantry Brigade H.Q. VERMAND.
17th. " " " Small Foot Wood. R.8.b.

(6) The 73rd. Infantry Brigade will remain at BERNES and HANCOURT in Corps Reserve. 73rd. Infantry Brigade H.Q. BERNES.

(7) Trench stores, photographs, defence schemes, plans of work in hand and projected will be taken over and receipts given.

(8) Other details of relief will be arranged direct between Os.C. Field Companies and Os. C. Field Squadrons concerned.

(9) (a) Command of front held by Dismounted Divisions will pass to B.Gs.C. 72nd. and 17th. Infantry Brigades on completion of Infantry reliefs.

(b) G.O.C. 24th. Division assumes command of the front now held by Dismounted Divisions at 10 a.m. on 14th. March.

(10) Headquarters 24th. Division close at MERAUCOURT and open at BOUVINCOURT AT 10 a.m. 14th. March.

(11) Completion of reliefs to be reported by Field Companies to C.R.E. by wire.

P.T.O.

(12) ACKNOWLEDGE.

J.R. Grant
Capt. & Adjt. R.E.
for C.R.E. 24th. Division.

Issued at 3.30 p.m.
10.3.1918.

DISTRIBUTION.

Copy No.1. "G" 24th. Division.
" " 2. "Q" 24th. Division.
" " 3. 17th. Infantry Brigade.
" " 4. 72nd. Infantry Brigade.
" " 5. 73rd. Infantry Brigade.
" " 6. A.D.M.S. 24th. Division.
" " 7. O.C. 24th. Divisional Train.
" " 8. O.C. 12th. Sherwood Foresters (Pioneers).
" " 9. O.C. 103rd. Field Comany R.E.
" "10. O.C. 104th. Field Company R.E.
" "11. O.C. 129th. Field Company R.E.
" "12. O.C. 24th. Divisional Signal Company.
" "13. C.R.E. Dismounted Divisions.
" "14. War Diary.
" "15. Record.

MARCH TABLE "A". Reference 1/40000 Map 62 c.

To accompany C.R.E. Operation Order No.72. Dated March 10th, 1918.

Date.	Unit.	In Relief of	From.	To	Route.	Remarks.
March 11th.	Field Coy. R.E. 103rd.	Field Squadron R.E. 2nd.	DEVISE.	VERMAND.	Centimetre Rly.	Transport by Road. Personnel entrain at MONS-EN-CHAUSSEE.
11/12.	2 Sections 103rd.	do.	~~VILLECHOLLES.~~ VERMAND	VADENCOURT and MAISSEMY.	----	H.Q. & 2 Sections remain at VERMAND.
12th.	104th. Fd.Co.R.E.	Field Squadron R.E. 1st.	MONTECOURT.	BERNES.	Via VRAIGNES and HANCOURT.	To arrive BERNES by noon.
do.	do.	do.	BERNES.	Small Foot Wood and VADENCOURT.	Via VENDELLES.	Field Squadron to be clear of billets by 2 p.m. Transport remain at BERNES.
13th.	H.Q. R.E. 24th. Division.	H.Q. R.E. Dimounted Divisions.	MERAUCOURT.	BOUVINCOURT.	----	Billet at BOUVINCOURT to be vacated by 11 a.m.

NOTE. No movement of relieving troops East of MAISSEMY ridge or VADENCOURT before 8 p.m.
The following intervals will be maintained on the march - between Sections 200 yards - between each 6 transport vehicles 200 yards.

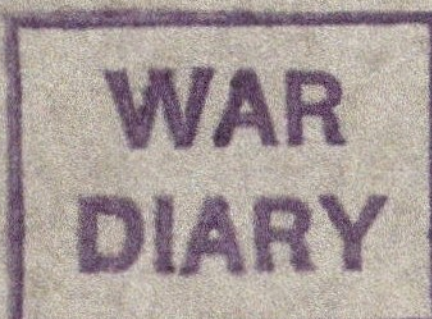

Headquarters,

ROYAL ENGINEERS, 24th Division.

A P R I L

1 9 1 8

Instructions regarding War Diaries and Intelligence Summaries are contained in F. S. Regs., Part II. and the Staff Manual respectively. Title pages will be prepared in manuscript.

WAR DIARY
or
INTELLIGENCE SUMMARY.
(*Erase heading not required.*)

Army Form C. 2118.

Place	Date	Hour	Summary of Events and Information	Remarks and references to Appendices
	1918			
	April			
COTTENCHY.	1		129th. Field Company R.E. returned to Horse Lines.	
			Major PRIOR appointed C.R.E. with temporary rank of Lieut. Col.	
	2		C.R.E. went round line with G.S.O. 1.	
	3		Division takes over more front. C.R.E. goes over new front with G.S.O.1.	
	4		Reconnoitred Bridges and Crossings at BOVES.	
BOUILLET.			Divisional Headquarters moved to BOUILLET.	
	5		Withdrawal of the Division from the line commenced.	
ST. VALERY.	6		Division moves to rest in ST. VALERY Area.	
	8		C.R.E. visited 103rd. 104th. and 129th. Field Companies R.E. and 17th. 72nd. & 73rd. Infantry Brigades.	
	10		103rd. 104th. and 129th. Field Companies R.E. moved to MIANNAY.	
	11		C.R.E. visited 103rd. 104th. and 129th. Field Companies R.E.	
	13		C.R.E. visited 103rd. 104th. and 129th. Field Companies R.E.	
	15		C.R.E. visited 103rd. 104th. and 129th. Field Companies R.E.	
LA THIEULOYE	17		Divisional Headquarters moved to LA THIEULOYE.	

D. D. & L., London, E.C. (A7883) Wt W809/M1672 350,000 4/17 Sch. 52a Forms/C/2118/14

Instructions regarding War Diaries and Intelligence Summaries are contained in F. S. Regs., Part II. and the Staff Manual respectively. Title pages will be prepared in manuscript.

WAR DIARY
or
INTELLIGENCE SUMMARY.
(*Erase heading not required.*)

Army Form C. 2118.

Place	Date	Hour	Summary of Events and Information	Remarks and references to Appendices
	18		C.R.E. visited 103rd. and 129th. Field Companies R.E.	
	19		C.R.E. visited 104th. Field Company R.E.	
	20		C.R.E. visited C.E. XV111 Corps.	
	21		C.R.E. visited Brigades and 103rd. & 129th. Field Companies R.E.	
	22		Conference of R.E. Officers at which C.E. XV111 Corps was present and lectured.	
	23		Visited C.E. XV111 Corps.	
	24		Visited 72nd. Brigade Baths at OURTON.	
			Captain J.R.GRANT vacated position of Adjutant and proceeded to take over command of 2nd. Field Company R.E.	
			Lieut. E.H.FORD takes over duties of Adjutant.	
	25		Visited Field Companies R.E. in training with G.O.C. 24th. Division and G.S.O.1.	
	26		Conference of R.E. Officers and Lecture by C.E. XV111 Corps.	
	27		C.R.E. visited 72nd. and 73rd. Infantry Brigades and 103rd. Field Companies R.E.	
	28		Went with C.E. XV111 Corps who lectured at Conference of Officers of 12th. Sherwood Foresters (Pioneers).	

D. D. & L., London, E.C.
(A7833) Wt W809/M1672 350,000 4/17 Sch. 52a. Forms/C/2118/14

Instructions regarding War Diaries and Intelligence Summaries are contained in F. S. Regs., Part II. and the Staff Manual respectively. Title pages will be prepared in manuscript.

WAR DIARY
or
INTELLIGENCE SUMMARY.
(Erase heading not required.)

Army Form C. 2118.

Place	Date	Hour	Summary of Events and Information	Remarks and references to Appendices
	29		Orders received for 73rd. Infantry Brigade to move subsequently cancelled.	
	30th.		Visited C.R.E. 3rd. Canadian Division with reference to taking over from him.	
			J. H. Prior Lieut. Col. R.E.	
			8th. May 1918. C.R.E. 24th. Division.	

D. D. & L., London, E.C.
(A7883) Wt. W809/M1672 350,000 4/17 Sch. 52a Forms/C/2118/14

Confidential

Vol 33

War Diary.

Month of May 1918

H.Q. R.E.

Army Form C. 2118.

Instructions regarding War Diaries and Intelligence Summaries are contained in F. S. Regs., Part II. and the Staff Manual respectively. Title pages will be prepared in manuscript.

WAR DIARY
or
INTELLIGENCE SUMMARY.
(*Erase heading not required.*)

Place	Date	Hour	Summary of Events and Information	Remarks and references to Appendices
	1918. MAY.			
LA THIEULOYE.	1		Went to see C.R.E. 3rd. Canadian Division re taking over from him.	
	2		ditto. ditto.	
SAINS EN GOHELLE.	3		Divisional Headquarters R.E. move to SAINS EN GOHELLE.	
	4		Went round portion of Line with G.O.C. and G.S.O.1.	
			Saw Officer i/c. XV111 Corps Dump re Stores for Divisional R.E. Dump.	
	5		Went up the Line with C.E. XV111 Corps and O.C. 3rd. Australian Tunnelling Company. Visited HYTHE TUNNEL.	
	6		Went round FOSSE 7 Defences with C.E. XV111 Corps and O.C. 104th. Field Company R.E.	
	7		Went to see Staff Officer, R.E. XV111 Corps with reference to several Stores questions.	
	8		Went with A.D.M.S. to Divisional Main Dressing Station, FOSSE 10; and arranged for the erection of a shed for anti-gas treatment.	
			Arranged with 12th. Sherwood Foresters (Pioneers) for work on ST. JOHNS WOOD TRENCH.	
	9		Went round portion of the Line with B.G. 17th. Infantry Brigade and G.S.O. 2.	
			Visited 103rd., 104th., & 129th. Field Companies R.E. to see that they knew Special Instructions.	
	10		Went with O.C. 104th. Field Company R.E. round FOSSE 7 Defences.	
	11		Went with A.D.M.S. to see improvements required at FOSSE 11 Advanced Dressing Station. Also	

D. D. & L., London, E.C. (A7883) Wt. W809/M1672 350,000 4/17 Sch. 52a Forms/C/2118/14

Instructions regarding War Diaries and Intelligence Summaries are contained in F. S. Regs., Part II. and the Staff Manual respectively. Title pages will be prepared in manuscript.

WAR DIARY
or
INTELLIGENCE SUMMARY.
(*Erase heading not required.*)

Army Form C. 2118.

Place	Date	Hour	Summary of Events and Information	Remarks and references to Appendices
			CONTINUED.	
			saw progress of work at Main Dressing Station, FOSSE 10.	
	12		Went with G.S.O. 1 to N. end of Village Defences and FOSSE 7 Defences.	
	13		Office Routine.	
	14		Visited FOSSE 7 Defences with O.C. 129th. Field Company R.E.	
			Reconnoitred Road proposal in nieghbourhood of FOSSE 11 and BULLY GRENAY with O.C. 331st.	
			Road Construction Company R.E.	
	15		Went up the Line with G.S.O. 1 and reconnoitred LONDON ROAD SWITCH.	
	16		With O.C. 3rd. Australian Tunnelling Company reconnoitering Divisional Headquarters as to	
			possibilities of underground accommodation.	
	17		Went round work in progress in 72nd. Infantry Brigade Area with O.C. 103rd. Field Company R.E.	
			Work on Dugout accommodation at Divisional Headquarters commenced.	
	18		Went with O.C. 12th. Sherwood Foresters (Pioneers) round the work they have in hand up the Line.	
	19		With O.C. 3rd. Australian Tunnelling Company and O.C. 129th. Field Company R.E. ~~Visited~~	
			Visited Puits 14 Bis re O.P. and L.G. Emplacement.	
	20		~~With~~ Went with G.S.O. 1 to ELVASTON CASTLE with reference to accommodation for Gunners and 73rd.	

D. D. & L., London, E.C. (A7883) Wt. W809/M1672 350,000 4/17 Sch. 52a Forms/C/2118/14

Instructions regarding War Diaries and Intelligence Summaries are contained in F. S. Regs., Part II. and the Staff Manual respectively. Title pages will be prepared in manuscript.

WAR DIARY
or
INTELLIGENCE SUMMARY.
(*Erase heading not required.*)

Army Form C. 2118.

Place	Date	Hour	Summary of Events and Information	Remarks and references to Appendices
			CONTINUED.	
			Infantry Brigade Headquarters. Also visited Village Line in front of MAROC.	
	21		Went round Village Line with C.E. XV111 Corps.	
	22		C.E. 1st. Army came to see C.R.E.	
			Went with B.G.C. 72nd. Infantry Brigade and G.S.O. 1 to see Defences in vicinity of COUGAR POST.	
	23		Went up the Line with G.S.O. 1 and O.C. 12th. Sherwood Foresters (Pioneers).	
			Went round Reserve Line - FOSSE 7 Defences - with O.C. 129th. Field Company R.E.	
	24		Went round work in forward area with O.C. 104th. Field Company R.E.	
	25		Went with G.S.O. 1 round Village Line from EDGWARE ROAD to PICCADILLY POST.	
	26		Saw O.C. SUSSEX and NORTHANTS Regiments re ST. PATRICK being turned into Battalion H.Q. in place of HACKETT.	
			Visited B.G.C. 72nd. Infantry Brigade and C.C. Forward Battalion re provision of tunnelled accommodation for latter.	
	27		Went round line noting progress of work on PICCADILLY and LONDON ROAD SWITCH.	
	28		Went with G.S.O. 1 round a portion of MAROC DEFENCES.	
	29		Went round LENS ROAD SWITCH and ST. PIERRE SWITCH with G.S.O. 1.	

D. D. & L., London, E.C. (A7883) Wt. W809/M1672 350,000 4/17 Sch. 52a Forms/C/2118/14

Instructions regarding War Diaries and Intelligence Summaries are contained in F. S. Regs., Part II. and the Staff Manual respectively. Title pages will be prepared in manuscript.

WAR DIARY
or
INTELLIGENCE SUMMARY.
(Erase heading not required.)

Army Form C. 2118.

Place	Date	Hour	Summary of Events and Information	Remarks and references to Appendices
			CONTINUED.	
	30		Went with G.O.C. and G.S.O. 1 round a portion of MAROC DEFENCES.	
	31		Went with G.S.O. 1 round BLUE LINE in 72nd. Infantry Brigade Area.	
			J. H. Prior Lieut. Col. R.E.	
			3.6.1918. C.R.E. 24th. Division.	

D. D. & L., London, E.C. (A7883) Wt. W809/M1672 350,000 4/17 Sch. 52a Forms/C/2118/14

S E C R E T.

Copy No. 11

C.R.[illegible] ORDER NO. 441.

With reference to 24th. Division Order No. 240 d/11.5.18.

(1) On the 12/13th. May the 104th. Field Company R.E. will take over from the 129th. Field Company R.E. the R.E. services in the area taken over by 17th. Infantry Brigade from 73rd. Infantry Brigade.

(2) On the 13/14th. the 104th. Field Company R.E. will take over from the 103rd. Field Company R.E. the R.E. services in the area taken over by the 17th. Infantry Brigade from 72nd. Infantry Brigade.

(3) Work on [illegible] Defences will be handed over from 104th. Field Company R.E. to 129th. Field Company R.E. on the 13th. inst.

(4) Details of handing over will be arranged between O.C. Companies.

(5) All Maps, Plans, ~~xx other~~ and other details of work in hand will be handed over.

(6) ACKNOWLEDGE.

Lieut. Col. R.E.
C.R.E. 24th. Division.

11th. May 1918.

Copies to :-

1. "G" 24th. Division.
2. "Q" 24th. Division.
3. 17th. Infantry Brigade.
4. 72nd. Infantry Brigade.
5. 73rd. Infantry Brigade.
6. O.C. 103rd. Field Company R.E.
7. O.C. 104th. Field Company R.E.
8. O.C. 129th. Field Company R.E.
9. O.C. 3rd. Australian Tunnelling Company R.E.
10. File.
11. War Diary.

Confidential.

95/3

H.Q. R.E.

War diary for month of June 1918.

Army Form C. 2118.

Instructions regarding War Diaries and Intelligence Summaries are contained in F. S. Regs., Part II, and the Staff Manual respectively. Title pages will be prepared in manuscript.

WAR DIARY
or
INTELLIGENCE SUMMARY.
(*Erase heading not required.*)

Place	Date	Hour	Summary of Events and Information	Remarks and references to Appendices
	1918. June			
SAINS EN	1st.		Went round FOSSE 7 Reserve Line with G.O.C. and O.C. 129th. Field Company R.E.	
GOHELLE.	2nd.		Accompanied Corps Commander, Divisional Commander, and B.G.C. 17th. Infantry Brigade round 17th.	
			Brigade area.	
			Attended C.E's Conference.	
	3rd.		Visited "CUP" R.E. Dump to see new R.A.O.P.	
	4th.		Went round 17th. Brigade forward system with G.S.O.1 and G.S.O.3.	
			Conference of Os.C. Field Companies R.E.	
	5th.		Went round CRASSIER SWITCH with G.S.O.1.	
	6th.		Went round part of VILLAGE LINE.	
			C.E. XV111 Corps came to see C.R.E.	
	7th.		Visited FOSSE 7 Defences. With O.C. 129th. Field Company R.E. and O.C. 12th. Sherwood Foresters	
			(Pioneers) re work on MAROC Defences.	
	8th.		Went with G.S.O.3 round portion of GREEN LINE.	
	9th.		Visited LENS ROAD SWITCH, ST. PIERRE SWITCH & ELVASTON CASTLE with C.E. 18th. Corps.	
	10th.		Visited the Line with G.O.C., G.S.O.1., and O.C. 3rd. Australian Tunnalling Company re Shelters	
			to be put in LENS ROAD SWITCH.	

D. D. & L., London, E.C. (A7883) Wt W809/M1672 350,000 4/17 Sch. 52a Forms/C/2118/14

Instructions regarding War Diaries and Intelligence Summaries are contained in F. S. Regs., Part II. and the Staff Manual respectively. Title pages will be prepared in manuscript.

WAR DIARY
or
INTELLIGENCE SUMMARY.
(Erase heading not required.)

Army Form C. 2118.

Place	Date	Hour	Summary of Events and Information	Remarks and references to Appendices
CONTINUED.	11th.		Visited the Line with G.S.O.1., O.C. 24th. Battn. M.G.C. and O.C. 129th. Field Company R.E. re position of Pill Boxes.	
	12th.		Attended Conference of B.G.C's with G.O.C. & G.S.O.1.	
			With G.S.O.1. and O.C. 24th. M.G.Battn. re sites for M.G's in 17th. and 72nd. Brigade areas.	
	13th.		Went with G.S.O.1 round RED LINE.	
	14th.		Visited Baths at SAINS EN GOHELLE, BULLY GRENAY and LES BREBIS.	
			Visited O.C. 12th. Sherwood Foresters (Pioneers), 72nd. Infantry Brigade Rear H.Q., 3rd. Australian Tunnelling Company and 24th. Divisional R.E.Dump.	
	15th.		Went with G.S.O.3. round Shelters being constructed in LENS ROAD SWITCH.	
	16th.		Went to "CUP" R.E. Corps Dump with O.C. 129th. Field Company re material and camouflage for Pillboxes.	
	17th.		With G.S.O.1., and O.C. 104th. Field Company R.E. visiting parts of LENS ROAD SWITCH and VILLAGE LINE. Also visited future H.Qrs. of 72nd. Infantry Brigade at FOSSE 11.	
	18th.		With O.C. 3rd. Australian Tunnelling Company at place for Road Mine at ST. PIERRE. Also at proposed Battalion H.Q.	
	19th.		Went up the Line with G.S.O.1.	

D. D. & L., London, E.C. (A7883) Wt. W809/M1672 350,000 4/17 Sch. 52a Forms/C/2118/14

Instructions regarding War Diaries and Intelligence Summaries are contained in F. S. Regs., Part II. and the Staff Manual respectively. Title pages will be prepared in manuscript.

WAR DIARY
or
INTELLIGENCE SUMMARY.
(Erase heading not required.)

Army Form C. 2118.

Place	Date	Hour	Summary of Events and Information	Remarks and references to Appendices
CONTINUED.	20th.		Went with Lieut. DALTON round work being done for R.A.	
	21st.		Went to Tank Demonstration.	
	22nd.		With Lieut. DAVISON, 350th. Electrical & Mechanical Company re lighting of 72nd. Infantry Brigade H.Q.	
	23rd.		Went with G.O.C. and G.S.O.1 round LENS ROAD SWITCH, RUPERT TRENCH and Pill Boxes at PREVITE CASTLE and COPSE POST.	
	24th.		Went through HYTHE TUNNEL with G.S.O.1.	
	25th.		Visited 129th. Field Company R.E., 12th. Sherwood Foresters (Pioneers) and 72nd. Brigade H.Q.	
	26th.		Took Major HEATH round portion of work in 73rd. Brigade area.	
	27th.		Went with C.E. XVlll Corps to a demonstration of LANd Mines.	
	28th.		Went with B.G.C. 72nd. Infantry Brigade, Major HEATH, and O.C. 12th. Sherwood Foresters (Pioneers) round work being done by Pioneers in 72nd. Brigade area.	
	29th.		Office routine and handing over to Major HEATH.	
			Visited Lieut. DAVISON, 350th. Electrical & Mechanical Company re Lighting of 72nd. Brigade new Advanced H.Q.	

D. D. & L., London, E.C. (A7883) Wt. W809/M1672 350,000 4/17 Sch. 52a Forms/C/2118/14

Army Form C. 2118.

Instructions regarding War Diaries and Intelligence Summaries are contained in F. S. Regs., Part II. and the Staff Manual respectively. Title pages will be prepared in manuscript.

WAR DIARY
or
INTELLIGENCE SUMMARY.
(*Erase heading not required.*)

Place	Date	Hour	Summary of Events and Information	Remarks and references to Appendices
CONTINUED.	30th.		Visited BLACK LINE in 72nd. Brigade and 17th. Brigade areas. Also visited 72nd. Infantry Brigade (with reference lighting new H.Q., FOSSE 11.) and 73rd. Infantry Brigade.	
			fo Heath Major, R.E.	
			2nd. July 1918. A/C.R.E. 24th. Division.	

D. D. & L., London, E.C.
(A7883) Wt. W809/M1672 350,000 4/17 Sch. 52a Forms/C/2118/14

Army Form C. 2118.

WAR DIARY of C.R.E.24th Division or ~~INTELLIGENCE SUMMARY.~~

(Erase heading not required.)

Instructions regarding War Diaries and Intelligence Summaries are contained in F. S. Regs., Part II. and the Staff Manual respectively. Title pages will be prepared in manuscript.

Vol 35

Place	Date	Hour	Summary of Events and Information	Remarks and references to Appendices
	1918. July			
MAINS-EN-GOHELLE.	1		Visited MAISTRE Line in MAROC Area. Also visited L.G.Emplacement and Pill Box under construction near FOSSE 16.	
	2		Visited 72nd. Infantry Brigade to discuss work required on new dugouts in COWDEN TRENCH. (BLACK LINE). Allotted two dugouts to 12th. Sherwood Foresters (Pioneers) and one to 103rd. Field Company R.E.	
	3		Visited COWDEN TRENCH, 72nd. Brigade area to fix sites for dugouts with O.C. 12th. Sherwood Foresters (Pioneers) and O.C. 103rd. Field Company R.E.	
	4		Visited work being done by 3rd. Australian Tunnelling Company on RUPERT TRENCH. Conference of Os. C. Field Companies R.E. to discuss "Battle" dispositions.	
	5		Visited ST. PIERRE with G.S.O.2 to decide on defence of right flank ST. PIERRE SWITCH.	
	6		Went round S.MAROC Line with O.C. 12th. Sherwood Foresters (Pioneers) and pointed out required work. Also looked at proposed Battle Battalion H.Q. in Quarry outside wall S. MAROC.	
	7		Went round 73rd. Infantry Brigade back area - AEROPLANE TRENCH - RUPERT TRENCH - LENS ROAD SWITCH - visiting Pill Boxes under construction.	
	8		Visited CUPIGNY DUMP to meet C.E. VIIIth. Corps to discuss material question. Visited O.C. Electrical & Mechanical Company, GOUY SERVINS.	
	9		Visited VILLAGE LINE with O.C. 12th. Sherwood Foresters (Pioneers).	
	10		Went round VILLAGE LINE ~~with~~ 8.2.Gun Positions with Lieut. DEAN - AIX NOULETTE - CORONS D'AIX - BULLY GRENAY - MAZINGARBE. Also new R.A. H.Q. at FOSSE 11.	
	11		Took C.E. VIIIth. Corps round S.MAROC Line - VILLAGE Line - M.G.E's. south of FOSSE 16.	
	12		Went to LENS ROAD SWITCH with G.S.O.3 and O.C. 12th. Sherwood Foresters (Pioneers) to decide on deviation required just N. of LENS - BETHUNE ROAD.	
	13		Routine work.	
	14		Visited MAROC to make out Scheme for "localities" for defence of Village.	
	15		C.R.E. visited 17th. Infantry Brigade - BLACK LINE - with Major HEATH.	
	16		Visited Pill Boxes in 73rd. Infantry Brigade area with O.C. 129th. Field Company R.E.	
	17		Went round M.G.Emplacements in 72nd. Infantry Brigade area with O.C. 103rd. Field Company R.E.	
	18		Visited CANTEEN TUNNEL with G.S.O.1.	
	20		Conference of Os. C. Field Companies R.E. at C.R.E's Office.	
	21		Conference of C.R.E's at C.E's Office.	
	23		C.R.E. went round LONDON ROAD SWITCH and part of FOSSE 7 with G.S.O.1.	
	24		Visited FOSSE 11 and AIX NOULETTE with A.D.M.S.	
	25		Went to see B.G.C. 73rd. Infantry Brigade with Corps Camouflage Officer.	
	26		Went to see C.E. VIIIth. Corps.	

D. D. & L., London, E.C. (A8004) Wt. W1771/M2031 750,000 5/17 Sch. 52 Forms C2118/14

Instructions regarding War Diaries and Intelligence Summaries are contained in F. S. Regs., Part II. and the Staff Manual respectively. Title pages will be prepared in manuscript.

WAR DIARY of C.R.E.24th Division (Contd.) ~~or INTELLIGENCE SUMMARY.~~

(*Erase heading not required.*)

Army Form C. 2118.

Place	Date	Hour	Summary of Events and Information	Remarks and references to Appendices
CONTINUED.	27		Went round work proceeding on M.G. and LEWIS GUN Emplacements MAROC with O.C. 12th. Sherwood Foresters (Pioneers).	
	28		Office Routine.	
	29		Went with G.O.C., B.G.C. 73rd. Infantry Brigade and G.S.O.1. round 73rd. Infantry Brigade Forward area.	
	30		C.R.E. went to see C.E. Vlllth. Corps.	
	31		C.R.E. went round line with G.S.O.1.	
			J. H. Prior Lieut. Col. R.E. C.R.E. 24th. Division.	
			4.8.1918.	

D. D. & L., London, E.C. (A8001) Wt. W1771/M2031 750,000 5/17 Sch. 52 Forms C2118/14

~~Con~~fidential

War Diary

H.Q. 2B

August 1918.

Army Form C. 2118.

Instructions regarding War Diaries and Intelligence Summaries are contained in F. S. Regs., Part II. and the Staff Manual respectively. Title pages will be prepared in manuscript.

WAR DIARY
or
INTELLIGENCE SUMMARY.

(Erase heading not required.)

Place	Date 1918	Hour	Summary of Events and Information	Remarks and references to Appendices
	Aug:			
SAINS EN GOHELLE.	1		C.R.E. went to 1st. Pontoon Park.	
	2		C.R.E. went to see C.E. V111th. Corps.	
	3		Visited 72nd. Infantry Brigade Forward Area with B.G.C.72nd. Infantry Brigade, Major GAWTHORP, 24th. M.G.C. and Major GREATHEAD, O.C. 103rd. Field Company R.E.	
	5		Went to "CUP" Dump. Also visited 103rd. Field Company R.E.	
	6		Went with A.D.M.S. to Divisional Rest Station.	
	7		Went with G.S.O.1 up the line to various M.G.Positions.	
	10		Went to see C.E. V111 Corps.	
	11		Went up the line with A.D.M.S.	
	12		C.R.E. went to Lecture by Inspector General of Training.	
	13		C.R.E. went to 1st. Army Rifle Meeting.	
	14		Went up the line with G.S.O.1.	
	15		Went with C.E. V111th. Corps to MONO rail demonstration.	
	16		Visited V111th. Corps School with Divisional "Q".	
	17		C.R.E. went to see C.E. 1st. Corps.	
	18		C.R.E. went to 1st. Army Workshops re M.G.Mountings.	
	19		C.R.E. went round area taken over from 20th. Division with C.R.E. 20th. Division, O.C.103rd. Field Company R.E. and Brigade Major, 72nd. Infantry Brigade.	
	20		Went round trenches in new area with O.C. 103rd. Field Company R.E. with a view to considering drainage scheme.	
	21		C.R.E. attended lecture by Corps Commander; afterwards attended Conference of C.R.E's at C.E's.	
	22		C.R.E. visited Divisional Reception Camp with G.S.O.2 with a view to improvements.	
	23		C.R.E. went to see C.E. V111th. Corps; also went to VERDREL re improvements.	
	25		C.R.E. visited 104th. and 129th. Field Companies R.E.	
	26		C.R.E. proceeded to 1st. Army H.Q. to be invested with LEGION of HONOUR.	
	27		C.R.E. 15th. Division came and discussed details of handing over. Visited C.E.V111th. Corps.	
	28		129th. Field Company R.E. moved to new area.	
	29		C.R.E. lectured at V111th. Corps School to Pioneer Class.	
	30		Visited new area with C.R.E. 20th. Division.	
	31		Went with B.G.C. 17th. Infantry Brigade and O.C. 103rd. Field Company reconnoitring for a Forward Track for 17th. Infantry Brigade.	

4.9.18.

J. H. Prior
Lieut. Col. R.E.
C.R.E. 24th. Division.

D. D. & L., London, E.C. (A8001) Wt. W1771/M2031 750,000 5/17 Sch. 52 Forms C2118/14

Confidential

W.D. 37

War Diary.

H.Q. R.E. 24th Division

September 1918.

Army Form C. 2118.

WAR DIARY
or
INTELLIGENCE SUMMARY.
(*Erase heading not required.*)

Instructions regarding War Diaries and Intelligence Summaries are contained in F. S. Regs., Part II. and the Staff Manual respectively. Title pages will be prepared in manuscript.

Place	Date	Hour	Summary of Events and Information	Remarks and references to Appendices
	1918 Sept.			
SAINS-EN-GOHELLE.	1		Visited 3rd. Australian Tunnelling Company re arrangements for Booby Traps.	
	2		C.R.E. went round Forward Roads with C.E. Vlllth. Corps. Visited 129th. Field Company R.E. and B.G.C. 73rd. Infantry Brigade.	
	3		Reconnoitring Forward Roads in 72nd. Infantry Brigade area with O.C. 103rd. Field Company R.E.	
	4		Visited tunnel at Hill 65.	
	5		C.R.E. visited 73rd. Infantry Brigade Forward Area with "Q" and A.D.M.S.	
	6		Went to 1st. Army R.E. Park. Capt. Ford (Adjutant) proceeded on leave.	
	7		C.R.E. visited 73rd. Infantry Brigade H.Q. and 24th. Divisional Train. Also visited FOSS 11.	
	8		Field Company Transport inspected.	
	9		Conference of C.R.E's. at C.E's. Office, Vlll Corps.	
	10		Conference at Divisional Headquarters. Conference of Company Commanders.	
	11		Visited 17th. Infantry Brigade, 103rd. and 104th. Field Companies R.E.	
	12		Went with O.C. 103rd. Field Company R.E. round Forward Roads and Tracks.	
	13		Visited 103rd & 104th. Field Companies R.E. and 12th. Sherwood Foresters (Pioneers).	
	14		Attended Conference at 72nd. Infantry Brigade H.Q.	
	15		Went round Forward Roads with "Q".	
	16		Visited Divisional Wing, also went to 1st. Army R.E. Park.	
	17		Went round Forward Roads with Major MAITLAND, Field Engineer to C.E. Vlllth. Corps.	
	18		Conference of O.C. 12th. Sherwood Foresters (Pioneers), 103rd. and 104th. Field Companies R.E.	
	19		Went to see C.E. Vlllth. Corps. C.E. 20th. Division came to see C.R.E. re KINGSTON ROAD.	
	20		Visited 12th. Sherwood Foresters (Pioneers) and 72nd. Infantry Brigade.	
	21		Went round Forward Roads with C.E. Vlllth. Corps.	
	22		Visited Divisional Rest Station VERDREL with D.A.Q.M.G.	
	23		Went to GREEN CRASSIER with O.C. 129th. Field Company R.E.	
	24		Office Routine.	
	25		ditto.	
	26		Visited NO.1 PONTOON PARK, also C.E. 1st. Army and C.E. Vlllth. Corps.	
	27		Preparing for handing over.	
	28		C.R.E. 58th. Division visited area and went to H.Qrs. of 103rd. & 104th. Field Companies R.E.	
	29		Handing over to C.R.E. 58th. Division.	
	30		Divisional H.Q. moved to LUCHEUX.	

5.10.1918.

J.H. Prior
Lieut. Col.
C.R.E. 24th. Division.

D. D. & L., London, E.C. (A8001) Wt. W1771/M2031 750,000 5/17 Sch. 52 Forms C2118/14

H.Q. R.E.
24th. Division.

W A R   D I A R Y.

O C T O B E R.

1 9 1 8.

9

Army Form C. 2118.

Instructions regarding War Diaries and Intelligence Summaries are contained in F. S. Regs., Part II. and the Staff Manual respectively. Title pages will be prepared in manuscript.

WAR DIARY
or
~~INTELLIGENCE SUMMARY.~~

(Erase heading not required.)

Place	Date 1918.	Hour	Summary of Events and Information	Remarks and references to Appendices
	Oct:			
LUCHEUX.	1		Office Routine.	
	2		C.R.E. visited Field Companies and 72nd. Infantry Brigade.	
	3		Tactical Exercises 72nd. Brigade. C.R.E. acted as Umpire. 103rd. Field Company R.E. built 2 Bridges.	
	4		C.R.E. visited Forward Light Railway Tramway School and arranged for party of Pioneers to attend.	
	5		Field Companies R.E. Training.	
MOEUVRES.	6		Moved from Rest to 17th. Corps. Divisional Headquarters moved to MOEUVRES.	
CANTAING MILL.	7		Divisional Headquarters moved to CANTAING MILL.	
NINE WOOD.	8		Divisional Headquarters moved to NINE WOOD. Field Companies working on Forward Roads, Water Supply and Bridges.	
MOUNT SUR L'OEUVRE.	9		Divisional Headquarters moved to MOUNT SUR L'OEUVRE. Field Companies working on Forward Roads, Water Supply and Bridges.	
CAMBRAI.	10		Divisional Headquarters moved to outskirts of CAMBRAI. Field Companies working on Forward Roads, Water Supply and Bridges.	
	11		Attack by 17th. Infantry Brigade. Field Companies engaged on Water Supply and Roads.	
	12		Field Companies moved to AVESNES.	
AVESNES.	13		Divisional Headquarters moved to AVESNES.	
	14		Old German Baths at AVESNES put into working order.	
	15		Bridging River SELLE with small Infantry Bridges.	
	16		" " " " " " " C.R.E. 19th. Division came to discuss handing over.	
	17		Handed over to C.R.E. 19th. Division.	
CAMBRAI.	18		Left forward area AVESNES for CAMBRAI.	
	19		Field Companies R.E. in training.	
	20		" " " " "	
	21		" " " " "	
	22		" " " " " G.O.C. inspected Billets of 12th. Sherwood Foresters (Pioneers) and 104th. Field Company R.E. Also saw 104th. Field Company R.E. at training (Bridging).	
	23		Field Companies R.E. in training.	
	24		Conference at Divisional Headquarters.	
	25		" " " " C.R.E. had interview with C.E. 17th. Corps.	
ST.AUBERT.	26		Divisional Headquarters moved to ST.AUBERT. Interviewed C.R.E. of the 61st. Division.	

D. D. & L., London, E.C. (A6034) Wt. W1771/M2031 750,000 5/17 Sch. 52 Forms/C2118/14

CONTINUED.

Instructions regarding War Diaries and Intelligence Summaries are contained in F. S. Regs., Part II. and the Staff Manual respectively. Title pages will be prepared in manuscript.

WAR DIARY

or

~~INTELLIGENCE SUMMARY.~~

(Erase heading not required.)

Army Form C. 2118.

Place	Date	Hour	Summary of Events and Information	Remarks and references to Appendices
	27		C.R.E. reconnoitred Forward Area.	
	28		C.R.E. visited 104th. and 129th. Field Companies.	
	29		C.R.E. visited 12th. Sherwood Foresters (Pioneers) and C.R.A.	
	30		C.R.E., O.C. 129th Field Company R.E. and O.C. 103rd. Field Company R.E. visited DUFOUR PARK to see various types of Light Infantry Bridges.	
	31		C.R.E. attended Tactical exercises of 73rd. Infantry Brigade. Conference at Divisional Headquarters.	

1.11.1918.

J. H. Prior

Lieut. Col.
C.R.E. 24th. Division.

D. D. & L., London, E.C. (A8001) Wt. W1771/M2031 750,000 5/17 Sch. 52 Forms/C2118/14

November 1918

War Diary

H Q R E

24th Divn

November 1918

Army Form C. 2118.

Instructions regarding War Diaries and Intelligence Summaries are contained in F. S. Regs., Part II. and the Staff Manual respectively. Title pages will be prepared in manuscript.

WAR DIARY
or
INTELLIGENCE SUMMARY.
(Erase heading not required.)

Place	Date	Hour	Summary of Events and Information	Remarks and references to Appendices
	Nov.			
In the Fld.				
	1.		Visited C.R.E. 19th Divn. with C.R.E. 61st Divn.	
	2.		Visited B.G.C.,73rd Inf.Bde., C.R.E.61st Divn. and O.C.129 Fld.Co with C.E.17th Corps	
	3.		H.Q. moved to BERMERAIN.	
	4.		H.Q. moved to SEPMERIES, Division attacked.129 Fld.Co. with leading Bde.	
	5.		Div.H.Q. moved to WARGNIES-le-GRAND. 103 Fld.Co. with leading Bde.	
	6.		Divisionm made slight advance. Working on forward roads.	
	7.		Division advanced to E. of BAVAY	
	8.		129 Fld.Co.working with 72nd Inf.Bde., 104 Fld.Co. with 73rd Inf.Bde in advance,103 Fld.Co in reserve	
	9.		Field Coys. worked with Brigades during advance as on 8th. Div.H.Q. moved to BAVAY	
	10.		Arranging work with C.R.E. 20th Divn. as per C.Es. instruction.	
	11.		Armistice	
	12.		Conference at Office of C.E.17th Corps	
	13.		Conference at Divn. H.Q.	
	14.		Office routine	
	15.		" "	
	16.		Field Coys. commenced move to new area.	
	17.		Office routine etc.	
	18.		Lt.Col.Prior proceeded on 3 mths special leave. Div.H.Q. moved to MASNY.	
	19.		Major Heath took over C.R.Es work.	
	20.		Visited Bdes. and 104 Fld.Co. Decided on work required at Div.Reception Camp SOMAIN and detailed 104 Fld.Co to do work.	
	21.		Visited 129 Fld.Co re baths at ANICHE and 104 Fld.Co. re baths at SOMAIN.	
	22.		Visited 104 Fld.Co. and 12th Sherwood Foresters.	
	23.		Visited 103 Fld.Co and 129 Fld.Co.	
	24.		Routine work	
	25.		Routine work.	
	26.		H.Q. 24th Divn. moved to SAMEON. Visited Inf.Bdes and Fld.Coys .on the move.	
	27.		Visited TOURNAI to see what billets were available for C.R.Es.Office and Field Companies.	
	28.		Visited TOURNAI and area generally with G.S.O.2. Cavalry Barracks TOURNAI allotted to Fld.Coys	
	29.		and Pioneer Bn. as billets.	
	29.		Billeting parties for 12th Sherwoods and 3 Fld.Coys went to TOURNAI.	
	30		Advance parties of Fld.Coys moved to TOURNAI. Visited 104 Fld.Coy. at LECELLES. Attended Conference at Office of C.E. 1st Corps ROSNY re organisation of Technical re-education. Visited 104 Fld.Coy. to be carried out near LECELLES.	

J. Heath
Major.R.E.
C.R.E.24 th Divn.

D. D. & L., London, E.C. (A8001) Wt. W1771/M2031 750,000 5/17 Sch. 52 Forms/C2118/14

Dec/18

Vol 40

WAR DIARY

HQ RE

24TH
DIV

Army Form C. 2118.

Instructions regarding War Diaries and Intelligence Summaries are contained in F. S. Regs., Part II. and the Staff Manual respectively. Title pages will be prepared in manuscript.

WAR DIARY
or
~~INTELLIGENCE~~ SUMMARY.

(Erase heading not required.)

Place	Date 1918	Hour	Summary of Events and Information	Remarks and references to Appendices
	Dec.			
In the Fld.	1.		Visited MAULDE - R.E.Dump, ANTOING, Fld.Coys. at TOURNAI, 12th Sher.Fotesters at COBRIEUX	
	2.		Office Routine - Visited work in progress at LECELLES.	
	3.		Office Routine.	
	4.		H.Q.R.E. moved to TOURNAI - 53 Rue Beyaert.	
	5.		Selecting R.E.Workshops etc at TOURNAI.	
	6.		R.E.Workshops fixed - Collecting material to form Dump	
	7.		Visited Office of C.E.1st Corps	
	8.		Office Routine etc.	
	9.		Office Routine etc.	
	10.		Office Routine etc.	
	11.		Visited VAULX les TOURNAI R.E.Dump and arranged to move machinery to R.E.Workshops TOURNAI.	
	12.		Visited VAULX les TOURNAI R.E.Dump	
	13.		Visited 17th 72nd and 73rd Infantry Brigades and C.R.A. re re-educational scheme.	
	14.		Visited Dumps in neighbourhood of TOURNAI.	
	15.		Visited VAULX les TOURNAI R.E.Dump.	
	16.		Visited 1st Corps Concentration Camp to estimate work required for repairs etc.Visited C.R.E. 8th Division.	
	17.		Visited 17th Inf.Bde.- C.E.1st Corps - TEMPLEUVE Dump - 72nd Inf.Bde. 73rd Inf.Bde. - C.R.A.	
	18.		Office Routine and R.E.Workshops etc.	
	19.		Visited E.and M. Coy at RAISMES re circular saws.	
	20.		Visited C.E.1st Corps and TEMPLEUVE DUmp.Interviewed M.KONINGS re construction of bridge over river at TOURNAI.	
	21s		Handing over to Major E.M.Marvin Visited Div.Workshops - Pioneers H.Q. - "Q" - "G" - 24th Division	
	22.		Office routine etc.	
	23.		Visited B.H.Qs 73rd and 17th Inf.Bdes. and "G" 24th Divn.	
	24.		Workshops closed down until 28-12-18.	
	25.		Christmas Day - Holiday.	
	26.		Holiday	
	27.		Office Routine.	
	28.		Visited B.H.Q. 73rd Inf.Bde. - C.E.1st Corps - "G" & "Q" 24th Division.Office Routine etc.	
	29,		Office Routine etc.	
	30.		Visited "Q" - Collected electrical stores from LILLE - Office Routine etc.	
	31.		Office Routine etc. Visited Workshops.	

Major.

D. D. & L., London, E.C.
(A8001) Wt. W1771/M2031 750,000 3/17 Sch. 52 Forms C2118/14

Instructions regarding War Diaries and Intelligence Summaries are contained in F. S. Regs., Part II. and the Staff Manual respectively. Title pages will be prepared in manuscript.

24/ 16/3

WAR DIARY C·R·E· 24th Division

or

~~INTELLIGENCE SUMMARY.~~

(*Erase heading not required.*)

Army Form C. 2118.

WO 95/2198 (handwritten: 41)

Place	Date	Hour	Summary of Events and Information	Remarks and references to Appendices
	Jan.			
In the Fld.	1.		Holiday	
	2		)	
	3		)	
	4		) Office Routine	
	5		)	
	6		)	
	7		)	
	8		Major F·P·HEATH took over C·R·E·	
	9		Office Routine	
	10		Visited 17 Bde· and work in Div'l area·Visited C·E·1st Corps, TEMPLEUVE Dump and 73rd Bde·	
	11		R·E·Train arrives - arranging for siding and off-loading	
	12		Sunday·	
	13		)	
	14		)	
	15		)	
	16		)	
	17		) Office Routine	
	18		)	
	19		)	
	20		)	
	21		)	
	22		)	
	23		Confidential reports on officers sent in·	
	24		Honours list submitted to Divn·	
	25		)	
	26		)	
	27		) Office Routine	
	28		)	
	29		)	
	30		Lieut·Col·J·H·PRIOR returned from leave and took over C·R·E·	
	31		Visited Divn· and Field Coys·	

J.H. Prior

Lieut·Col·R·E·
C·R·E 24th Divn·

D. D. & L., London, E.C. (A8001) Wt. W1771/M2031 750,000 5/17 Sch. 52 Forms/C2118/14

Instructions regarding War Diaries and Intelligence Summaries are contained in F. S. Regs., Part II. and the Staff Manual respectively. Title pages will be prepared in manuscript.

Army Form C. 2118.

WAR DIARY of C.R.E 24th Division or ~~INTELLIGENCE SUMMARY.~~

(Erase heading not required.)

Vol 42

Place	Date	Hour	Summary of Events and Information	Remarks and references to Appendices
TOURNAI	Feb 1919			
	1		Visited Field Companies & went round barracks	
	2		Office routine	
	3		C.E. 1st Corps came to see C.R.E	
	4		Conference at Divisional H.Q.	
	5		C.R.E. went to ANTOING to see condition of road	
	6		G.O.C. 24th Division went round Field Coy Barracks	
	7		Visited VAUX ammunition dumps with B.G.C 72 Bde re [illegible]	
	8		Conference of Field Company Commanders	
	9		Office routine.	
	10		Visited BACHY dump	
	11		Conference of Field Coy Commanders	
	12		Office routine.	
	13		Visited 73rd Infantry Bde re Work in hand.	
	14		" 17th "	
	15		Captain Skrimshire joined & took over command of 103 Fd Coy	
	16th to 25		Office routine.	
	26		Visited VAULX dump with Stores Officer	
	27 28		Office routine.	

J. H. Prior
Lt. COL. R.E.
C. R. E. 24th DIV.
4/3/19

D. D. & L., London, E.C. (A8001) Wt. W1771/M2031 750,000 5/17 Sch. 52 Forms C2118/14

Instructions regarding War Diaries and Intelligence Summaries are contained in F. S. Regs., Part II. and the Staff Manual respectively. Title pages will be prepared in manuscript.

WAR DIARY of C.R.E 24th Division
or
INTELLIGENCE SUMMARY.
(Erase heading not required.)

Army Form C. 2118.

Vol 43

Place	Date	Hour	Summary of Events and Information	Remarks and references to Appendices
TOURNAI	March 1919			
	1st		Office routine.	
	2		Conference Field Coy Commanders	
	3			
	4		Office routine.	
	5		C.R.E went to see C.E Ist Corps	
	6		Draft of 43 retainable O.R. from Field Coys to 26 Field Coy Ist Division	
	7		Office routine	
	8		C.E Ist Corps came to see C.R.E	
	9		Office routine	
	10			
	11			
	12		C-in-C visited H.Q 24th Div	
	13		Office routine	
	14			
	15			
	16		Conference Divisional H.Q	
	17		Office routine	
	18			
	19			
	20			
	21		103 & 104 Field Coys moved from TOURNAI to S.A.N	
	22		Lt Col Prior handed over to Major Heath & proceeded to VIth Corps	

J. H. Prior
22/3/19

Lt. COL. R.E.
C. R. E. 24th DIV.

D. D. & L., London, E.C.
(A8001) Wt. W1771/M2031 750,000 5/17 Sch. 52 Forms/C2118/14

Instructions regarding War Diaries and Intelligence Summaries are contained in F. S. Regs., Part II. and the Staff Manual respectively. Title pages will be prepared in manuscript.

WAR DIARY
or
~~INTELLIGENCE SUMMARY.~~
(Erase heading not required.)

Army Form C. 2118.

C.R.E. 24th Division —

Place	Date	Hour	Summary of Events and Information	Remarks and references to Appendices
Tournai	23rd		Office routine —	
	24th		(as above)	
	25th		129th Field Company and H.Q.R.E. moved to SYN.	
	26th		Visited C.E. Corps to discuss clearing of Audry Barracks Tournai of R.E. Stores —	
	27th		Office routine — Companies clearing equipment	
	28th		(as above)	
	29th		(as above)	
	30th		(as above)	
	31st		(as above)	

3/4/19

[illegible] Heath [illegible]
Cdr 24th Division

D. D. & L., London, E.C.
(A8001) Wt. W1771/M2031 750,000 5/17 Sch. 52 Forms/C2118/14

Army Form C. 2118.

WAR DIARY
or
INTELLIGENCE SUMMARY.
(Erase heading not required.)

OF. C.R.E. 24 DIV. GROUP.

MONTH OF APRIL 1919.

Vol 44

Place	Date	Hour	Summary of Events and Information	Remarks and references to Appendices
SIN. (FRANCE)	1/4/19.		Visit to Dumps under administration of CRE.	C.R.E., 24TH DIVISION. No. ...... Date ......
	2 – 6		Office Routine	
	7.		VAULX LES TOURNAI. Dump taken over by the 3rd Aust. Tunnelling Coy RE	
	8.		visit Brigades in Div area to value stores as returned by them under D.R.O. No 4717.	
	9.		Guard placed on [illegible] Dump TOURNAI.	
	10.		All retainable men volunteers for the army of occupation transferred to 409. Field Coy RE. of Western Div.	
	11 – 13		Office Routine	
	14		visit [illegible] Camp TOURNAI. to value German Huts & RE Stores. Lt F.G. [illegible] RE transferred from 103 Fld Coy to 129 Fld Coy RE to complete Cadre establt vice Lt. A.H. PORTER RE. transferred to 217 A.T. Coy RE	
	15.		visit VAULX LES TOURNAI Dump. to value Stores	
	16 – 17		Office Routine	
	18		visit Cavalry Barracks. TOURNAI. RE Dump to value wood	
	19 – 21.		Office Routine	
	22.		VAULX LES TOURNAI. Dump taken over from the 3rd Aust. Tunnelling Coy RE.	
	23		Office Routine	
	24		Inspection of unit Equipment by D.D.O.S. at BAISIEUX	
	25		Office Routine	
	26		TO GENECH. value 7 German Hangars.	
	27 – 30		Office Routine.	

C.S. [illegible] Capt RE
Cadre Officer
H.Q. RE. 24 DIV. Group

2/5/19.

Army Form C. 2118.

Instructions regarding War Diaries and Intelligence Summaries are contained in F. S. Regs., Part II. and the Staff Manual respectively. Title pages will be prepared in manuscript.

WAR DIARY
or
~~INTELLIGENCE SUMMARY.~~
(Erase heading not required.)

OF. C.R.E. 24 DIV. GROUP. A.

MONTH OF MAY 1919.

WR 45

Place	Date	Hour	Summary of Events and Information	Remarks and references to Appendices
SIN. (FRANCE.)	1 to 3		Routine Work. Visit Dumps under C.R.E.'s Administration.	
	4.		Orders Received to Reduce R.E. Field Coy Cadres to 2 Off. & 40. O. Rs	
	5 to 10		Office Routine. Personnel withdrawn from Dump Cavalry Barracks	
	10		Wire Received giving Dispersal Stations in U.K for Cadres of 103 + 104 Field Coy. R.E	
	11.		Orders Received giving dates & time of entraining for cadres proceeding to U.K.	
	12		Orders Received, cancels above order.	
	13		G.O.C. inspects unit Registers of Field Coy. RE	
	14.		Office Routine	
	15		Personnel guarding Hutting Dump Tournai, withdrawn.	
	16.		Received Provisional Warning "RE units will be broken up in France	
	17.		Visit C.R.E. Douai. Cadres	
	18.		Office Routine	
	19.		Visit C.E. No 1 Area	
	20		Office Routine	
	21.		E.C. Sgt. Dodds transferred to C.E. No 1. Area	
	22 to 31.		Office Routine	

[signature]
Capt RE
Cmdr C.RE 24 Div. GR.

C.R.E.
24TH DIVISION.
No.
Date.

D. D. & L., London, E.C. (A5001) Wt. W1 71/M2031 750,000 5/17 Sch. 52 Forms/C2118/14

A. F. C. 2118

4

WAR DIARY OF. C.R.E. 24 DIV. GROUP

MONTH. OF. JUNE 1919

Ceased

Place	Date	Summary
SIN (FRANCE)	1. to 12.	Office Routine
	12.	all stores as laid down in MOB TABLE (G.1098) handed in to I.C.S. TOURNAI.
	13 to 16	Office Routine
	17	all vehicles loaded on TRAIN BAISIEUX STATION
	18.	above vehicles despatched to Ordnance Calais.
	19 to 25	Office Routine
	25.	all personnel of H.Q.R.E. also Field Coys forwarded to No 8 Conc. Camp SOMAIN for Demobilisation. 24 DIV. R.E. ceased to exist from 09.30 Hours on the 25.6.19

C. H. Hus[illegible]
Capt R.E.

www.ingramcontent.com/pod-product-compliance
Lightning Source LLC
Chambersburg PA
CBHW080828010526
44112CB00015B/2474

* 9 7 8 1 4 7 4 5 1 2 7 8 7 *